Studies in Educational Learning Environments

An International Perspective

METROPOLITAN COLLEGE
OF NEW YORK LIBRARY
75 Varick Street 12th Fl.
New York, NY 10013

Studies in Educational Learning Environments

An International Perspective

Edited by

Swee Chiew Goh
Myint Swe Khine

National Institute of Education
Nanyang Technological University
Singapore

World Scientific
New Jersey • London • Singapore • Hong Kong

Published by

World Scientific Publishing Co. Pte. Ltd.
P O Box 128, Farrer Road, Singapore 912805
USA office: Suite 1B, 1060 Main Street, River Edge, NJ 07661
UK office: 57 Shelton Street, Covent Garden, London WC2H 9HE

British Library Cataloguing-in-Publication Data
A catalogue record for this book is available from the British Library.

STUDIES IN EDUCATIONAL LEARNING ENVIRONMENTS
An International Perspective

Copyright © 2002 by World Scientific Publishing Co. Pte. Ltd.

All rights reserved. This book, or parts thereof, may not be reproduced in any form or by any means, electronic or mechanical, including photocopying, recording or any information storage and retrieval system now known or to be invented, without written permission from the Publisher.

For photocopying of material in this volume, please pay a copying fee through the Copyright Clearance Center, Inc., 222 Rosewood Drive, Danvers, MA 01923, USA. In this case permission to photocopy is not required from the publisher.

ISBN 981-238-145-7
ISBN 981-238-056-6 (pbk)

Printed by FuIsland Offset Printing (S) Pte Ltd, Singapore

Foreword

S. Gopinathan

National Institute of Education
Nanyang Technological University
Singapore

There is increasing recognition that many of the school reform initiatives currently under way in school systems everywhere will depend for their success on how well teachers and policymakers understand the classroom environments in which learning and teaching take place. A burgeoning literature has emerged which provides insights and data on such relationships as links between classroom environments and patterns of student learning, and the impact of innovations in curriculum and teaching strategies on learning. Researchers have also recognised that different disciplines and their particular ways of knowing reality will impose different demands upon learning environments. It can confidently be said that a robust knowledge base exists that will prove valuable in teacher preparation and professional development courses and policy making that seeks enhanced student achievement.

This volume *Studies in Educational Learning Environments: An International Perspective* represents an exciting advance in that it brings into one volume work by some of the leaders in the field, notably Barry Fraser, cross-cultural approaches and recent work from such Asian countries as Singapore, Taiwan, Korea and Brunei. The influence of culture is deservedly given an important place in these studies and will contribute to the emergence of models for classroom environment studies that will, by remaining sensitive to cultural variation, have greater explanatory power.

The co-editors, Swee Chiew Goh and Myint Swe Khine, are to be congratulated for their initiative and efforts in preparing this volume. Their efforts will, I am sure, be amply rewarded when learning environments research is more and more utilised in improving schooling.

Preface

Barry J. Fraser

Curtin University of Technology
Australia

"Constructive educational climates may be so vitally important that priorities should be drastically rearranged." (Riorden, 1982, p. 310)

This book is devoted to conceptualising, assessing and investigating what happens to students during their school and university education. In particular, the main focus is on important aspects of classroom learning environments. Clearly, having positive classroom environments is a valuable goal of education. But, it should not be assumed that the equally important issue of student outcomes is ignored. Rather, this book presents compelling evidence that the classroom environment so strongly influences student outcomes that it should not be ignored by those wishing to improve the effectiveness of schools and universities.

The curriculum of schools and universities consists not just of content and outcomes, but also of classrooms where the business of learning takes place. It is the quality of life lived in classrooms that determines many of the things that we hope for from education. As this book clearly shows, classroom climate can be assessed and studied. In fact, remarkable progress has been made in conceptualising, assessing and researching it.

In particular, over the years, researchers have developed quite a few questionnaires to assess students' perceptions of their classroom learning environments. These questionnaires have been used in different countries and at different grade levels. They have been translated into various languages. They have been used by hundreds of researchers, thousands of teachers and millions of students around the world.

Given the ready availability of questionnaires, the importance of classroom environment, the influence of classroom environment on student outcomes, and the value of environment assessments in guiding educational improvement, it seems very important that researchers and teachers give it greater priority. Although educators around the world pay great attention to student achievement and only a little attention to the environment of school and university classrooms, research on classroom environment should not be buried under a pile of achievement tests. Hopefully, this timely book will encourage and guide important research and practical applications involving classroom environment, especially in Asian countries.

From The Editors

This book on educational learning environments is conceptualised as a platform for researchers and educators to share the results of their work with others who are interested in the field of Learning Environments Research (LER). It is also hoped that the book, in bringing together recent research conducted in various parts of the world, will help consolidate the achievements and developments of the field for the past 30 years.

Background to LER

Historically, learning environments research began to attract attention from the late 1960s with the much publicised work of firstly, H.J. Walberg and colleagues in connection with the Harvard Physics Project and secondly, the work of R.H. Moos in clinical and family therapy that was later extended to education. The efforts of Walberg and Moos pioneered many major research studies in perceptions of classroom environments from the 1970s. There emerged a distinct tradition of research on students' perceptions of their classroom environment. The studies of B.J. Fraser and his associates in Australia, particularly the studies in science classrooms, contributed to the momentous growth of LER. In The Netherlands, Th. Wubbels and his colleagues worked on the model of teacher interpersonal behaviour to explain the significance of teacher–student relationship in the classrooms. Past research on classroom learning environments has been accompanied by the development and validation of several instruments over the last 30 years and these instruments formed the backbone of all studies in learning environments. Thus, LER has evolved into a field of study providing alternatives to explain students' learning success other than through students' examination performance.

As LER is carried out in many countries, it is our pleasant task to invite prominent scholars and educators from all over the world to contribute each a chapter on the research in their respective countries. This gives the book its international outlook. We would like to express our thanks to all the contributors for responding to this call of 'duty' and for making this book a reality. It is the only one of its kind and this book is our joint achievement.

Organisation of book

This book is organised in a special way. It contains 10 chapters. The first chapter is written by Professor Barry J. Fraser, a distinguished name linked to learning environments research. He has been greatly involved in the field for many years and is the best person to write on "Learning Environments Research: Yesterday, Today and Tomorrow". The chapter offers insights that will set directions and stimulate further growth in LER.

The remaining nine chapters are devoted to LER in nine countries. Each chapter presents LER in the context of the country concerned and is unique in its own way. Chapters 2 to 5 present LER in Australia, Canada, The Netherlands and the USA. Chapters 6 to 10 highlight LER in the Asian countries of Brunei, Indonesia, Korea, Singapore and Taiwan. Owing to restraints, studies documented in the various chapters are not exhaustive of LER carried out in their respective countries.

Currently, research in Asian countries is gaining impetus and this prompts the authors to not only present the significant findings of their research but also provide information on the educational systems in their countries. The "What is Happening in this Class" (WIHIC) questionnaire is used in a number of Asian studies and this book has the privilege of including translated versions of the WIHIC in the Indonesian, Korean and Chinese languages. This will enhance the understanding of learning environments in different educational, social and cultural contexts. All the LER documented in the chapters bear testimony to a vibrant field and it is no wonder that there are increasing publications and conference presentations at international levels. LER has attained a level of distinction in the field of educational research that we are all proud of.

We would also like to express our thanks to the Dean of Foundation Programmes, National Institute of Education, Professor S. Gopinathan, for his unstinting support throughout the publication of this book.

Indeed, we extend our big thank you to everyone who has assisted in the publication of the book.

Swee Chiew Goh
Myint Swe Khine
National Institute of Education
Nanyang Technological University
Singapore

About The Contributors

Jill M. Aldridge obtained her PhD from Curtin University of Technology, Australia. She collaborated with Professors Yang J.H. and Iris Huang in the cross-national study of learning environments in science classrooms in Taiwan and Australia.

Mieke Brekelmans is Associate Professor in a teacher training and educational research group of the Institute of Education (IVLOS) at Utrecht University (The Netherlands). Her research is in the field of teaching and teacher education. Currently, her focus is on the relation between teacher thinking and action, and the development of teaching during the professional teacher career.

Cristobal Carambo is a high school teacher in chemistry and physical science and a teaching mentor for students from the University of Pennsylvania's graduate school of education. He holds a master's degree from Florida State University. His current research focus is on the interrelationship between student agency, inquiry learning and scientific literacy in the science classroom.

Perry den Brok is Associate Professor in a teacher training and educational research group of the Institute of Education (IVLOS) at Utrecht University (The Netherlands). His research is in the field of teaching and teacher education. Currently his focus is on multicultural and intercultural studies on classroom environments, and factors that explain differences in student perceptions of teaching.

Rowhea Elmesky is a research associate at the University of Pennsylvania where she is undertaking research on the teaching and learning of science in urban high schools. Rowhea has her graduate and undergraduate degrees in science education, including her doctorate, from Florida State University.

Darrell Fisher is with the National Key Centre for Science and Maths Education in Curtin University, Perth, Australia. Professor Fisher's major research interests include classroom and school environments, and curriculum issues related to science, particularly curriculum evaluation. Currently, he is the Regional Editor for Asia and Australia of *Learning Environments Research: An International Journal*.

Barry J. Fraser is Professor and Director of the Science and Mathematics Education Centre at Curtin University of Technology in Perth, Australia. He is co-editor of the 72-chapter *International Handbook of Science Education* published by Kluwer, and editor-in-chief of the Kluwer journal *Learning Environments Research: An International Journal*. He is a fellow of the American Association for the Advancement of Science, Academy of Education, Academy of the Social Sciences in Australia and Australian College of Education. He is an eminent scholar in learning environments research.

Swee Chiew Goh is with the National Institute of Education, Nanyang Technological University, Singapore. Associate Professor Goh has been in teacher education for more than 20 years. She also undertakes supervision of Master in Education students in their research and dissertation. Her research interests include the studying of learning environment at the primary, secondary and tertiary levels and classroom management.

Iris Huang Tai-chu is a science educator from the Graduate Institute of Science Education, National Kaohsiung Normal University, Taiwan. The study of learning environments in science classrooms is one of her many research interests.

Myint Swe Khine is with the National Institute of Education, Nanyang Technological University, Singapore, where he teaches courses in classroom management, IT integration and instructional design at both undergraduate and postgraduate levels. One of his academic qualifications includes Doctor of Education from Curtin University of Technology, Australia. He has been a teacher educator for more than 20 years.

Heui Baik Kim is Professor at the Wonkwang University in Iksan, Korea. She is involved in teaching biology education courses for pre-

About the Contributors   xiii

service and in-service teacher education programmes. Her research interests include students' understanding of science concepts and the learning environment at secondary level.

Seon Uk Lee obtained her PhD from Curtin University of Technology, Australia. She is a science teacher registered at the Education Department of Western Australia and is also involved in Korean language teaching.

Eko S. Margianti is Professor and President of the Gunadarma University Jakarta, Indonesia. She is the Secretary-General of Indonesia Computer Society, the Chairperson of Funding and Development of Indonesia Private Association, Vice-President of Private Indonesia Tertiary Study of Computer Association, Board Member of SEARCC IT Professional Council in South East Asia and Chairperson of Computer Education Foundation in Jakarta, Indonesia.

Kenneth Tobin is Professor of Education in the Graduate School of Education at the University of Pennsylvania. His research interests are focussed on the teaching and learning of science in urban schools and co-teaching as a way of learning to teach in urban high schools. His recent publications include three co-authored books, Re/Constructing Elementary Science, At the Elbow of Another: Learning to Teach by Coteaching and Transforming Undergraduate Science Teaching: Social Constructivist Perspectives.

Bruce Waldrip has completed a great deal of research in classroom learning environment, especially in the science laboratory classroom and its relationship with learning outcomes, effect of culture on student learning, and teachers' and students' perceptions of their school-level environments. Currently, he is a senior lecturer in science education at La Trobe University, Bendigo campus, Victoria, Australia.

Theo Wubbels is Professor of Education and Director of the Institute of Educational Studies in the School of Social Sciences of Utrecht University (The Netherlands). He specialises in social psychology in education, teacher thinking and action.

Jong-Hsiang Yang is Professor of Science Education, National Taiwan Normal University, Taiwan. He organised the 2000 Second International Conference on Science, Mathematics and Technology Education at the NTNU, Taiwan, under the co-sponsorship of Curtin University of Technology, Australia. Professor Yang is a pioneer on qualitative research methodology in science education in Taiwan.

David B. Zandvliet is with the Faculty of Education, Simon Fraser University, Vancouver, Canada. He is Director of the faculty's Centre for Educational Technology over the past three years and has been deeply involved in teacher education. His research interests lie in the areas of science, technology and environmental education with a focus on students' perceptions of their learning environment.

Contents

Foreword v

Preface vii

From the Editors ix

About the Contributors xi

Chapter 1
Learning Environments Research: Yesterday, Today and Tomorrow 1
 Barry J. Fraser

Chapter 2
Measuring Culturally Sensitive Factors of Classroom Learning Environments with the CLEQ 27
 Darrell L. Fisher and Bruce G. Waldrip

Chapter 3
Learning Environments in Technology-Rich Classrooms 49
 David B. Zandvliet

Chapter 4
Teacher Experience and the Teacher–Student Relationship in the Classroom Environment 73
 Mieke Brekelmans, Theo Wubbels and Perry den Brok

Chapter 5
Learning Environments in Urban Science Classrooms: Contradictions, Conflict and Reproduction of Social Inequality 101
 Kenneth Tobin, Rowhea Elmesky and Cristobal Carambo

Chapter 6
Study of Learning Environment for Improving Science
Education in Brunei 131
Myint Swe Khine

Chapter 7
Learning Environment Research in Indonesia 153
Eko S. Margianti

Chapter 8
Curriculum Development and Learning Environment
Research in Korea 169
Seon Uk Lee and Heui Baik Kim

Chapter 9
Studies on Learning Environments in Singapore Classrooms 197
Swee Chiew Goh

Chapter 10
Investigating Factors that Prevent Science Teachers from
Creating Positive Learning Environments in Taiwan 217
Jong-Hsiang Yang, Iris Tai-Chu Huang and Jill M. Aldridge

Selected Bibliography 235

Index 239

Chapter 1

LEARNING ENVIRONMENTS RESEARCH: YESTERDAY, TODAY AND TOMORROW

Barry J. Fraser
Curtin University of Technology
Australia

Learning environments research has expanded remarkably over the past few decades on the international scene, with Asian researchers making important and distinct contributions particularly over the previous decade. Asian researchers have cross-validated the main contemporary classroom environment questionnaires that originated in the West and have undertaken careful translations and adaptations for use in the Chinese, Korean, Malay and Indonesian languages. Asian studies have replicated Western research in establishing consistent associations between the classroom environment and student outcomes, in using learning environment assessments in evaluating educational programs, and in identifying determinants of learning environments. Some desirable directions for future learning environment research in Asia include more use of qualitative research methods and using learning environment assessments to guide practitioners' attempts to improve their classrooms.

1. Introduction

The field of learning environments has undergone remarkable growth, diversification and internationalisation during the past 30 years (Fraser, 1998a). A striking feature of this field is the availability of a variety of economical, valid and widely-applicable questionnaires that have been developed and used for assessing students' perceptions of classroom environment (Fraser, 1998b). Although learning environment research originated in Western countries, Asian researchers in the last decade have made many major and distinctive contributions. In particular, some of the main questionnaires that were developed in the West have been adapted (sometimes involving translation into another language) and cross-validated for use in several Asian countries. In order to provide wide access to past research and to instruments that have proven valid and useful in Asian contexts, this chapter has a particular focus on studies undertaken in Asia. Through this focus, it is hoped that this chapter will stimulate and guide future research agendas in the field of learning environments in Asian countries.

2. Instruments for Assessing Classroom Environment

Because few fields of educational research can boast the existence of such a rich array of validated and robust instruments, this section describes four contemporary instruments that have been used in Asia: Questionnaire on Teacher Interaction (QTI); Science Laboratory Environment Inventory (SLEI); Constructivist Learning Environment Survey (CLES); and What Is Happening In This Class? (WIHIC) questionnaire. Before discussing each of these instruments below, some historically-important questionnaires are briefly considered.

2.1. Historically-Important Questionnaires

The Learning Environment Inventory (LEI) and Classroom Environment Scale (CES) were developed in the USA in the late 1960s. The initial development of the LEI began in conjunction with evaluation and research related to Harvard Project Physics (Walberg & Anderson, 1968). The CES (Moos & Trickett, 1987) grew out of a comprehensive program of research involving perceptual measures of a variety of human environments including psychiatric hospitals, prisons, university residences and work milieus (Moos, 1974).

The LEI was used in the Hindi language in a large study involving approximately 3000 tenth grade students in 83 science and 67 social studies classes (Walberg, Singh & Rasher, 1977). Student perceptions on the LEI accounted for a significant increment in achievement variance beyond that attributable to general ability. In Indonesia, Paige (1979) used the CES and three scales selected from the LEI to reveal that individual modernity was enhanced in classrooms perceived as having greater task orientation, competition and difficulty and less order and organisation, while achievement was enhanced in classes higher in speed and lower in order and organisation. Hirata and Sako (1998) used an instrument in the Japanese language that incorporated scales from the CES. Factor analysis of the responses of 635 students suggested a four-factor structure for this questionnaire (consisting of Teacher Control, Sense of Isolation, Order and Discipline, and Affiliation).

The My Class Inventory (MCI) is a simplified form of the LEI for use among children aged 8–12 years (Fisher & Fraser, 1981). In Singapore, Goh, Young and Fraser (1995) changed the MCI's original Yes-No response format to a three-point response format (Seldom, Sometimes and Most of the Time) in a modified version of the MCI which includes a Task Orientation scale. Goh *et al.* found the modified MCI to be valid and useful in research applications with 1512 primary mathematics students in 39 classes. In Brunei Darussalam, Majeed, Fraser and Aldridge (in press) used the original version of the MCI with 1565 mathematics students in 81 classes in 15 government secondary schools. When the Satisfaction scale was used as an attitudinal outcome variable, instead of as a measure of classroom environment, Majeed *et al.* (in press) found strong support for a three-factor structure for the MCI consisting of three of the four *a priori* scales, namely, Cohesiveness, Difficulty and Competitiveness.

Whereas the LEI, CES and MCI were designed for teacher-centred classrooms, the Individualised Classroom Environment Questionnaire (ICEQ) was the first learning environment instrument to focus on dimensions which distinguish individualised classrooms from conventional ones (Fraser, 1990). The ICEQ appears to have been used very little in the Asian context, but Asghar and Fraser (1995) used it in Brunei Darussalam to investigate associations between students' attitudes and their classroom environment perceptions at the lower secondary school level.

2.2. *Questionnaire on Teacher Interaction (QTI)*

Research which originated in The Netherlands focuses on the nature and quality of interpersonal relationships between teachers and students (Wubbels & Brekelmans, 1998; Wubbels & Levy, 1993). Drawing upon a theoretical model of proximity (cooperation-opposition) and influence (dominance-submission), the QTI was developed to assess student perceptions of eight behaviour aspects (Leadership, Helpful/Friendly, Understanding, Student Responsibility/Freedom, Uncertain, Dissatisfied,

Admonishing and Strict). Each item has a five-point response scale ranging from Never to Always. Typical items are "She/he gives us a lot of free time" (Student Responsibility and Freedom behaviour) and "She/he gets angry" (Admonishing behaviour). Research with the QTI has been completed at various grade levels in the USA (Wubbels & Levy, 1993) and Australia (Fisher, Henderson & Fraser, 1995).

The QTI has been used in several large-scale studies in Asia. Goh pioneered the use of the QTI in a simplified form in Singapore with a sample of 1512 primary mathematics students in 39 classes in 13 schools (Goh & Fraser, 1996, 1998, 2000). This study cross-validated the QTI for use in a new country and found it to be useful in several research applications. Also, further support for the validity and usefulness of the QTI in Singapore is provided by Quek, Fraser and Wong's (2001) study among 497 gifted and non-gifted chemistry students and by Fisher, Goh, Wong and Rickards' (1997) study involving 20 secondary science classes.

Scott and Fisher (2001) translated the QTI into Standard Malay and cross-validated it with 3104 primary school students in 136 classes in Brunei Darussalam. An English version of the QTI has been cross-validated for secondary schools in Brunei Darussalam for samples of 1188 science students (Khine & Fisher, 2002) and 644 chemistry students (Riah & Fraser, 1998). In Korea, Kim, Fisher and Fraser (2000) validated a Korean-language version of the QTI among 543 Grade 8 students in 12 schools, and Lee and Fraser (2001a) provided further cross-validation information for the QTI using a sample of 440 Grade 10 and 11 science students. In Indonesia, Soerjaningsih, Fraser and Aldridge (2001b) translated the QTI into the Indonesian language and cross-validated it with a sample of 422 university students in 12 research methods classes.

2.3. Science Laboratory Environment Inventory (SLEI)

Because of the importance of laboratory settings in science education, an instrument specifically suited to assessing the environment of science laboratory classes at the senior high school or higher education levels was developed (Fraser, Giddings & McRobbie, 1995; Fraser &

McRobbie, 1995). The SLEI has five seven-item scales (Student Cohesiveness, Open-Endedness, Integration, Rule Clarity and Material Environment) and the five response alternatives are Almost Never, Seldom, Sometimes, Often and Very Often. Typical items are "I use the theory from my regular science class sessions during laboratory activities" (Integration) and "We know the results that we are supposed to get before we commence a laboratory activity" (Open-Endedness). The SLEI was field tested and validated simultaneously with a sample of 5447 students in 269 classes in six different countries (the USA, Canada, England, Israel, Australia and Nigeria), and cross-validated with Australian students (Fisher, Henderson & Fraser, 1997; Fraser & McRobbie, 1995).

In Asia, the SLEI has been cross-validated and found useful in research involving both its original English form and translated versions. The validity of the English version of the SLEI has been established in Singapore by Wong and Fraser's (1995, 1996) study of 1592 Grade 10 chemistry students in 56 classes in 28 schools, and by Quek *et al.*'s (2001) study of 497 gifted and non-gifted chemistry students. Also, Riah and Fraser (1998) cross-validated the English version of the SLEI with 644 Grade 10 chemistry students in Brunei Darussalem.

A noteworthy program of research involving a Korean-language version of the SLEI has been initiated by Kim and built upon by Lee (Kim & Kim, 1995, 1996; Kim & Lee, 1997; Lee & Fraser, 2001b, 2002). For example, Lee and Fraser reported strong factorial validity for a Korean version of the SLEI and replicated several patterns from previous research in Western countries (e.g., low Open-Endedness scores and significant associations with students' attitudes).

2.4. *Constructivist Learning Environment Survey (CLES)*

According to the constructivist view, meaningful learning is a cognitive process in which individuals make sense of the world in relation to the knowledge which they already have constructed, and this sense-making process involves active negotiation and consensus building. The CLES (Taylor, Fraser & Fisher, 1997) was developed to assist researchers and teachers to assess the degree to which a particular classroom's environment is consistent with a constructivist epistemology, and to assist teachers to reflect on their epistemological assumptions and reshape their teaching practice. The CLES has 36 items, with five response alternatives ranging from Almost Never to Almost Always, which assess Personal Relevance, Uncertainty, Critical Voice, Shared Control, and Student Negotiation. Typical items are "I help the teacher to decide what activities I do" (Shared Control) and "Other students ask me to explain my ideas" (Student Negotiation).

In Singapore, Wilks (2000) expanded and modified the CLES for use among students studying English (a subject called General Paper) in junior colleges in Singapore. The revised GPCLES contains two new scales called Political Awareness (reflecting Habermas's notion of emancipatory interest and assessing the extent to which students analyse causes of social injustice and advocate political reform) and Ethic of Care (the degree of emotional warmth in the classroom), which are especially relevant in the teaching of General Paper. When Wilks administered the GPLES to 1046 students in 48 classes in junior colleges, the questionnaire displayed good factorial validity and internal consistency reliability and each scale differentiated significantly between the perceptions of students in different classrooms.

Kim, Fisher and Fraser (1999) translated the CLES into the Korean language and administered it to 1083 science students in 24 classes in 12 schools. The original five-factor structure was replicated for the Korean-language version of both an actual and a preferred form of the CLES. Similarly, Lee and Fraser (2001a) replicated the five-factor structure of a Korean-language version of the CLES among 440 Grade 10 and 11 science students in 13 classes. Furthermore, the CLES has been translated into Chinese for use in Taiwan (Aldridge, Fraser, Taylor & Chen, 2000). In this cross-national study, the original English version was administered to 1081 science students in 50 classes in Australia, while the new Chinese version was administered to 1879 science students in 50 classes in Taiwan. The same five-factor structure emerged for the CLES in the two countries and scale reliabilities were similar.

2.5. What Is Happening In This Class? (WIHIC) Questionnaire

The WIHIC questionnaire combines modified versions of salient scales from a wide range of existing questionnaires with additional scales that accommodate contemporary educational concerns (e.g. equity and constructivism). The original 90-item nine-scale version was refined by both statistical analysis of data from 355 junior high school science students, and extensive interviewing of students about their views of their classroom environments in general, the wording and salience of individual items and their questionnaire responses (Fraser, Fisher & McRobbie, 1996). Analysis of data from an Australian sample of 1081 students in 50 classes (Aldridge & Fraser, 2000) led to a final form of the WIHIC containing the seven eight-item scales (Student Cohesiveness, Teacher Support, Involvement, Investigation, Task Orientation, Cooperation, Equity). Response alternatives range from Almost Never to Very Often. Typical items are "I discuss ideas in class" (Involvement) and "I work with other students on projects in this class" (Cooperation).

Although the WIHIC is a relatively recent instrument, its take-up in Asia has been frequent. Already it has been translated into several Asian languages and cross-validated:

- An English version has been cross-validated in Brunei Darussalam with samples of 644 Grade 10 Chemistry students (Riah & Fraser, 1998) and 1188 Form 5 science students (Khine & Fisher, 2001).
- Two studies have used an English version of the WIHIC in Singapore. Fraser and Chionh (2000) report strong validity and reliability for both an actual and a preferred form of the WIHIC when it was responded to for the subjects of mathematics and geography by a sample of 2310 students in 75 senior high school classes. Khoo and Fraser (1998) used the WIHIC with a sample of 250 adults attending computer courses in 23 classes in four Singaporean computing schools.
- A Chinese version of the WIHIC has been developed for use in Taiwan and cross-validated with a sample of 1879 junior high school students in 50 classes (Aldridge & Fraser, 2000; Aldridge, Fraser & Huang, 1999).

- Chua, Wong and Chen (2001) developed a Chinese-language version of the WIHIC, based on the Taiwanese version of Aldridge, Fraser and Huang (1999). This is a bilingual instrument with every item presented in both English and Chinese. Detailed procedures were used to develop this Chinese version, which was cross-validated with a sample of 1460 students in 50 classes.
- The WIHIC has been translated into the Korean language and validated with a sample of 543 Grade 8 students in 12 schools (Kim et al., 2000).
- The WIHIC has been translated into the Indonesian language and used with university students in computing-related courses. The validity and usefulness of the WIHIC has been established for samples of 2498 university students in 50 computing classes (Margianti, Fraser & Aldridge, 2001a, 2001b) and 422 students in 12 research methods classes (Soerjaningsih, Fraser & Aldridge, 2001a).

3. Research Involving Classroom Environment Instruments

In order to illustrate the many and varied applications of classroom environment instruments, this section considers six types of past research which focus on (1) associations between student outcomes and environment, (2) evaluation of educational innovations, (3) differences between students' and teachers' perceptions of the same classrooms, (4) determinants of classroom environment, (5) use of qualitative research methods, and (6) cross-national studies.

3.1. Associations between Student Outcomes and Environment

The strongest tradition in past classroom environment research has involved investigation of associations between students' cognitive and affective learning outcomes and their perceptions of psychosocial characteristics of their classrooms. Fraser's (1994) tabulation of 40 past studies shows that associations between outcome measures and classroom environment perceptions have been replicated for a variety of cognitive and affective outcome measures, a variety of classroom environment instruments and a variety of samples (ranging across numerous countries and grade levels).

Asian researchers have undertaken a wide variety of valuable studies into associations between student outcomes and students perceptions of their classroom learning environment. These studies also cover a wide range of environment instruments, student outcomes, school subjects and grade levels. While some studies have involved English-language versions of questionnaires, other studies have involved learning environment questionnaires that have been translated into various Asian languages:

- In Singapore, relationships have been established between a variety of student outcomes and students' classroom environment perceptions as assessed by several instruments. In one of the early learning environment studies in Singapore, Wong and Fraser (1996) established links between students' attitudes and scores on SLEI scales for a sample of 1592 Grade 10 chemistry students in 56 classes. In another pioneering study in Singapore, Goh used both the MCI and the QTI with 1512 primary mathematics students in 39 classes to establish associations between the classroom environment and mathematics achievement and attitudes (Goh & Fraser, 1998, 2000). Fraser and Chionh's (2000) unusually comprehensive study established associations between WIHIC scales and three student outcomes (examination results, attitudes and self-esteem) among a large sample of 2310 mathematics and geography students in 75 classes. Using both the SLEI and QTI, Quek *et al.* (2001) reported links with student attitudes for a sample of 497 gifted and non-gifted secondary school chemistry students. Khoo and Fraser (1998) established links between student satisfaction and dimensions of the WIHIC for a sample of 250 adults attending 23 computing classes. Using an instrument suited for computer-assisted instruction classrooms, Teh and Fraser (1995) found associations between classroom environment, achievement and attitudes among a sample of 671 high school geography students in 24 classes in Singapore. Finally, Waldrip and Wong (1996) reported attitude-environment associations when they used the SLEI in both Singapore and Papua New Guinea.

- In Brunei Darussalam, outcome-environment associations have been established for: satisfaction and scales of the MCI for a sample of 1565 Form 2 mathematics students in 81 classes (Majeed *et al.*, in press); for science attitudes and scales of both the WIHIC and QTI for a sample of 1188 Form 5 students in 54 science classrooms (Khine, 2001; Khine & Fisher, 2001, 2002); achievement and attitudes and scales of the WIHIC, QTI and SLEI for a sample of 644 chemistry students in 35 classes from 23 government secondary schools (Riah & Fraser, 1998); and for enjoyment of science lessons with scales of a primary school version of the QTI that had been translated into Standard Malay and used with 3104 students in 136 classes in 23 private schools (Scott & Fisher, 2001).

- In Korea, outcome-environment associations have been reported for: students' attitudes to science and a Korean-language version of the SLEI, CLES and QTI (Lee & Fraser, 2001a, 2001b, 2002) for a sample of 440 Grade 10 and 11 science students in 13 classes; and student attitudes and Korean-language versions of the CLES for a sample of 1083 science students in 24 classes (Kim *et al.*, 1999) and of the QTI and WIHIC for 543 students in 12 schools (Kim *et al.*, 2000).

- In Taiwan, outcome-environment relationships have been found for student satisfaction and a Chinese-language version of scales for both the WIHIC and CLES for a sample of 1879 science students in 50 classes (Aldridge & Fraser, 2000; Aldridge *et al.*, 1999; Aldridge *et al.*, 2000).

- In Indonesia, Margianti *et al.* (2001a, 2001b) reported associations between the outcomes of achievement and attitudes and students' perceptions on an Indonesian-language version of the WIHIC for a sample of 2498 university students in 50 classes. Similarly, Soerjaningsih *et al.* (2001a, 2001b) used Indonesian language-versions of both the WIHIC and QTI to establish links with student outcomes (course achievement, leisure interest in computers, and attitude towards the internet) among 422 university students in 12 classes.

While many past learning environment studies have employed techniques such as multiple regression analysis, few have used multilevel analysis (Bryk & Raudenbush, 1992), which takes cognisance of the hierarchical nature of classroom settings. However, two studies in Singapore compared the results from multiple regression analysis with those from an analysis involving the hierarchical linear model. In Wong, Young, and Fraser's (1997) study involving 1592 Grade 10 students in 56 chemistry classes in Singapore, associations were investigated between three student attitude measures and a modified version of the SLEI. In Goh's study with 1512 Grade 5 mathematics students in 39 classes in Singapore, scores on modified versions of the MCI and QTI were related to student achievement and attitude. Most of the statistically significant results from the multiple regression analyses were replicated in the HLM analyses, as well as being consistent in direction (Goh *et al.*, 1995; Goh & Fraser, 1998).

Some research into outcome-environment associations has involved the use of more than one classroom environment questionnaire in the same study. Several Asian studies have employed more than one learning environment questionnaire and have used commonality analysis to ascertain the unique and joint contributions made by each questionnaire to the variance in student outcomes. In Singapore, Goh and Fraser (1998) used the MCI and QTI in a study involving the achievement and attitudes of 1512 primary mathematics students. The MCI and the QTI each uniquely accounted for an appreciable proportion of the variance in achievement, but not in attitudes. Much of the total variance in attitude scores was common to the two questionnaires. A conclusion from this study was that it is useful to include the MCI and QTI together in a future study of achievement, but not of attitudes.

Other studies in Asia have reported similar commonality analyses for the unique and joint influences of two questionnaires on student outcomes. Quek *et al.* (2001) used the SLEI and QTI together in a study of science students' attitudes in Singapore. Lee and Fraser (2001a,

2001b, 2002) used the Korean-language versions of the SLEI, QTI and CLES in a study of science students' attitudes in Korea. Generally, these studies also confirmed that each classroom environment instrument accounted for variance in student outcome measures that is independent of that accounted for by the other instrument.

3.2. Evaluation of Educational Innovations

Classroom environment instruments can be used as a valuable source of process criteria in the evaluation of educational innovations. For example, an evaluation of the Australian Science Education Project (ASEP) revealed that, in comparison with a control group, ASEP students perceived their classrooms as being more satisfying and individualised and having a better material environment (Fraser, 1979). Despite the potential value of evaluating educational innovations and new curricula in terms of their impact on transforming the classroom learning environment, only a small number of such studies have been carried out in Asian countries. However, in Singapore, Teh used his own classroom environment instrument (the Geography Classroom Environment Inventory) as a source of dependent variables in evaluating computer-assisted learning (Fraser & Teh, 1994; Teh & Fraser, 1994). Compared with a control group, a group of students using micro-PROLOG-based computer-assisted learning had much higher scores for achievement (3.5 standard deviations), attitudes (1.4 standard deviations) and classroom environment (1.0–1.9 standard deviations). Khoo and Fraser (1998) used the WIHIC in evaluating adult computer application courses in Singapore among a sample of 250 people in 23 classes. Generally students perceived their computing classes as being relatively high in involvement, teacher support, task orientation and equity, but the course was differentially effective for students of different sexes and ages.

3.3. Differences between Student and Teacher Perceptions of Actual and Preferred Environment

An investigation of differences between students and teachers in their perceptions of the same actual classroom environment and of differences between the actual environment and that preferred by students or teachers was reported by Fisher and Fraser (1983). Students preferred a more positive classroom environment than was actually present for all five environment dimensions. Also, teachers perceived a more positive classroom environment than did their students in the same classrooms on four of the dimensions. The pattern in which students prefer a more positive classroom learning environment than the one perceived as being currently present has been replicated using the WIHIC and QTI among Singaporean high school students (Fraser & Chionh, 2000; Wong & Fraser, 1996), and using the WIHIC among 2498 university students in Indonesia (Margianti et al., 2001b).

3.4. Determinants of Classroom Environment

Classroom environment dimensions have been used as criterion variables in research aimed at identifying how the classroom environment varies with such factors as teacher personality, class size, grade level, subject matter, the nature of the school-level environment and the type of school (Fraser, 1994). In Asia, learning environment scores have been used in numerous studies as dependent variables. Hirata and Sako (1998) found differences between the classroom environment perceptions of at-risk students (delinquent and non-attendees) and normal students in Japan. Quek et al. (2001) reported interesting differences in the perceived learning environments of gifted and non-gifted students in Singapore. In Brunei, Khine and Fisher (2001, 2002) reported cultural differences in students' classroom environment perceptions depending on whether the teacher was Asian or Western. In Korea, Lee and Fraser (2001a, 2001b, 2002) reported the use of the SLEI, CLES and QTI in investigating differences between streams (science-oriented, humanities-oriented) in student-perceived learning environment, whereas Kim et al. (1999) used the CLES in comparing the levels of perceived constructivism in Grade 10 with Grade 11. In Indonesia, differences in classroom environment were found for students in different university subjects, namely, statistics and linear algebra classes (Margianti et al., 2001a, 2001b) and in computer science and management classes (Soerjaningsih et al., 2001a, 2001b).

Undoubtedly, the determinant of classroom environment that has been most extensively researched in Asia is student gender. Generally within-class comparisons of students' perceptions reveal that females typically have more favourable views of their classroom learning environment than do males. These studies of gender differences have encompassed numerous Asian countries, including Singapore (Fraser & Chionh, 2000; Goh & Fraser, 1998; Khoo & Fraser, 1998; Quek *et al.*, 2001; Wong & Fraser, 1996), Brunei (Khine & Fisher, 2001, 2002; Riah & Fraser, 1998), Indonesia (Margianti *et al.*, 2001a, 2001b) and Korea (Kim *et al.*, 2000).

3.5. Use of Qualitative Research Methods

Significant progress has been made in using qualitative methods in learning environment research and in combining quantitative and qualitative methods within the same study of classroom environments (Fraser & Tobin, 1991; Tobin & Fraser, 1998). For example, Fraser's (1999) multilevel study of the learning environment incorporated a teacher-researcher perspective as well as the perspective of six university-based researchers. The research commenced with an interpretive study of a Grade 10 teacher's classroom at a school which provided a challenging learning environment in that many students were from working class backgrounds, some were experiencing problems at home, and others had English as a second language. Qualitative methods involved several of the researchers visiting this class each time it met over five weeks, using student diaries, and interviewing the teacher-researcher, students, school administrators and parents. A video camera recorded activities for later analysis. Field notes were written during and soon after each observation, and team meetings took place three times per week. The qualitative component of the study was complemented by a quantitative component involving the use of a classroom environment questionnaire.

Surprisingly, the use of quantitative methods has tended to dominate Asian research into learning environments. But there are some notable exceptions in which qualitative methods have been used to advantage. Quite a few Asian studies have used qualitative methods in a minor way, such as in interviews of a small group of students aimed at checking the suitability of a learning environment questionnaire and modifying it before using it in a large-scale study (e.g., Margianti *et al.*, 2001a, 2001b; Soerjaningsih *et al.*, 2001a, 2001b; Khine, 2001). For example, in Singapore, Khoo and Fraser (1998) randomly selected 46 students for interviews in order to cross-check students' questionnaire responses and to obtain richer insights into students' perceptions of their classroom environments. Similarly, in Brunei, Khine and Fisher (2001, 2002) conducted a pilot study in which students were interviewed concerning difficulties experienced in responding to classroom environment surveys.

Wilks' (2000) study of English classes at the senior high school level in Singapore used interpretative and narrative methods to support the validity of a modified version of the Constructivist Learning Environment Survey. Also these qualitative methods, in conjuction with the questionnaire survey, were used to investigate the extent to which the teaching and learning environment in English classes (a subject called General paper) is consistent with critical constructivism.

Lee's study in Korea involved a strong quantitative component involving the administration of the SLEI, CLES and QTI to 439 students in 13 classes (four classes from the humanities stream, four classes from the science-oriented stream and five classes from the science-independent stream) (Lee & Fraser, 2001a, 2001b, 2002). However, also, two or three students from each class were selected for face-to-face interview in the humanities stream and the science-oriented stream. In the case of students in the science-oriented stream, interviews were conducted via e-mail to overcome practical constraints. All of the face-to-face interviews were audiotaped and later transcribed in Korean and translated into English. When the Korean transcriptions were completed, they were shown to the students to obtain comments and feedback from them, in order to make sure that their voices had been clearly understood. Furthermore, one class from each stream was selected for observation. While the researcher was observing, she wrote down any salient events occurring in the classroom whenever possible. Some photographs were also taken. Field notes were made and translated into English in order to transfer the images into English.

Overall, the findings from interviews and observations replicated the findings from using the learning environment surveys. The information from interviews with students mainly contributed to clarifying their replies to the questionnaire, but the interviews with teachers also contributed to drawing conclusions by providing background information about the practical situation in classrooms and schools.

In Hong Kong, qualitative methods involving open-ended questions were used to explore students' perceptions of the learning environment in Grade 9 classrooms (Wong, 1993, 1996). This study found that many students identified the teacher as the most crucial element in a positive classroom learning environment. These teachers were found to keep order and discipline whilst creating an atmosphere that was not boring or solemn. They also interacted with students in ways that could be considered friendly and showed concern for the students.

3.6. Cross-National Studies

Educational research that crosses national boundaries offers much promise for generating new insights for at least two reasons (Fraser, 1997). First, there usually is greater variation in variables of interest (e.g. teaching methods, student attitudes) in a sample drawn from multiple countries than from a one-country sample. Second, the taken-for-granted familiar educational practices, beliefs and attitudes in one country can be exposed, made 'strange' and questioned when research involves two countries. In a cross-national study, six Australian and seven Taiwanese researchers worked together on a study of learning environments (Aldridge *et al.*, 1999, 2000; She & Fisher 2000). The WIHIC and CLES were administered to 50 junior high school science classes in Taiwan (1879 students) and Australia (1081 students). An English version of the questionnaires was translated into Chinese, followed by an independent back translation of the Chinese version into English again by team members who were not involved in the original translation (Aldridge *et al.*, 2000).

Qualitative data, involving interviews with teachers and students and classroom observations, were collected to complement the quantitative information and to clarify reasons for patterns and differences in the means in each country. Data from the questionnaires guided the collection of qualitative data. Student responses to individual items were used to form an interview schedule to clarify whether items has been interpreted consistently by students and to help to explain differences in questionnaire scale means between countries. Classrooms were selected for observations on the basis of the questionnaire data, and specific scales formed the focus for observations in these classrooms. The qualitative data provided valuable insights into the perceptions of students in each of the countries, helped to explain some of the differences in the means between countries, and highlighted the need for caution when interpreting differences between the questionnaire results from two countries with cultural differences (Aldridge et al., 1999, 2000).

Researchers from Singapore and Australia also have carried out a cross-national study of secondary science classes (Fisher, Goh et al., 1997). The QTI was administered to students and teachers from a sample of 20 classes from 10 schools in each of Australia and Singapore. Australian teachers were perceived as giving more responsibility and freedom to their students than was the case for the Singapore sample, whereas teachers in Singapore were perceived as being stricter than their Australian counterparts. These differences are not surprising given the different cultural backgrounds and education systems in the two countries.

4. Conclusion: Looking Ahead

The history of the first two decades of learning environments research in Western countries shows a strong emphasis on the use of a variety of validated and robust questionnaires that assess students' perceptions of their classroom learning environment (Fraser, 1998a). The past decade of research into learning environments in Asian countries shows a very similar pattern. Asian researchers have completed numerous impressive studies that have cross-validated the main contemporary classroom environment questionnaires (the Questionnaire on Teacher Interaction, Science Laboratory Environment Inventory, Constructivist Learning Environment Survey, and What Is Happening In This Class?) that were originally developed in English. Not only have these questionnaires been validated for use in English in countries such as Singapore and Brunei, but Asian researchers also have undertaken painstaking translations and have validated these questionnaires in the Chinese, Indonesian, Korean and Malay languages. These researchers have laid a solid foundation for future learning environment research in Asia by making readily accessible a selection of valid, reliable and widely-applicable questionnaires for researchers and teachers to use in a range of languages for a variety of purposes.

While Asian researchers have an impressive record in terms of cross-validating and/or translating questionnaires that originated in English, they have been less active in the development of new instruments. In the future, there is scope for Asian researchers to make internationally significant contributions to the field by developing new questionnaires that tap the nuances and uniqueness of Asian classrooms, and/or which focus on the various information technology-rich learning environments (e.g., web-based, online learning) that currently are sweeping education worldwide. Similarly, there is scope to adapt currently widely-used paper-and-pencil questionnaires to online formats.

As in the case for Western research, the most common line of learning environment research in Asia has involved investigating associations between students' outcomes and their classroom environment perceptions. This impressive series of studies has been carried out in Singapore, Brunei, Korea and Indonesia in a variety of subject areas (science, mathematics, geography, English and computing), at various grade levels (primary, secondary and tertiary), and using numerous student outcome measures (achievement, attitudes, self-efficacy) and different learning environment questionnaires. Overall, these Asian studies provide consistent support for the existence of associations between the nature of the classroom environment and a variety of valued student outcomes. These findings hold hope for improving student outcomes through the creation of the types of classroom environments that are empirically linked to favourable student outcomes.

Whereas the use of questionnaires in Asian learning environment research has been prolific, studies which include qualitative methods such as interview and observation have been less common. Although some recent Asian studies demonstrate the benefits of combining qualitative and quantitative methods in learning environment research (Lee & Fraser, 2002; Wilks, 2000), it is desirable for learning environment research in Asia to make greater use of qualitative methods.

Feedback information based on student or teacher perceptions of actual and preferred environment has been employed in Western countries in a five-step procedure as a basis for reflection upon, discussion of, and systematic attempts to improve classroom environments (Thorp, Burden & Fraser, 1994; Yarrow, Millwater & Fraser, 1997). Surprisingly, this important practical benefit has not yet been realised in Asia as no published article could be located that reported teachers' attempts to use learning environment assessments to guide improvements in their classroom environments.

Finally, there is scope for Asian researchers to adopt, adapt or create new theoretical frames to guide the next generation of learning environment studies. For example, this could build upon Roth's (1999) advice against conceptualising the environment as being independent of the person, and on his use of lifeworld analysis as a new theoretical underpinning. Roth, Tobin and Zimmermann (in press) break with past traditions by taking researchers into the front lines of the daily work of schools, thereby assisting in bringing about change. They propose coteaching as an equitable inquiry into teaching and learning processes in which all members of a classroom community participate — including students, teachers, student teachers, researchers and supervisors. Roth and colleagues articulate coteaching in terms of activity theory and the associated first-person methodology for doing research on learning environments that is relevant to practice.

References

Aldridge, J.M. & Fraser, B.J. (2000). A cross-cultural study of classroom learning environments in Australia and Taiwan. *Learning Environments Research, 3*, 101–134.

Aldridge, J.M., Fraser, B.J. & Huang, T.-C.I. (1999). Investigating classroom environments in Taiwan and Australia with multiple research methods. *Journal of Educational Research, 93*, 48–62.

Aldridge, J.M., Fraser, B.J., Taylor, P.C. & Chen, C.-C. (2000). Constructivist learning environments in a cross-national study in Taiwan and Australia. *International Journal of Science Education*, 22, 37–55.

Asghar, M. & Fraser, B. (1995). Classroom environment and attitudes to science in Brunei Darussalam. *Journal of Science and Mathematics Education in Southeast Asia*, XVIII(2), 41–47.

Bryk, A.S. & Raudenbush, S.W. (1992). *Hierarchical linear models: Applications and data analysis method*. Newbury Park, CA: Sage.

Chua, S.L., Wong, A.F.L. & Chen, D.-T. (2001, December). *Validation of the Chinese Language Classroom Environment Inventory (CLCEI) for use in Singapore secondary schools*. Paper presented at the annual conference of the Australian Association for Research in Education, Fremantle, Australia.

Fisher, D.L. & Fraser, B.J. (1981). Validity and use of My Class Inventory. *Science Education*, 65, 145–156.

Fisher, D.L. & Fraser, B.J. (1983). A comparison of actual and preferred classroom environment as perceived by science teachers and students. *Journal of Research in Science Teaching*, 20, 55–61.

Fisher, D.L., Goh, S.C., Wong, A.F.L. & Rickards, T.W. (1997). Perceptions of interpersonal teacher behaviour in secondary science classrooms in Singapore and Australia. *Journal of Applied Research in Education*, 1(2), 2–13.

Fisher, D.L., Henderson, D. & Fraser, B.J. (1995). Interpersonal behaviour in senior high school biology classes. *Research in Science Education*, 25, 125–133.

Fisher, D., Henderson, D. & Fraser, B. (1997). Laboratory environments & student outcomes in senior high school biology. *American Biology Teacher*, 59, 214–219.

Fraser, B.J. (1979). Evaluation of a science-based curriculum. In H. J. Walberg (Ed.), *Educational environments and effects: Evaluation, policy, and productivity* (pp. 218–234). Berkeley, CA: McCutchan.

Fraser, B.J. (1990). *Individualised Classroom Environment Questionnaire*. Melbourne, Australia: Australian Council for educational Research.

Fraser, B.J. (1994). Research on classroom and school climate. In D. Gabel (Ed.), *Handbook of research on science teaching and learning* (pp. 493–541). New York: Macmillan.

Fraser, B.J. (1997). NARST's expansion, internationalization and cross-nationalization (1996 Annual Meeting Presidential Address). *NARST News*, 40(1), 3–4.

Fraser, B.J. (1998a). Science learning environments: Assessment, effects and determinants. In B.J. Fraser & K.G. Tobin (Eds.), *International handbook of science education* (pp. 527–564). Dordrecht, The Netherlands: Kluwer.

Fraser, B.J. (1998b). Classroom environment instruments: Development, validity and applications. *Learning Environments Research, 1,* 7–33.

Fraser, B. (1999). 'Grain sizes' in learning environment research: Combining qualitative and quantitative methods. In H. Waxman & H.J. Walberg (Eds.), *New directions for teaching practice and research* (pp. 285–296). Berkeley, CA: McCutchan.

Fraser, B.J. & Chionh, Y.-H. (2000, April). *Classroom environment, self-esteem, achievement, and attitudes in geography and mathematics in Singapore.* Paper presented at the annual meeting of the American Educational Research Association, New Orleans, LA.

Fraser, B.J., Fisher, D.L. & McRobbie, C.J. (1996, April). *Development, validation, and use of personal and class forms of a new classroom environment instrument.* Paper presented at the annual meeting of the American Educational Research Association, New York.

Fraser, B.J., Giddings, G.J. & McRobbie, C.J. (1995). Evolution and validation of a personal form of an instrument for assessing science laboratory classroom environments. *Journal of Research in Science Teaching, 32,* 399–422.

Fraser, B.J. & McRobbie, C.J. (1995). Science laboratory classroom environments at schools and universities: A cross-national study. *Educational Research and Evaluation, 1,* 289–317.

Fraser, B.J. & Teh, G.P.L. (1994). Effect sizes associated with micro-PROLOG-based computer-assisted learning. *Computers in Education, 23,* 187–196.

Fraser, B.J. & Tobin, K. (1991). Combining qualitative and quantitative methods in classroom environment research. In B.J. Fraser & H.J. Walberg (Eds.), *Educational environments: Evaluation, antecedents and consequences* (pp. 271–292). London: Pergamon.

Goh, S.C. & Fraser, B.J. (1996). Validation of an elementary school version of the Questionnaire on Teacher Interaction. *Psychological Reports, 79,* 512–522.

Goh, S.C. & Fraser, B. (1998). Teacher interpersonal behaviour, classroom environment and student outcomes in primary mathematics in Singapore. *Learning Environments Research, 1,* 199–229.

Goh, S.C. & Fraser, B.J. (2000). Teacher interpersonal behavior and elementary students' outcomes. *Journal of Research in Childhood Education, 14,* 216–231.

Goh, S.C., Young, D.J. & Fraser, B.J. (1995). Psychosocial climate and student outcomes in elementary mathematics classrooms: A multilevel analysis. *Journal of Experimental Education, 64*, 29–40.

Hirata, S. & Sako, T. (1998). Perceptions of school environment among Japanese junior high school, non-attendant, and juvenile delinquent students. *Learning Environments Research, 1*, 321–331.

Khine, M.S. (2001). *Associations between teacher interpersonal behaviour and aspects of classroom environment in an Asian context.* Unpublished doctoral thesis, Curtin University of Technology, Perth, Australia.

Khine, M.S. & Fisher, D.L. (2001, December). *Classroom environment and teachers' cultural background in secondary science classes in an Asian context.* Paper presented at the annual meeting of the Australian Association for Research in Education, Perth, Australia.

Khine, M.S. & Fisher, D.L. (2002, April). *Analysing interpersonal behaviour in science classrooms: Associations between students' perceptions and teachers' cultural background.* Paper presented at the annual meeting of the National Association for Research in Science Teaching, New Orleans, LA.

Khoo, H.S. & Fraser, B.J. (1998, April). *Using classroom environment dimensions in the evaluation of adult computer courses.* Paper presented at the annual meeting of the American Educational Research Association, San Diego, CA.

Kim, H.-B., Fisher, D.L. & Fraser, B.J. (1999). Assessment and investigation of constructivist science learning environments in Korea. *Research in Science and Technological Education, 17*, 239–249.

Kim, H.B., Fisher, D.L. & Fraser, B.J. (2000). Classroom environment and teacher interpersonal behaviour in secondary school classes in Korea. *Evaluation and Research in Education, 14*, 3–22.

Kim, H.B. & Kim, D.Y. (1995). Survey on the perceptions towards science laboratory classroom environment of university students majoring in education. *Journal of the Korean Association for Research in Science Education, 14*, 163–171.

Kim, H.B. & Kim, D.Y. (1996). Middle and high school students' perceptions of science laboratory and their attitudes in science and science subjects. *Journal of the Korean Association for Research in Science Education, 16*, 210–216.

Kim. H.B. & Lee, S.K. (1997). Science teachers' beliefs about science and school science and their perceptions of science laboratory learning environment. *Journal of the Korean Association for Research in Science Education, 17*, 210–216.

Lee, S.S.U. & Fraser, B.J. (2001a, March). *High school science classroom learning environments in Korea.* Paper presented at the annual meeting of the National Association for Research in Science Teaching, St. Louis, MO.

Lee, S.S.U. & Fraser, B. (2001b, December). *Science laboratory classroom environments in Korea.* Paper presented at the annual conference of the Australian Association for Research in Education, Fremantle, Australia.

Lee, S.S.U. & Fraser, B.J. (2002, April). *High school science classroom learning environments in Korea.* Paper presented at the annual meeting of the American Educational Research Association, New Orleans, LA.

Majeed, A., Fraser, B.J. & Aldridge, J.M. (in press). Learning environment and its associations with student satisfaction among mathematics students in Brunei Darussalam. *Learning Environments Research.*

Margianti, E.S., Fraser, B.J. & Aldridge, J.M. (2001a, April). *Classroom environment and students' outcomes among university computing students in Indonesia.* Paper presented at the annual meeting of the American Educational Research Association, Seattle, WA.

Margianti, E.S., Fraser, B. & Aldridge, J. (2001b, December). *Investigating the learning environment and students' outcomes in university level computing courses in Indonesia.* Paper presented at the annual conference of the Australian Association for Research in Education, Fremantle, Australia.

Moos, R.H. (1974). *The Social Climate Scales: An overview.* Palo Alto, CA: Consulting Psychologists Press.

Moos, R.H. & Trickett, E.J. (1987). *Classroom Environment Scale manual* (2nd ed.). Palo Alto, CA: Consulting Psychologists Press.

Paige, R.M. (1979). The learning of modern culture: Formal education and psychosocial modernity in East Java, Indonesia. *International Journal of Intercultural Relations, 3,* 333–364.

Quek, C.L., Fraser. B. & Wong, A.F.L. (2001, December). *Determinants and effects of perceptions of Chemistry classroom learning environments in secondary school gifted education classes in Singapore.* Paper presented at the annual conference of the Australian Association for Research in Education, Fremantle, Australia.

Riah, H. & Fraser, B. (1998, April). *Chemistry learning environment and its association with students' achievement in chemistry.* Paper presented at the annual meeting of the American Educational Research Association, San Diego, CA.

Roth, W.-M. (1999). Learning environments research, lifeworld analysis, and solidarity in practice. *Learning Environments Research, 2,* 225–247.

Roth, W.-M., Tobin, K. & Zimmermann, A. (in press). Coteaching/cogenerative dialoguing: Learning environments research as classroom praxis. *Learning Environments Research.*

Scott, R. & Fisher, D. (2001, December). *The impact of teachers' interpersonal behaviour on examination results in Brunei.* Paper presented at the Annual conference of the Australian Association for Research in Education, Fremantle, Australia.

She, H.C. & Fisher, D.L. (2000). The development of a questionnaire to describe science teacher communication behavior in Taiwan and Australia. *Science Education, 84,* 706–726.

Soerjaningsih, W., Fraser, B.J. & Aldridge, J.M. (2001a, April). *Achievement, satisfaction and learning environment among Indonesian computing students at the university level.* Paper presented at the annual meeting of the American Educational Research Association, Seattle, WA.

Soerjaningsih, W., Fraser, B. & Aldridge, J. (2001b, December). *Learning environment, teacher-student interpersonal behaviour and achievement among university students in Indonesia.* Paper presented at the annual conference of the Australian Association for Research in Education, Fremantle, Australia.

Taylor, P.C., Fraser, B.J. & Fisher, D.L. (1997). Monitoring constructivist classroom learning environments. *International Journal of Educational Research, 27,* 293–302.

Teh, G. & Fraser, B.J. (1994). An evaluation of computer-assisted learning in terms of achievement, attitudes and classroom environment. *Evaluation and Research in Education, 8,* 147–161.

Teh, G. & Fraser, B.J. (1995). Associations between student outcomes and geography classroom environment. *International Research in Geographical and Environmental Education, 4*(1), 3–18.

Thorp, H., Burden, R.L. & Fraser, B.J. (1994). Assessing and improving classroom environment. *School Science Review, 75,* 107–113.

Tobin, K. & Fraser, B.J. (1998). Qualitative and quantitative landscapes of classroom learning environments. In B.J. Fraser & K.G. Tobin (Eds.), *International handbook of science education* (pp. 623–640). Dordrecht, The Netherlands: Kluwer.

Walberg, H.J. & Anderson, G.J. (1968). Classroom climate and individual learning. *Journal of Educational Psychology, 59,* 414–419.

Walberg, H.J., Singh, R. & Rasher, S.P. (1977). Predictive validity or student perceptions: A cross-cultural replication. *American Educational Research Journal, 14,* 45–49.

Waldrip, B.G. & Wong, A.F.L. (1996). Association of attitudes with science laboratory environments in Singapore and Papua New Guinea. *Journal of Science and Mathematics in South East Asia*, *14*, 26–37.

Wilks, D.R. (2000). *An evaluation of classroom learning environments using critical constructivist perspectives as a referent for reform.* Unpublished doctoral thesis, Curtin University of Technology, Perth, Australia.

Wong, A.F.L. & Fraser, B.J. (1995). Cross-validation in Singapore of the Science Laboratory Environment Inventory. *Psychological Reports*, *76*, 907–911.

Wong, A.L.F. & Fraser, B.J. (1996). Environment-attitude associations in the chemistry laboratory classroom. *Research in Science and Technological Education*, *14*, 91–102.

Wong, A.F.L., Young, D.J. & Fraser, B.J. (1997). A multilevel analysis of learning environments and student attitudes. *Educational Psychology*, *17*, 449–468.

Wong, N.Y. (1993). Psychosocial environments in the Hong Kong mathematics classroom. *Journal of Mathematical Behavior*, *12*, 303–309.

Wong, N.Y. (1996). Students' perceptions of the mathematics classroom in Hong Kong. *Hiroshima Journal of Mathematics Education*, *4*, 89–107.

Wubbels, Th. & Brekelmans, M. (1998). The teacher factor in the social climate of the classroom. In B.J. Fraser & K.G. Tobin (Eds.), *International handbook of science education* (pp. 565–580). Dordrecht, The Netherlands: Kluwer.

Wubbels, Th. & Levy, J. (Eds.). (1993). *Do you know what you look like: Interpersonal relationships in education.* London: Falmer Press.

Yarrow, A., Millwater, J. & Fraser, B.J. (1997). Improving university and primary school classroom environments through preservice teachers' action research. *International Journal of Practical Experiences in Professional Education*, *1*(1), 68–93.

Chapter 2

MEASURING CULTURALLY SENSITIVE FACTORS OF CLASSROOM LEARNING ENVIRONMENTS WITH THE CLEQ

Darrell L. Fisher
Curtin University
Perth, Western Australia

Bruce G. Waldrip,
La Trobe University
Bendigo, Victoria, Australia

The purpose of this chapter is to describe the development and validation of an instrument designed to assess culturally-sensitive factors of science students' learning environments, and to examine associations between these factors, students' achievement of problem-solving skills, students' abilities to utilise literacy skills into science, and students' enjoyment of their science lessons. The development of a measure of culturally-sensitive factors of the learning environment, namely the Cultural Learning Environment Questionnaire (CLEQ), is described. The instrument, which was influenced by Hofstede's four dimensions of culture (Power–Distance, Uncertainty–Avoidance, Individualism, and Masculinity–Femininity) and past learning environment research, contained seven scales. With a large sample of students, the reliability and validity of the CLEQ scales were confirmed. The CLEQ confirmed the diversity of classrooms, indicated by examining the standard deviations of each scale for different classrooms. Associations were found between the CLEQ scales and problem-solving skills, students' abilities to utilise literacy skills into science and with students' enjoyment of their science lessons. The chapter concludes with a consideration of the implications for teachers.

1. Introduction

The purpose of this chapter is to describe the development and application of an instrument specifically designed to assess aspects of science students' learning environments that might be culturally sensitive. According to Phelan, Davidson, and Cao (1991), culture is the norms, values, beliefs, expectations, actions and emotional responses of a group. In fact, culture is learned, people are not born with a culture

(Stull & Von Till, 1994). Many students come from communities with widely differing cultural practices and at times the teaching and learning strategies adopted in science classrooms can be perceived as being in conflict with the natural learning strategies of the learner. However, teachers can often find it difficult to understand the "nature, causes and consequences of cultural conflicts in minority populations" (Delgado-Gaiten & Trueba, 1991, p. 24). Since teachers can use practices that may inadvertently conflict with students' previous learning patterns, home environment, mores and values, there is an increasing need for teachers to be sensitive to the important cultural milieu in which their teaching is placed (Thaman, 1993).

Increasingly, culturally-related issues are being addressed within science education in response to the fact that the student population is becoming more culturally and linguistically diverse. "Science is embedded in, and influenced by, society and culture" (Aikenhead, 1997a, p. 419). Teachers are finding that traditional approaches need to be re-considered for this changed student population. Solano-Flores and Nelson-Barber (2001) argued that assessment can be culturally biased. Lee (1999) argued that assessment and consequently science content, learning, and teaching need to be addressed for teachers to be able to cope with this increased diversity. It has further been argued that these culturally-diverse students bring a rich array of thinking, communicating and interacting that may create differences from the typical classroom (Lee, 2001). It is apparent that today's teachers need to fully understand an individual student's culture and worldviews so that learning can be made more meaningful for all students (Lee & Fradd, 1998). Aitkenhead and Jegede (1999) referred to border-crossing as the ability to make the transition from students' life-worlds into the science classroom and proposed that teachers are assisted in addressing some of these difficulties when they acknowledge students' border-crossings; help students through their border-crossing experiences; recognise that Western science is a cultural entity; and consider how students might make sense out of cultural conflicts. Science can be viewed as a cultural artefact. While there are a number of research studies in science concerning culture and education generally (Aikenhead, 1997a, 1997b; Atwater, 1993, 1996; Cobern, 1996; Maddock, 1981), comparatively little research examines the interaction that occurs between culturally sensitive factors of students' learning environment and their learning in science.

Therefore, as schools are becoming increasingly diverse in their scope and clientele, any examination of the interaction of culturally sensitive factors of students' learning environments with learning processes is timely and could be of critical importance.

2. Development of the Cultural Learning Environment Questionnaire (CLEQ)

The new instrument utilised in this study was based on previous learning environment scales that a review of research literature indicated could be culturally important (Fisher & Waldrip, 1997, 1999). The selection of these scales was guided further by an examination of literature from the fields of anthropology, sociology and management theory. The initial development of the instrument, named the Cultural Learning Environment Questionnaire (CLEQ), (Fisher & Waldrip, 1999) was guided by the following criteria:

1. Grashna (1972) argued that there are three contrasting styles of learning: dependent–independent, competitive–collaborative and avoidant–participant. Authority figures feature strongly with dependent students while independent students like to think and work on their own but do not mind listening to others. Competitive students view learning as a competitive process but collaborative students prefer cooperative learning approaches. Finally, avoidant students try to avoid becoming involved in the class while participant students look for opportunities to socialise and interact in the class context. Consistency with the important learning style dimensions identified by Grashna was one criterion.

2. Hofstede (1984) identified the important cultural dimensions of the unique environments of multicultural organisations. After collecting information with a detailed questionnaire from thousands of individuals working in multi-national corporations operating in 40 countries, Hofstede analysed the data and identified four dimensions

of culture, namely, Power Distance, Uncertainty Avoidance, Individualism, and Masculinity/Femininity. Consistency with Hofstede's cultural dimensions was another criterion.

3. In his research on human environments, Moos (1979) found that three general categories can be used in characterising diverse learning environments. This finding emerged from Moos' work in a variety of environments including hospital wards, school classrooms, prisons, military companies, university residences and work milieus. The three dimensions are: relationship dimensions which identify the nature and intensity of personal relationships within the environment and assess the extent to which people are involved in the environment and support and help each other; personal development dimensions which assess personal growth and self-enhancement; and system maintenance and system change dimensions which involve the extent to which the environment is orderly, clear in expectations, maintains control, and is responsive to change. Scales for the CLEQ were chosen to include at least one scale from each of Moos' three dimensions.

4. It was considered important that this new questionnaire should be consistent with previously developed learning environment questionnaires. Therefore, all relevant scales contained in relevant existing instruments designed for assessing the learning environment were examined for guidance in identifying suitable scales.

5. By interviewing teachers and students, an attempt was made to ensure that the CLEQ's scales and individual items were considered salient by students and teachers.

6. In order not to consume too much valuable classroom time, the CLEQ was designed to have a relatively small number of reliable scales, each containing a small number of items.

The result was a questionnaire containing 35 items in seven scales: Equity, Collaboration, Deference, Competition, Teacher Authority, Modelling, and Congruence. Each scale contains five items that are responded to on a five-point scale with the extreme alternatives of Disagree — Agree. Students are asked to indicate to what extent they agree that each item describes their science classroom. A description of each of these scales, together with a sample item from each is provided in Table 1.

Table 1. Descriptive information for each scale of the CLEQ.

Scales	Description	Sample Item	Grashna's Learning Styles	Moos' Dimension
Equity	The extent to which students perceive males and females are treated equally.	I feel that comments in class by male and female students are equally important. (+)	Competitive–Collaborative	Relationship
Collaboration	The extent to which students perceive they collaborate with other students rather than act as individuals.	I feel that it is important for the class to work together as a team. (+)	Competitive–Collaborative	Relationship
Deference	The extent to which students feel they defer to the opinions of others.	I try to say what I think the teacher wants rather than give my own opinions. (+)	Avoidant–Participant	Relationship
Competition	The extent to which the students are competitive with each other.	I like to compete against the other students. (+)	Competitive–Collaborative	Personal Development
Teacher Authority	The extent to which students perceive the teacher has authority in the classroom.	It is OK for me to disagree with the teacher. (–)	Dependent – Independent	System Maintenance & Change
Modelling	The extent to which the students expect to learn by a process of modelling.	I like teachers to show me what to do. (+)	Dependent – Independent	Personal Development
Congruence	The extent to which the students perceive learning at school matches their learning at home.	What I learn in this class helps me at home. (+)	Avoidant–Participant	System Maintenance & Change

3. Validation of the CLEQ

In order to provide validation information, the CLEQ was given to 3,785 school students in 186 classes in 67 schools. The refinement and validation of the CLEQ involved a series of principal component analyses, the purpose of which was to examine the internal structure of the set of 35 items. A principal components analysis with oblique rotation was used to generate the factors. Since the instrument was designed with seven scales, a seven-factor solution was considered. The principal component analyses, depicted in Table 2 supported the 35-item 7-scale version of CLEQ. Table 2 shows the factor loadings obtained for the sample of 3,785 school students. The percentage variances extracted and eigenvalues associated with each factor also are recorded at the bottom of each scale. The only factor loadings included in this table are those greater than or equal to the conventionally accepted value of 0.4. The conceptual distinction among the scales was justified by the principal component analysis and supported by the mean scale correlations referred to below.

In keeping with previous learning environment research, the reliability and validity of the CLEQ was also established by examining the internal consistency reliability (Cronbach alpha reliability coefficient) and discriminant validity (mean correlation with other scales) of each of the CLEQ scales. These are shown in Table 3 which indicates that for the sample of students, the alpha coefficients ranged from 0.69 to 0.86 using the individual as the unit of analyses and from 0.73 to 0.90 when the class mean was used. This suggests that each CLEQ scale has acceptable reliability, especially for scales containing a relatively small number of items. The mean correlation of a scale with other scales was used as a convenient measure of the discriminant validity of the CLEQ. The mean correlations ranged from 0.08 to 0.18 and from 0.19 to 0.30 for the two units of analysis indicating that the CLEQ measures distinct, although somewhat overlapping, aspects of the learning environment. Another desirable characteristic of the CLEQ is that it is capable of differentiating between perceptions of students in different classrooms. This characteristic was explored by analysis using one-way ANOVA, with class membership as the main effect and using the individual as the unit of analysis. The results in Table 3 indicate that each scale differentiated significantly between classrooms (p<0.01). The eta^2 statistic represents the amount of variance in environment scores accounted for by class membership and ranged from 0.08 to 0.13.

Table 2. Factor loadings for items in 35-item version of personal form for the individual student as the unit of analysis.

Item No	Equity	Collaboration	Teacher Authority	Competition	Deference	Modelling	Congruence
1.	.72						
2.	.74						
3.	.72						
4.	.71						
5.	.48						
6.		.82					
7.		.68					
8.		.63					
9.		.40					
10.		.82					
11.			.74				
12.			.52				
13.			.77				
14.			.56				
15.			.46	.40			
16.				.78			
17.				.81			
18.				.67			
19.				.80			
20.				.79			
21.					.69		
22.					.81		
23.					.77		
24.					.63		
25.					.65		
26.						.68	
27.						.73	
28.						.63	
29.						.59	
30.						.53	
31.							.72
32.							.79
33.							.79
34.							.73
35.							.77
% Variance	17.6	7.0	3.1	11.2	4.0	3.2	6.6
Eigenvalue	7.0	2.8	1.2	4.5	1.6	1.3	2.7

Factor Loadings smaller than 0.4 have been omitted.

Table 3. Scale item mean, Cronbach Alpha reliability and discriminant validity (mean correlation with other scales) and Eta^2 for each scale of the CLEQ.

Scale	No of items	Unit of analysis	Alpha reliability	Mean correlation with other scales	Scale item mean	Scale item SD	ANOVA results Eta^2
Equity	5	Individual	0.74	0.09	4.53	0.56	0.12 *
		Class	0.81	0.19	4.61	0.21	
Collaboration	5	Individual	0.74	0.12	4.08	0.70	0.08 *
		Class	0.73	0.24	4.05	0.20	
Deference	5	Individual	0.69	0.18	2.98	0.83	0.13 *
		Class	0.78	0.30	2.98	0.26	
Competition	5	Individual	0.86	0.17	3.03	1.07	0.09 *
		Class	0.90	0.24	3.01	0.41	
Teacher Authority	5	Individual	0.78	0.08	3.02	0.98	0.09 *
		Class	0.84	0.18	3.04	0.36	
Modelling	5	Individual	0.72	0.17	3.10	0.80	0.13 *
		Class	0.78	0.24	3.05	0.24	
Congruence	5	Individual	0.83	0.16	3.43	0.89	0.10 *
		Class	0.89	0.28	3.45	0.29	

n=3,785 *$p<0.01$

The scale item means for this sample are also presented in Table 3. The high means for Equity and Collaboration suggest that the students believed that the males and females were treated equally in their classes that there was a high degree of collaborative learning occurring. The slightly lower mean for Deference possibly suggests that students were willing to give their own opinions in class.

To investigate the construct validity of the CLEQ, an interpretative approach (Erickson, 1997) was adopted to investigate students' perceptions of the items and scales within the CLEQ. Using a stratified random sampling technique, schools were chosen to be involved in the interview component of this study. Three students from each school were interviewed for a maximum of 15 minutes in a fully visible position where student confidentiality could be assured, for example, in an interview or counselling room, an open classroom, on school playground seating, or library annex. After ensuring them of the confidentiality of their responses, their approval for audio-recording was obtained. A semi-structured interview was used. Students were asked for their perceptions about the nature of the classroom they would like to be in. Secondly, the interview focused on their perceptions of the scales used and thirdly, on their responses to individual items. They were asked to explain any differences between their current interview response and their written responses to the CLEQ. Finally, more detailed explanations were sought about students' perceptions about key concepts by focussing on consistency in their answers. Overall, the construct validity of the questionnaire was confirmed through these interviews with students. Detailed information on this interview process and its results have been reported previously (Waldrip & Fisher, 2000).

Thus, the CLEQ has been shown to be a valid and reliable instrument (Fisher & Waldrip, 1997, 1999, Waldrip & Fisher, 2000). The CLEQ contains 35 items, which have been construct and content validated by teachers, students and fellow researchers. The remainder of this paper describes three separate applications in which the CLEQ was used to examine the associations of its scales with students' learning outcomes in science, associations with teacher–student interactions, and differences between classrooms in metropolitan and country schools.

4. Associations between CLEQ Scales and Learning Outcomes

Past environment research has often investigated associations between student outcomes and the nature of the classroom environment (Fraser, 1994). In order to permit an examination of the predictive validity (i.e. the ability to predict student learning outcomes) of the CLEQ, 3,031 secondary science students completed the CLEQ and two outcome measures. A simple Likert-type questionnaire based on the Test of Science-Related Attitudes (Fraser, 1981) was used to assess students' attitudes towards science. In this application, the Cronbach alpha reliability of this attitude scale was 0.79 as a cognitive measure, students' enquiry skills were examined using selected items from the Test of Enquiry Skills (Fraser, 1979). Again in the application, the reliability of this measure of enquiry skills was 0.69.

Simple correlation analysis was used in examining the degree of association between each of the CLEQ scales and attitude to science and between the CLEQ scales and achievement of enquiry skills. Overall, as depicted in Table 4, most of the scales of the CLEQ were found to be associated with students' attitudes and achievement of enquiry skills. Furthermore, it can be seen that all of the significant correlations were positive except for two cases in which greater levels of perceived Deference were associated with lower scores on attitude towards science and greater levels of Teacher Authority were associated with lower scores on enquiry skills. It should be noted that in these cases, the sizes of the correlations were quite small.

Table 4. Student outcomes — simple and multiple correlation between attitudes, enquiry skills and CLEQ scales.

CLEQ scale	simple correlation(r)		standardised regression weight (β)	
	Attitudes	Enquiry skills	Attitudes	Enquiry Skills
Equity	0.25 *	0.22 *	0.14 *	0.21 *
Collaboration	0.08 *	0.06 *	-0.01	-0.01
Deference	-0.08 *	0.06 *	-0.09 *	0.07 *
Teacher authority	0.05 **	-0.06 *	-0.01	-0.11 *
Competition	0.17 *	0.11 *	0.12 *	0.11 *
Modelling	-0.04	-0.03	-0.14 *	-0.04 **
Congruence	0.32 *	0.12 *	0.24 *	0.06 *
Communication	0.31 *	0.13 *	0.20 *	0.04 *
Multiple correlation, R	0.62 *			0.31 *
R^2	0.38			0.10
Sample size	3,031	3,031	3,031	3,031

* $p<0.01$ ** $p<0.05$

These associations were further investigated using multiple regression. The magnitude and statistical significance of the regression coefficient provides a measure of the association between the outcomes and input variable when scores on the other input variables are held constant. The multiple regression analysis helps reduce the Type I error associated with simple correlational analysis. The multiple regression results were obtained when the whole set of eight learning environment predictors were separately regressed on attitudes and enquiry skills. Beta weights and significance levels are reported in Table 4 for each CLEQ scale and it is noteworthy that there is a high degree of congruence with the results of the simple correlations. Table 4 shows that the number of significant regression weights for the multiple correlation analysis was six for attitudes and seven for enquiry skills. On examination of the signs of the significant beta weights in Table 4, it can be seen that the regression weight is positive in all cases, except for Deference and Modelling with student attitude and Teacher Authority and Modelling with enquiry skills. An examination of the multiple correlations indicates that 38% of the variance in students' attitudes to their science classes could be attributed to their perceptions of the cultural factors of their learning environments. Similarly, these factors contributed to 10% of the variance in cognitive outcomes.

5. Associations between CLEQ Scales and Teacher–Student Interactions

The second application involved an investigation of the associations between the CLEQ scales and the interactions that occur between teachers and their students. Researchers in The Netherlands focused their classroom environment research specifically on the interpersonal behaviour between teachers and their students (Wubbels, Créton, & Hooymayers, 1985). The Dutch researchers investigated teacher interpersonal behaviour in classrooms from a systems perspective, adopting a theory on communication processes developed by Watzlawick, Beavin, and Jackson (1967). Within the systems perspective on communication, it is assumed that the behaviours of participants influence each other mutually. The behaviour of the teacher is influenced by the behaviour of the students and in turn influences student behaviour. Circular communication processes develop which not only consist of behaviour, but determine behaviour as well.

With the systems perspective in mind, Wubbels, Creton, and Hooymayers (1985) developed a model to map the interpersonal behaviour of teachers and their students extrapolated from the work of Leary (1957). In the adaptation of the Leary model, teacher behaviour is mapped with a Proximity dimension (Cooperation, C — Opposition, O) and an Influence dimension (Dominance, D — Submission, S) to form eight sectors, each describing different behaviour aspects. Wubbels, Créton, and Hooymayers (1985) labeled these sectors to describe the type of teacher interpersonal behaviour in each section: Leadership, Helping/Friendly, Understanding, Student Responsibility and Freedom, Uncertain, Dissatisfied, Admonishing and Strict. From this, they developed the Questionnaire on Teacher Interaction (QTI) composed of eight scales, each of six items, corresponding to the eight sectors.

The QTI has been shown to be a valid and reliable instrument (Fisher, Henderson, & Fraser, 1995; Wubbels & Levy, 1993) and it was used to assess the interactions between students and teachers in this study.

Past research has examined the associations between QTI sector scores and learning environment scores (Fisher, Henderson & Fraser, 1995; Fisher & Rickards, 1998; Rawnsley & Fisher, 1995). Preliminary data have indicated a weak relationship between school environment and QTI scores (Fisher, Fraser, Wubbels, & Brekelmanns, 1993) but there are virtually no published studies that investigate the relationship of the QTI to classroom learning environment. In this application, associations between QTI and CLEQ scales were investigated using simple correlations and multiple regression. To allow for this, a sample of 3,785 science students in 186 classes in 67 Australian secondary schools responded to both the CLEQ and the QTI. In this study, the alpha coefficients of the QTI scales ranged from 0.67 to 0.88. These figures are comparable with previously published results for the QTI in Australia where the range was from 0.63 to 0.83 (Fisher, Henderson, & Fraser, 1995).

Table 5 shows the results of these simple correlations and the more conservative mutiple regression analysis between the QTI and the CLEQ scales. Overall, as depicted in Table 5, most of the scales of the QTI were found to be associated with CLEQ scales. The QTI scale with the least associations was Student Responsibility while Admonishing, Dissatisfied and Strict had the most associations. Table 5 shows that the number of significant regression weights for the multiple correlation analysis were three to six for each CLEQ scale.

For example, an examination of Table 5 indicates that students who were more likely to see congruence between what they learned at school and home tended to have teachers who displayed more leadership, were friendlier and more helpful or strict. Students were less likely to see a congruence between school and home with teachers who they perceived to be uncertain and dissatisfied.

Equity was enhanced by teachers who were helping and friendly but retarded by too much freedom. Collaboration was more likely to occur when teachers who showed leadership were admonishing, or strict. Students were more likely to give their own opinions when the teacher was helping and friendly but were likely to defer to others when the teacher showed leadership, was uncertain, or strict. Competition was more likely to occur when teachers showed leadership, strict or uncertain behaviour or gave students more responsibility and freedom. Students deferred to the teacher's authority more when they were given more responsibility or the teacher was helping and friendly, and appeared uncertain or admonishing. Modelling tended to occur when students had responsibility and the teacher was admonishing, strict or a strong leader.

6. Differences between Metropolitan and Rural Schools

The aim of this application was to investigate differences in students' perceptions of culturally sensitive factors of the classroom learning environments in metropolitan, provincial, rural, and mining town schools. The four types of communities were defined in the following way: metropolitan schools were in the Perth city area of Australia; provincial towns were defined as communities outside the Perth metropolitan area with a population greater than 20,000; rural towns were generally centres which had a population base of less than 5,000; and mining towns were rural communities which were mining based and often had a largely transient population.

Table 5. Associations between QTI scales and CLEQ scales — simple correlations (r) and multiple correlation (β).

QTI scales	Equity r	Equity β	Collaboration r	Collaboration β	Deference r	Deference β	Competition r	Competition β	Teacher authority r	Teacher authority β	Modelling r	Modelling β	Congruence r	Congruence β
Leadership	.24*	.05	.13*	.07*	.08*	.21*	.10*	.11*	-.13*	-.02	.10*	.13*	.31*	.22*
Helping/Fr	.26*	.12*	.12*	.09*	.03#	.02	.08*	.06#	-.12*	.04	.08*	.08*	.28*	.14*
Understanding	.23*	.04	.11*	.03	.01	-.08*	.08*	.03	-.10*	.01	.08*	.02	.25*	.03
Student Resp/Fr	-.02	-.04#	.03	.02	.07*	.07*	.11*	.10*	.19*	.15*	.14*	.13*	.05*	.01
Uncertain	-.19*	-.03	-.05*	-.01	.09*	.02	.06*	.07*	.23*	.05*	.08*	.07*	-.10*	-.07*
Admonishing	-.22*	-.04	-.02	.06#	.07*	.12*	.06*	.06*	.25*	.17*	.09*	.08*	-.12	.03
Dissatisfied	-.23*	-.08*	-.04#	-.01	.07*	.00	.04#	-.01	.24*	.10*	.08*	.02	-.15*	-.05#
Strict	-.09	.01	.05*	.08*	.12*	.11*	.13*	.16*	.11*	.02	.16*	.18*	.04#	.11*
Multiple Correlation, R		.29*		.17*		.22*		.24*		.33*		.29*		.34*

# $p < 0.05$ * $p < 0.01$ n = 3,785

Measuring Culturally Sensitive Factors with CLEQ 41

The sample used contained 1,123 secondary school students in 15 metropolitan schools, 414 students in eight provincial schools, 439 students in 11 rural schools, and 102 students in 5 mining schools. All students completed the CLEQ and significant differences in CLEQ scales, due to type of school, were shown using a MANOVA.

Table 6 shows the means for metropolitan, provincial, rural and mining town students. The means of Equity and Collaboration suggest that the students believed that the males and females were treated equally in their classes and that there was a high degree of collaborative learning occurring. The lower means for Deference, Competition and Teacher Authority suggest that students were willing to give their own opinions in class, were less likely to be driven by competition and more likely to disagree with the teacher.

Table 6. Means and standard deviations of metropolitan, provincial, rural and mining town students' perceptions for CLEQ scales.

Scale	Metropolitan students mean (s.d.)	Provincial students mean (s.d.)	Rural students mean (s.d.)	Mining students mean (s.d.)
Equity	4.54 (0.55)	4.60 (0.48)	4.56 (0.57)	4.63 (0.57)
Collaboration	4.12 (0.67)	4.15 (0.69)	4.12 (0.63)	4.22 (0.63)
Deference	3.01 (0.81)	3.03 (0.81)	3.04 (0.79)	3.23 (0.82)
Competition	3.14* (1.06)	2.99 (0.95)	2.95* (1.01)	3.07 (0.94)
Teacher authority	2.98 (1.01)	3.02 (0.93)	3.09 (0.90)	2.91 (0.85)
Modelling	3.09* (0.78)	3.13 (0.77)	3.13 (0.74)	3.33* (0.78)
Congruence	3.46 (0.90)	3.49 (0.83)	3.43* (0.90)	3.70* (0.82)

* $p < 0.01$

A further examination of Table 6 indicates that mining students were more likely to model teachers than metropolitan students, but were more likely to perceive congruence between home and school. Metropolitan students were the most competitive and significantly more so than rural students who were the least likely to be competitive. Otherwise, on a collective but not individual basis, the students in classrooms in rural, provincial, and mining towns had similar perceptions of culturally sensitive factors of the learning environment.

7. Discussion

This paper is concerned with the culturally sensitive factors of the learning environments of secondary school science students. The underlying premise of this research is that if we can identify the culturally sensitive factors of the learning environments of multicultural classes, then it follows that we have an opportunity to optimise the teaching strategies to be utilised. The chapter has described the development, validation and the CLEQ and it a application in classrooms.

Associations between students' culturally sensitive learning environment and their attitudes and enquiry skills were found. Regression analysis suggested that more positive student attitudes are associated with more Equity, Competition and Congruence, and less Deference and Modelling. The development of student enquiry skills is associated with more Equity, Competition, Deference and Congruence, and less Modelling. It is apparent that highly-structured lessons which encourage students to model exactly what they have been shown are associated with lower students' attitudes towards science and achievement of enquiry skills.

The associations between teacher–student interactions and CLEQ scales were investigated using simple correlations. Overall, most of the QTI scales were found to be associated with CLEQ scales. The QTI scale with the least associations was Student Responsibility while Admonishing, Dissatisfied and Strict had the most associations. Particular teacher interactions were associated with distinct CLEQ scales. For example, students who are more likely to see congruence between what they learn at school and home tend to have teachers who display more leadership, are friendlier and more helpful or strict. Students are less likely to see a congruence between school and home with teachers who they perceive to be uncertain and dissatisfied. With a helping and friendly teacher, students perceive more equity, collaboration in their work, congruence between school and home learning, learn by modelling learn and are more likely to challenge the teacher.

The paper also has described metropolitan, provincial, rural and mining students' perceptions of culturally sensitive factors affecting their learning environments. While some aspects of the learning environment were similar, differences were found between the students from metropolitan, provincial, rural and mining areas. Mining town students were more likely to defer, model learning methods and see congruence between what was learned at home and in school. Mining students had a distinctly different perception of teacher–student interpersonal behaviours. The paper has provided information on what differences occur between metropolitan and country schools rather than why they occur. However, where there are such differences between schools, the achievement of students will most likely differ. These issues would be a worthwhile focus for future research.

Teachers need to consider how different learning conditions are utilised given students' different perceptions of learning environments. Teachers can utilise this new information to better match the teaching strategies they select for that class with the cultural expectations of their students. In practice, this would mean that the teacher, acting in the role of a school-based manager of learning, can select a balanced set of strategies and instructional approaches appropriate to the profile that has been determined by the teacher.

References

Aikenhead, G.S. (1997a). Student views on the influence of culture on science. International Journal of Science Education, 19(4), 419–428.

Aikenhead, G.S. (1997b). Towards a First Nations cross-cultural science and technology curriculum. Science Education, 81, 217–238.

Aitkenhead, G.S. & Jegede, O.L. (1999). Cross-cultural science education: A cognitive explanation of a cultural phenomenon. Journal of Research in Science Teaching, 36(3), 269–287.

Atwater, M. (1993). Multicultural science education: Assumptions and alternative views. The Science Teacher, 60(3), 32–38.

Atwater, M. (1996). Social constructivism: Infusion into the multicultural science education research agenda. Journal of Research in Science Teaching, 33(8), 821–837.

Cobern, W.W. (1996). Constructivism and non-western science education research. International Journal of Science Education, 18(3), 295–310

Delgado-Gaitan, C. & Trueba, H. (1991). Crossing cultural borders. London: The Falmer Press.

Erickson, F. (1997). Qualitative research methods in science education. In Fraser, B.J. & Tobin, K.G. (Eds.), The international handbook of science education (pp. 1155–1173). Dordrecht, The Netherlands: Kluwer.

Fisher, D., Fraser, B., Wubbels, T. & Brekelmans, M. (1993) Associations between school learning environment and teacher interpersonal behaviour in the classroom. In D. Fisher (Ed.), The study of learning environments, Volume 7 (pp. 32–42). Perth, WA: Science and Mathematics Education Centre, Curtin University of Technology.

Fisher, D. & Rickards, T. (1998). Associations between teacher-student interpersonal behaviour and student achievement and attitudes in mathematics, Mathematics Education Research Journal, 10 (1), 3–15.

Fisher, D., Henderson, D. & Fraser, B. (1995). Interpersonal behaviour in senior high school biology classes. Research in Science Education, 25(2), 125–133.

Fisher, D.L. & Waldrip, B.G. (1997). Assessing culturally sensitive factors in the learning environment of science classrooms. Research in Science Education, 27(1), 41–49.

Fisher, D.L. & Waldrip, B.G. (1999). Cultural factors of science classroom learning environments, teacher-student interactions and student outcomes. Research in Science & Technological Education, 17(1), 83–96.

Fraser, B.J. (1979). Test of enquiry skills. Melbourne: Australian Council for Educational Research.

Fraser, B.J. (1981). Test of science-related attitudes (TOSRA). Melbourne: Australian Council for Educational Research.

Fraser, B.J. (1994). Research on classroom and school climate. In D. Gabel (Ed.), Handbook of research on science teaching and learning (pp. 493–541). New York: Macmillan.

Grashna, A. (1972). Observations on relating teaching goals to student response styles and classroom methods. American Psychologist, 27, 144–147.

Hofstede, G. (1984). Culture's consequences. Newbury Park, CA: Sage Publications.

Leary, T. (1957). An interpersonal diagnosis of personality. New York: Ronald-Press.

Lee, E. (2001). Culture and language in science education: What do we know and what do we need to know? Journal of Research in Science Teaching, 38(5), 400–501.

Lee, O. & Fradd, S.H. (1998). Science for all, including students from non-English language backgrounds. Educational Researcher, 27(4), 12–21.

Lee, O. (1999). Equity implications based on the conceptions of science achievement in major reform documents. Review of Educational Research, 69(1), 83–115.

Maddock, M.N. (1981). Science education: An anthropological viewpoint. Studies in Science Education, 8, 1–26.

Moos, R.H. (1979). Evaluating educational environments: Procedures, measures, findings and policy implications. San Francisco: Jossey-Bass.

Phelan, P., Davidson, A. & Cao, H. (1991). Students' multiple worlds: Negotiating the boundaries of family, peer, and school cultures. Anthropology and Education Quarterley, 22, 224–250.

Rawnsley, D. & Fisher, D. (1997). Teacher-student relationships: Do they affect student outcomes? EQ Australia, 3, 34–35.

Solano-Flores, G. & Nelson-Barber, S. (2001). On the cultural validity of science assessments. Journal of Research in Science Teaching, 38(5), 553–573.

Stull, J.B. & Von Till, B. (1994, February). Determinants of ethnocentrism: A study of the relationship between students' exposure to other cultures and their attitudes towards cultural values. Paper presented at the annual meeting of the Western States Communication Association, San Jose, CA.

Thaman, K.H. (1993). Culture and the curriculum in the South Pacific. Comparative Education, 29(3), 249–260.

Waldrip, B.G. & Fisher, D.L. (2000). The development and validation of a learning environment questionnaire using both quantitative and qualitative methods. Journal of Classroom Interaction, 35(2), 25–37.

Watzlawick, P., Beavin, J. & Jackson, D. (1967). The pragmatics of human communication. New York: Norton.

Wubbels, T, Creton, H. & Hooymayers, H. (1985). Discipline problems of beginning teachers. Paper presented at annual meeting of the American Educational Research Association, Chicago, Il. (ERIC Document 260040).

Wubbels, T. & Levy, J. (1993). Do you know what you look like? Interpersonal relationships in education. London: Falmer Press.

Cultural Learning Environment Questionnaire (CLEQ)

This questionnaire asks you to describe you and your perceptions about your class.

This is **NOT** a test

Your opinion is what is wanted.

The questionnaire has 35 sentences about your class. For each sentence, circle the number corresponding to your response. For example:

	Disagree				Agree
I like working in groups.	0	1	2	3	4

If you agree that you like working in groups, circle 4. If you disagree and do not like working in groups, circle 0. You can also choose the numbers 1, 2 and 3 which are in-between. If you want to change your answer, cross it out and circle a new number. Thank you for your cooperation.

Item	Disagree				Agree
1. I think that both females and males make excellent teachers.	0	1	2	3	4
2. I like being taught by both male and female teachers	0	1	2	3	4
3. I feel that comments in class by male and female students are equally important.	0	1	2	3	4
4. I feel that female teachers should be shown the same amount of respect as male teachers.	0	1	2	3	4
5. I feel that male students are just as capable as female students in all class activities.	0	1	2	3	4
6. I like working in groups.	0	1	2	3	4
7. I feel that it is important for the class to work together as a team.	0	1	2	3	4
8. I would rather decide what to do as a group than to make a decision by myself.	0	1	2	3	4
9. It is important for me to be involved in class discussions.	0	1	2	3	4
10. I like to work with other students	0	1	2	3	4
11. I try to say what I think the teacher wants rather than give my own opinions.	0	1	2	3	4
12. I like to listen to what other students say before I answer a question	0	1	2	3	4
13. I try to say what the class thinks rather than give my own opinion.	0	1	2	3	4
14. It is important that I am able to answer all the questions teachers ask me.	0	1	2	3	4
15. It is important to me that I give the right answers to questions in class.	0	1	2	3	4
16. It concerns me if I don't do as well as the other students.	0	1	2	3	4
17. It is very important that I do better than the other students.	0	1	2	3	4
18. I like to compete against the other students.	0	1	2	3	4
19. I worry if I don't perform as well as other students.	0	1	2	3	4
20. I like to do my work better than other students in the class.	0	1	2	3	4

Item	Disagree				Agree
21. I like asking the teachers questions that might be hard for them to answer.	0	1	2	3	4
22. I feel that I can challenge or question what teachers say.	0	1	2	3	4
23. I like to question what teachers tell me in class.	0	1	2	3	4
24. It is OK for me to disagree with teachers.	0	1	2	3	4
25. It is OK for me to argue with teachers.	0	1	2	3	4
26. I like teachers to show me what to do.	0	1	2	3	4
27. I like to learn by copying what teachers show me.	0	1	2	3	4
28. I like to see how other students attempt problems.	0	1	2	3	4
29. I like to have teachers tell me how to work in class.	0	1	2	3	4
30. I like to watch how my classmates tackle a problem before I start.	0	1	2	3	4
31. What I learn at home helps me to do things at school.	0	1	2	3	4
32. What I learn in school helps me to do things at home.	0	1	2	3	4
33. I feel that ideas I learn at school are similar to those I learn at home.	0	1	2	3	4
34. What I learn in this class agrees with what I learn at home.	0	1	2	3	4
35. What I learn in this class helps me at home.	0	1	2	3	4

Chapter 3

LEARNING ENVIRONMENTS IN TECHNOLOGY-RICH CLASSROOMS

David B. Zandvliet
Simon Fraser University
Canada

The study of learning environments has gained considerable and widespread use as a research model suitable for investigating the effects and affects of educational innovations. An important new area for inquiry on student perceptions of the learning environment would then be the study of these in the newly emerging "information technology-rich" classrooms which are being implemented throughout the world. This chapter will report on a number of investigations into the use of Internet technologies in high school classrooms in Australia and Canada. Specifically, it combines studies of the physical and psychosocial learning environments operating within these "technological settings" and investigates interactions among the selected physical and psychosocial factors in influencing students' satisfaction with their learning. Further, the chapter will describe how both the physical and psychosocial domains may effectively enable, or alternatively, constrain the teaching methodologies used in these classrooms. The chapter reports on two phases of investigation. The first, involves a broad examination of the learning environment as measured with a questionnaire containing items measuring aspects of the psychosocial learning environment and with ergonomic site evaluations. The second phase studied interactions among physical and psychosocial variables in these measures through the use of selected and detailed case studies from the original sample. Case studies included a more detailed assessment of the physical classroom environment in tandem with classroom observations and student/teacher interviews. The studies offer insight into varied approaches to technology implementation and teaching practice.

1. Introduction

Much technological change is occurring in schools around the world and parents and educators alike have increasingly looked at new information and communications technologies (ICTs) as a technical aid in developing new models for teaching and learning. This trend towards implementing ICT in schools is related to many contemporary ideas about teaching and learning further trends towards greater individualisation in learning, the use of cooperative learning groups, integration of subject areas and an increasing focus on higher order thinking skills (Duffy & Cunningham, 1996). Continuing research in this area suggests that the successful use of computers means involving students and educators in the learning process in new ways. As with any medium, the vitality of computer use depends on good teaching. Professional knowledge about student learning, curricula, and classroom organisation go hand in hand with other information on effective computer use. Learning environment studies then may provide us with useful data in describing and improving these new technology-rich classroom environments.

The foundation for contemporary studies of classroom learning environments was developed in the independent work of Walberg and Moos over two decades ago. Over the years, many studies built on this work and applied its use to a variety of educational settings (Fraser, 1991, 1994, 1998). While methods vary greatly, many useful instruments have been developed which measure the perceptions of students and teachers of a variety of aspects of the environment (Fraser, Fisher & McRobbie, 1996). Many of these instruments include scales, which have proven to be effective predictors of student achievement, behaviours and attitudes. This work has recently been extended to an investigation of computer-assisted learning environments (see for example Khoo & Fraser, 1997; Maor & Fraser, 1996; Teh & Fraser, 1994; Zandvliet & Fraser, 1998).

Still, technological change has affected many sectors of our society outside of the educational field, including a wide variety of environments within business and industry. These changes were accompanied by the development of the science of ergonomics, which describes the physical, physiological and psychosocial factors which influence worker productivity or health (see Kroemer & Grandjean, 1997). While scattered reports from a variety of disciplines have begun to explore this idea in classrooms, until recently only a few comprehensive studies had been undertaken. New research in this area applies an ergonomic approach to the study of school classrooms and involves looking at a wide range of physical and psychosocial factors together and determining how they are influenced by new ICTs (see for example Zandvliet & Fraser, 1998; Zandvliet & Straker, 2001).

The apparent research analogies between ergonomics in workplace environments and investigations of the learning environment in schools has inspired the conceptual view used for this study of computer networked learning environments. Ultimately, the use of an educational productivity model such as that espoused by Walberg (1991) is also useful when considering a wide range of factors operating within schools. In this study, it was assumed that a variety of factors taken together influence students' satisfaction with their learning. This approach also mirrors studies undertaken in workplace environments and reflects the true complexity of today's computerised classroom environments by considering students, teachers and classroom design.

In considering the complex nature of change in any technological setting, many researchers have considered the aspects contributing to or maintaining change (e.g. Gardiner, 1989). Gardiner's model has been adapted as the conceptual framework for this study (see Figure 1). This model proposes the joint consideration of physical and psychosocial factors in the environment while considering information about the specific educational context.

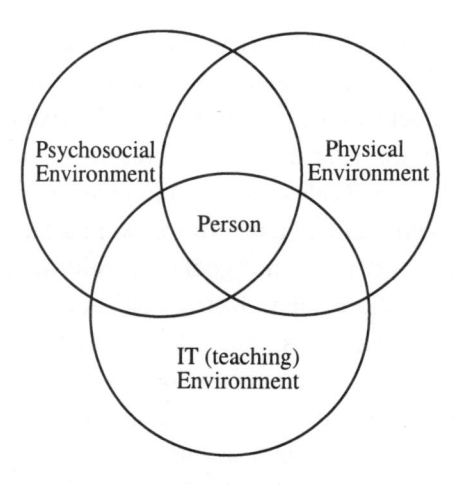

Fig. 1. A conceptual model for studying educational change.

2. Methodology

2.1. Sample Selection

A sample of 81 senior high school classes in Australia and Canada were selected for this study. The classrooms had a number of networked computers, with Internet resources that were used substantially in delivering the curriculum. For each classroom, a general profile of the learning environment was constructed by evaluating a number of psychosocial and physical factors. The results were then validated by intensive investigation of a small subset of eight classes from the original larger sample. A number of methodologies were used, including the use of questionnaires and an ergonomic inventory, student and teacher interviews, classroom observations and in-depth environmental monitoring. Student satisfaction was seen as the major dependent variable in the study as it was considered an important measure. Also, satisfaction has been shown to be a good predictor of learning in school settings and has also been shown to be an important predictor of productivity in conventional ergonomic workplace studies.

2.2. Questionnaires Assessing Psychosocial Factors

The psychosocial measures in the first phase of this study were obtained by administering five scales selected and adapted from a learning environment instrument entitled the *What is Happening in this Class* (WIHIC) questionnaire (Fraser, 1998; Fraser, Fisher & McRobbie, 1996). Specifically, the scales measuring *cohesiveness, involvement, autonomy, task orientation* and *cooperation* were selected for this study, as they are consistent with the goals of reform efforts aimed at individualising curriculum and instruction and increasing student interactions. These constructs are also consistent with variables considered important by ergonomists (Grandjean, 1988; Kroemer & Grandjean, 1997). The "actual" form was administered and the unit of statistical analysis was the class mean. Additionally, questionnaires included items assessing students' satisfaction with their learning in that environment. This was based on items selected and modified from the *Test of Science Related Attitudes* (Fraser, 1981).

2.3. Ergonomic Worksheets and Inventories

The study also initially investigated a selection of physical environmental factors through the use of a specially developed ergonomic inventory called the *Computerised Classroom Ergonomic Inventory* (CCEI) and a corresponding worksheet the *Computerised Classroom Ergonomic Worksheet* (CCEW). The inventory employed a hierarchical rating scale (scored out of five), which gave an estimate of a classroom's degree of "fit" within current published ergonomic guidelines (Kroemer & Grandjean, 1997).

The inventory includes a variety of general physical variables discretely measured or noted by the researcher, then grouped into the domains of *workspace, computer, visual* and *spatial environments,* and a rating of *overall air quality*. These considerations are those most usually noted by ergonomists (Grandjean, 1988; Kroemer & Grandjean, 1997). In order to ensure consistency, the same researcher in each setting completed inventories and worksheets and the unit of analysis was the individual classroom setting (sometimes shared by several class groupings).

2.4. Collection of Ergonomic Data

Undertaking school visits completed a general description of each physical learning environment and conducting evaluations of these computerised settings. On average, the evaluations took between 45–60 minutes to complete and were done outside of normal class time to facilitate the various physical measures needed for the ergonomic worksheets and inventories. Two instruments, the CCEI and CCEW were developed specifically for this purpose. In total, 43 evaluations were completed for this portion of the study. Each evaluation yielded scores of between 0 and 5 on each of the dimensions of *Workspace Environment, Computer Environment, Visual Environment, Spatial Environment* and the estimate, *Overall Air Quality* for that setting. In addition, the number of computers in each setting and the type of room layout were noted. An effort was also made to explore associations with the other data collected in the questionnaire portion of the study including associations between the psychosocial factors and other aspects of the physical (ergonomic) environment obtained using the Computerised Classroom Ergonomic Inventory. To do this, the class mean data for the five psychosocial scales and *Satisfaction* scale were related by using the cover sheets completed by teachers indicating locations where each class completed the questionnaires. The relevant data was then added for each of these data sets in preparation for the statistical analyses, which followed.

2.5. Case Studies of Selected Classrooms

In the second phase of this study, a small sub-sample of eight classrooms was selected from the original sample for more intense study. These case studies included detailed classroom observations of in-class behaviours followed by focused student and teacher interviews. The purpose of these was to explore, qualitatively, questions that emerged in the earlier quantitative portion of the study. More detailed physical environmental monitoring was also undertaken along with the classroom observations and interviews. These included factors of noise load as well as measures of ambient air temperature and carbon dioxide levels. Their inclusion with earlier inventory and questionnaire data completed a detailed profile for the physical and psychosocial environments in each of the selected classrooms.

3. Quantitative Results and Discussion

3.1. Validation of Scales

Initially, the five scales of the learning environment questionnaire were tested for their internal consistency (alpha reliability), discriminant validity (mean correlation of a scale with other scales) and ability to differentiate between classrooms (ANOVA eta^2 statistic). Reliability and validity data for the administration of the questionnaire to the present sample of 1404 students in 81 classes are provided in Table 1. All analyses of questionnaire data were completed using a statistical software package (SPSS version 6.1) and computed using both the individual and the class as the unit of analysis. Sample items from the questionnaire used in this study are provided as an appendix.

The analysis presented in Table 1 demonstrates that the five WIHIC scales selected for use in this study demonstrated good reliability (with values between .86 and .95 at the class level). A similar analysis of the TOSRA satisfaction scale also yielded high reliability (with a value of .74 at the class level). The discriminant validity of the WIHIC scales ranged between .16 and .52 demonstrating that these scales measured distinct, though somewhat overlapping, aspects of the psychosocial environment. Further, ANOVA methods indicated that each scale was useful in discriminating among the different classes.

Table 1. Internal Consistency (Cronbach Alpha Reliability), Discriminant Validity (Mean Correlation with Other Scales) and Ability to Differentiate Between Classes (ANOVA Results) for the five scales selected from the What is Happening in this Class (WIHIC) Questionnaire.

WIHIC Scale	Unit of Analysis	Cronbach Alpha	Discriminant Validity	ANOVA eta^2
Student Cohesiveness	Individual	.86	.46	.27*
	Class Mean	.94	.47	
Involvement	Individual	.86	.51	.23*
	Class Mean	.92	.50	
Autonomy / Independence	Individual	.77	.25	.27*
	Class Mean	.86	.16	
Task Orientation	Individual	.87	.44	.27*
	Class Mean	.95	.48	
Cooperation	Individual	.89	.50	.24*
	Class Mean	.94	.52	

*($p < .0001$)
The eta^2 statistic measures the ability of a scale to distinguish among classes.

After determining the validity and reliability of these scales, the data from all settings were pooled for further statistical analysis. As in the validation of the questionnaire, all analyses were completed using a statistical software package (SPSS version 6.1).

3.2. Descriptive Information for Scales

The completion of questionnaires by students and teachers in a wide variety of computerised learning environments provided some good descriptive information about how these learning environments were perceived. Mean scores, standard deviations, minimum and maximum values scores (for the student sample) for each questionnaire scale are provided in Table 2.

Overall, the study indicates that students viewed their learning environments positively and that these environments were characterised by relatively high levels of student cohesion, involvement, task orientation and cooperation. However, students rated the amount of autonomy and independence in these settings as low. This low rating may be in part due to any number of constraining factors, including physical (ergonomic) factors, curriculum constraints, or perhaps the inexperience of teachers working in this relatively new "technology rich" teaching context.

Table 2. Descriptive Statistics for Learning Environment Scales (WIHIC) and Student Satisfaction (TOSRA).

Questionnaire Scale	Mean	Std Dev	Minimum	Maximum
WIHIC Scales				
Social Cohesiveness	3.56	.33	2.84	4.32
Involvement	3.24	.32	2.62	3.98
Autonomy / Independence	2.29	.30	1.65	2.98
Cooperation	3.35	.35	2.51	4.24
Task Orientation	3.61	.34	2.72	4.43
TOSRA Scale				
Satisfaction	3.49	.26	2.95	4.13

N = 1404

Also, students rated their satisfaction with their learning in these computerised settings as high. When taken with the other measures of classroom environment, these data describe a generally positive learning environment. A comparison of teacher means with mean scores for students revealed a similar pattern with teachers reporting high levels of student cohesion, involvement, task orientation, cooperation and satisfaction in these classrooms. Teachers also shared the perception that students perceived relatively low levels of autonomy/independence in these classes. While the precise reasons for this trend are not known at this time, a number of hypotheses are offered later in this chapter and will help direct further research in this area.

3.3. Associations of Psychosocial Scales with Student Satisfaction

Student satisfaction with learning was an important measure for this study. Using satisfaction as the dependent variable, simple and multiple correlation analyses were used in exploring potential associations between student satisfaction and aspects of the psychosocial learning environment. Regression coefficients may provide information about the relationship between satisfaction and a particular environmental scale when all other environmental scales are mutually controlled. These data are presented in Table 3.

Table 3. Associations between five WIHIC Scales and Student Satisfaction (for class means) in terms of Simple Correlations (r) and Standardised Regression Coefficients (ß).

WIHIC Scale	r	ß
Student Cohesion	.35*	.13
Involvement	.35*	.00
Autonomy / Independence	.35*	.32*
Task Orientation	.53*	.46*
Cooperation	.31*	.11
Multiple correlation (R)	.61*	

N = 81 classes   *p < .01

As has been previously noted, students' satisfaction with learning in computerised settings was rated as high by both teachers and students. However, this study also indicates that students' satisfaction may be further influenced in a positive way by a variety of psychosocial factors.

Although many relationships were demonstrated with the simple correlation statistic, regression analyses revealed that strong independent associations were found between the factor of autonomy/independence and student satisfaction. As autonomy/independence was rated as less than optimal in these settings, this association becomes an important one. Further, a strong independent association was noted between task orientation and satisfaction. Together, these factors may influence students' satisfaction (and hence productivity) with learning.

3.4. Summary of Physical Data

Completion of classroom design evaluations using the Computerised Classroom Ergonomic Inventory (CCEI) revealed much descriptive information about computerised settings in schools. Overall, they tended to rate high on the quality of the computer equipment selected and for the quality of the spatial environment. However, ratings of *Workspace environment* in these settings were rated as fairly low. This would seem to indicate that this feature of computerised classrooms is in need of further attention by educators.

The collection of ergonomic data collected in computerised classrooms reveals important trends in the implementation of ICT in schools. These data indicated that schools rated highest in their choice of computer equipment (*Computer environment*) and the proper arrangement of this equipment throughout the room (*Spatial Environment*). On average, the studied schools were evaluated as deficient in the student work spaces where these computers are used (*Work Space Environment*) and other physical measures (*Visual Environment* and *Air Quality*) varied widely by location but were frequently also found to be less than adequate.

Further, the evaluation of computer settings in schools also indicated that the average number of computer work stations in a setting was 22. The preferred room layout was categorised as a 'peripheral lab' (27 out of a total 43 settings), which is described as typically featuring computers located along the peripheral walls of a classroom with working students facing away from the centre of the room. Next in popularity was a layout described as a 'linear layout' (9 settings), which had students and machines in rows with students facing the front of the classroom. A smaller number of classrooms had computers arranged in smaller 'clusters' around the classroom.

3.5. Associations Between Number of Workstations and Physical Factors

After considering the overall suitability of the computerised settings in question, an effort was made to explore associations with the number of computers in each setting and ergonomic data. Using multiple linear regression techniques and a computer statistical software package (SPSS Version 6.1) the *Number of work stations* was identified as a dependent variable against the set of five physical variables obtained from the CCEI (*Workspace, Computer, Visual and Spatial Environments* and *Overall Air Quality*). These statistics are presented in Table 4.

Table 4. Associations between Physical Variables (from CCEI) and Number of Workstations in terms of Simple Correlations (r) and Standardised Regression Coefficients (ß).

Physical factor	r	ß
Workspace environment	-.26*	-.02
Computer environment	-.60**	-.65**
Visual Environment	-.02	.12
Spatial Environment	-.36**	-.13
Overall Air Quality	-.05	.19
Multiple correlation (R)	.66**	

N = 43 locations
$p < .05*$, $p < .01**$

Interpretation of the results presented in Table 4 demonstrates a fairly strong (though negative) association between the *Computer Environment* (suitability of computing equipment) and increasing numbers of computers work stations in the learning environment. Simple correlations between the number of workstations and the quality of the workspace and visual environments are also noted.

The strong negative association between the number of computers in a setting and the measure *Computer Environment* (the quality of equipment) is an interesting one. This association probably reveals a common-sense economic relationship involving the purchase of computer equipment. For example, if a school has a fixed amount of funding for computers, it follows that if they buy more equipment, the quality of that equipment would be lower. This point is an important one as this is a trade off that schools are often forced to make.

3.6. Associations Between Number of Workstations and Psychosocial Factors

A similar multiple and linear regression analysis was repeated using *Number of work stations* as a dependent variable regressed against five psychosocial variables and *Satisfaction* scale derived from the questionnaire data. These statistics are presented in Table 5.

Table 5. Associations between Psychosocial Scales and Satisfaction with Number of Workstations in terms of Simple Correlations (r) and Standardised Regression Coefficients (ß).

WIHIC Scale	r	ß
Autonomy / Independence	-.27*	-.21
Cooperation	.01	.16
Involvement	-.15	-.38**
Satisfaction	-.17	-.18
Social Cohesion	.09	.15
Task Orientation	.03	.22
Multiple correlation (R)	.40*	

N = 81 classes
$p < .05^*$, $p < .01^{**}$

The data presented in Table 5 indicate that the psychosocial scale *Involvement* was negatively associated with increasing numbers of computer workstations in a setting. While other comparisons were made, no positive associations were demonstrated between increasing numbers of computers and the psychosocial scales described or with the attitudinal scale *Satisfaction*. Also, an additional simple (though negative) correlation with autonomy independence was noted.

The negative associations noted between the number of computers and the psychosocial scale, *Involvement* is important. This relationship would seem to advise that increasing the number of computers in a setting (beyond some optimal number) is potentially counter-productive. This idea gains greater importance when it is considered that no positive associations with the number of computers were described in this research, or in the larger study. From these data, it would appear that the more individualised computing becomes, the less involved students are with their lessons.

3.7. Associations between Physical and Psychosocial Factors

While ergonomic evaluations of physical learning spaces revealed much about the learning environment, relating this information with the psychosocial questionnaire data also revealed a number of surprising associations among physical and psychosocial measures. Simple correlations and multiple linear regression analyses were computed to explore possible associations between the measured physical and psychosocial factors. Each of the five psychosocial factors in turn was used as a dependent variable and then related to the set of five physical variables recorded during the ergonomic evaluations. These data are presented in Table 6.

Results of the regression analysis between the physical factors on the CCEI and the psychosocial variable *Involvement* at the class level revealed no significant associations. However, a number of other important and unexpected associations between the physical (ergonomic) factors and psychosocial factors were found.

In the first instance, a number of significant independent associations between the "work space environment" and student autonomy, cooperation and task orientation were noted. Further, significant independent associations between the "visual environment" and student autonomy, student cohesion and task orientation were also noted. These data suggest that the physical attributes of a learning space may influence the psychosocial environment within it and, further, may indirectly influence students' satisfaction with learning.

Table 6. Associations between Physical Classroom Variables (from the CCEI) and Psychosocial Variables (WIHIC) in terms of Simple Correlations (r) and Standardised Regression Coefficients (ß).

Physical variables	Student Cohesion		Autonomy Independence		Involvement		Task Orientation		Cooperation	
	r	ß	r	ß	r	ß	r	ß	r	ß
Workspace Environment	.08	.26	.28*	.30*	.17	.15	.22	.28*	.38**	.43**
Visual Environment	.27*	.31*	.12	.36**	.22	.24	.31**	.38**	.05	-.10
Spatial Environment	.03	-.03	.04	.13	.04	-.03	.07	.05	.17	.06
Computer Environment	.00	-.14	.18	.10	.09	.01	-.08	-.29*	.06	-.18
Overall Air Quality	.03	-.19	.22	.25	.05	-.13	.04	-.05	.18	.06
Multiple correlation (R)	.37		.44*		.27		.45**		.42*	

N = 81 classes
**$p < .01$ *$p < .05$

4. Case Study Findings and Discussion

In an effort to obtain more detailed qualitative descriptions of the learning environment, a small sub-sample of classrooms (8) was selected from the original sample for more intense case study. These included detailed classroom observations of in-class behaviours coupled with focused student and teacher interviews. The purpose of these was to further explore questions, which developed in the earlier quantitative portion of the study. More detailed physical environmental monitoring was also undertaken along with the classroom observations and interviews. These included measuring factors of noise load as well as ambient air temperature and quality. Their inclusion with earlier inventory and questionnaire data completed a detailed profile for the physical and psychosocial environments in each of the selected classrooms while also allowing for comparisons among case study locations.

4.1. Types of Data

The detailed case study of computerised learning environments in schools yielded much descriptive information about the educational context of these settings. The methodologies employed for these case studies included classroom observations with task analysis, detailed monitoring of physical environmental factors and, finally, focused interviews with students and teachers. These methods were adapted from those used in ergonomic evaluations (see Chapanis, 1996) and from previous studies of classroom learning environments.

In order to organise and synthesise the diverse data recorded for each of the study locations and to facilitate discussion about the relationships among these data, the use of a case study "template" was used to present this descriptive and contextual data (see sample in appendix). This template gives some categorical information about the study location (e.g. government or independent school, country, and school identification number), and then it continues to detail the data collected about each setting. A sample case study "template" is included as appendix.

4.2. Synthesis of Physical Findings

The eight locations selected for case study varied greatly in size, shape and number of computers. They included computer laboratories with many computers, classrooms with computers installed and one library setting. Overall, the number of computers in these locations ranged from a minimum of 10 machines in one library setting to a maximum of 30 in a class setting. The average number of computers per class was 23.

Throughout the larger study, a number of different, though typical, room layouts were noted during the completion of ergonomic evaluations. These layouts are represented in the sample case studies and illustrated in diagrams. The most common layout is described as a "peripheral lab" in this study. This type of lab is characterised by computer workstations positioned along the outer wall of a room. A second common layout was termed the "linear" arrangement and featured workstations in rows so that seated students would face the front of the room.

4.3. Synthesis of Task Analyses

Each of the eight case study locations was subjected to a task analysis, which involved sampling student and teacher behaviours (or tasks) during each minute of observation. Each classroom analysis involved two observation sessions of 50 minutes each where the tasks and behaviours of both students and teachers were noted and categorised on a coded observation sheet (see Chapanis, 1996). When these data are tabulated and summed across the eight cases, a time analysis of the types of activities typically occurring in computerised classrooms can be described. The data related to student tasks are presented in Fig. 2 whereas the data related to teacher tasks is presented in Fig. 3.

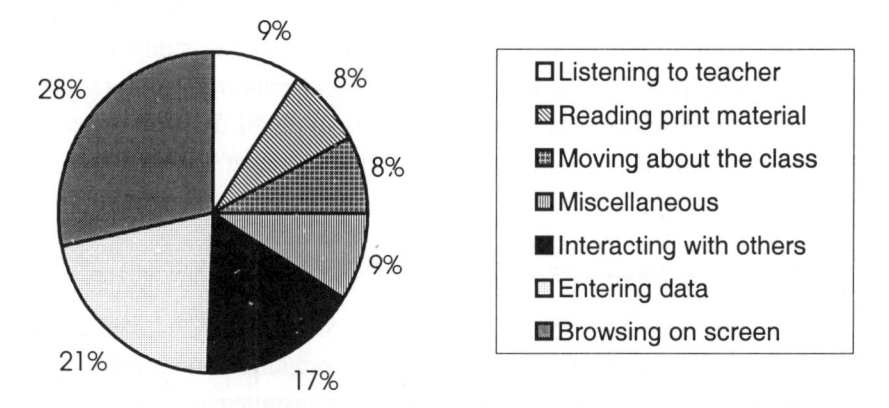

Fig. 2. Student Tasks in Computerised Classrooms (summary of all cases)

An interpretation of the chart presented in Fig. 2 indicates that, overall, students spend most of their time interacting directly with the computer (the tasks of "browsing on screen" and "entering data" together account for nearly 50% of the total time spent in class). Interacting with other students was also an important portion of a class — occupying about 18% of the total time. Miscellaneous or off-task behaviours were also notable and occupied on average, 9% of class time. Finally, students spent the least amount of their time listening to the teacher lecture, reading print or moving about in the class.

Technology-Rich Classrooms

The manner in which teachers spend their time in computerised settings (Fig. 3) was markedly different from students and is also of interest. An interpretation of the chart presented in Fig. 2 indicates that overall, teachers spend most of their time interacting one-on-one with students as they work on computers (the tasks of "moving about the room" and "interacting with students" account for fully 63% of a teacher's total time in class). Of next importance in teacher tasks was lecturing, although this activity occupied only 11% of a teacher's time. The remainder of time was spent doing a number of different tasks including entering data into computers, reading print materials or browsing on the internet. Interestingly, teachers too were observed in miscellaneous off-task behaviours and these on average occupied 5% of their time.

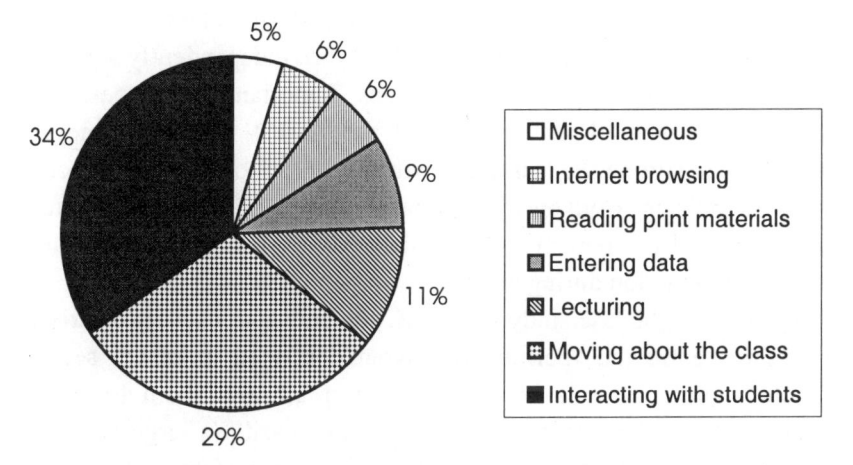

Fig. 3. Teacher Tasks in Computerised Classrooms (summary of all cases).

4.4. Interview Data

A number of trends may also be noted from a synthesis of the comments provided in the student and teacher interviews. While individuals were asked questions directly related to the use of IT in that setting, they were also asked to comment on aspects of their physical and psychosocial environments. These data were the last type to be considered in the case study portion of the study.

The type of course delivered in each of the settings varied to include information technology courses and science courses, as well as a humanities and business management course. Despite the range of curricula, most teachers had assigned to their students project or assignment work for which information or ideas were to be derived from browsing or searching on the internet. In one location, course information, assignments and other resources were also provided on-line. In some locations, the assignments given were individualised or open-ended (or based on a theme). One teacher (from case study one) allowed students to browse the internet as a reward for completing other course work. Many of the described settings had teachers and students who reported a positive learning environment in the class. These environments were characterised by cooperative groups of students who were permitted to interact freely with others during class periods. Both students and teachers described a need to work independently sometimes and at other times work in small groups. Importantly, the "peripheral" type layouts were those, which had the fewest number of negative comments regarding the learning environment, but one teacher described these as noisier. Conversely, "linear" layouts studied seemed to be characterised by comments from students or teachers indicating a desire for more interaction during classes.

Over the eight case study locations, students and teachers clearly had a preference for the "peripheral" layout described in earlier sections. Teachers preferred this arrangement as it allowed them to monitor student work and move about the room more easily (a large percentage of their tasks in these settings). Students also preferred this type of arrangement as it allows for easy movement and interaction among students as they work on individual projects or assignments. In one "linear" type layout (case study 2), students indicated that they were restricted from moving around and talking to other people. Their teacher expressed a desire to change the layout as it prevented students from working in groups.

Another factor, which was an issue for some locations, was the number of workstations present in that setting. In one location (case study 6), the number of computers (10) was considered insufficient by students and contributed to some frustration as students were denied opportunities to access the Internet. In another location (case study 3), the number of workstations was deliberately limited (to 17) in an attempt to stimulate more cooperation and interaction among students while they worked (despite more machines being readily available at the school).

Also, concerns about monitor height were described in two locations where some monitors were placed to be viewed from a standing position or from an elevated stool rather than from a chair. Students and/or teachers in half of the locations further described inadequacies in the ventilation or climate control of a setting, with three of these commenting that the room was too hot and stuffy. In one location, it was pointed out that the ventilation system caused excessive down drafts.

4.5. Discussion and Summary

The case study data presented and synthesised in this section reveals a great deal about the educational context of the larger study of Internet classrooms. First, it describes a range of ways in which educators are using these settings across a range of subject disciplines. Second, it highlights variations and potential deficiencies found in these environments (in both the physical and psychosocial sense). Also, the inclusion of qualitative data from this portion of the study complements the largely quantitative description of the psychosocial and physical learning environments in computerised classrooms.

The common link that teachers drew between the physical environment of a classroom setting (in particular its layout) and the teaching and learning environment within it suggests that the way in which a room is arranged or 'layed out' is an important (and often overlooked) consideration. Many case studies were characterised by room layouts, which were conducive to, or restricted, the activities performed in those settings. Teachers and students consistently preferred peripheral type layouts and expressed the need for adequate workspaces and for freedom to move around a room.

Task analyses conducted in the case study locations revealed a pattern of tasks and behaviours, which are likely to be familiar to teachers working in computerised settings. Students were largely involved in individual or small-group project work, with their teachers constantly moving about the room and interacting with the students. Such patterns of behaviour indicate a largely student-centred approach to teaching and learning, with an emphasis on process and problem solving. In such settings, teachers more closely resemble "project facilitators" rather than their traditional role as "providers of information".

Finally, it is most important to restate that a number of important physical environmental measures conducted during the case studies revealed deficiencies in the working environment of students and teachers (in both countries). These included problems with lighting and workspace requirements in addition to concerns about air quality (carbon dioxide levels) of a classroom setting.

The deficiencies noted are most likely due to the limited consideration on the part of schools to the physical classroom environment when implementing computer technology. Such concerns are often overruled by decisions regarding the type or quantity of equipment purchased for schools and its cost-effective set-up, and its ongoing security. Such concerns may ultimately negate potential positive aspects of computer use in schools.

5. Conclusions and Summary

The work presented in this chapter provides a significant contribution to the literature in that it jointly considered physical and psychosocial learning environments in a single study while combining both qualitative and quantitative methods. The research is distinctive because of its holistic and ecological approach to the study of an important new learning environment: the technological classroom. By including questionnaire data with case studies and evaluations of physical classroom factors, its approach mirrors ergonomic methods, which have proven effective in a wide variety of research in other settings, including technological settings within business and industry. Finally, this study identifies some important physical and psychosocial factors for inclusion in a new and developing model of educational productivity.

Case study data in this study provided important, detailed information about the psychosocial environments in these locations.

They also may be considered "typical" or representative of the broader range of locations involved in the administration of the learning environment questionnaire in the first portion of the study. Questionnaire data revealed quantitative associations between student satisfaction and the psychosocial variables of autonomy/independence and task orientation. To some extent these finding were also triangulated by comments obtained in the student and teacher interviews.

The representative case study data also provided important information about the physical (or ergonomic) environments found in the studied classrooms and should be considered "typical" of the broad range of locations in the larger sample. When linked to the questionnaire data, significant associations were revealed between the visual and work environments and the psychosocial factors of student cohesion, autonomy, task orientation and cooperation. This would seem to point out that the consideration of workspace and classroom design in computerised classrooms is an important educational endeavour and may significantly influence the learning environment in these settings.

References

Chapanis, A. (1996). *Human factors in systems engineering*. New York: John Wiley and Sons.

Duffy, T.M. & Cunningham, D.J. (1996). *Constructivism: Implications for the Design and Delivery of Instruction*. In D. Jonassen (Ed.), *Handbook of Research for Educational Communications and Technology*. New York, NY: Simon & Shuster Macmillan.

Fraser, B.J. (1981). *Test of science related attitudes*. Melbourne: Australian Council for Educational Research.

Fraser, B.J. (1991). *Two decades of classroom environment research*. In B.J. Fraser and H.J. Walberg, (Eds.), *Educational environments: Evaluation, antecedents and consequences*. London: Pergamon, 3–27.

Fraser, B.J. (1998). *Science learning environments: Assessment, effects and determinants*. In B.J. Fraser and K.G. Tobin, (Eds.), *International handbook of science education*. Dordrecht, Netherlands: Kluwer Academic Publishers, 527–564.

Fraser, B.J. (1994) *Research on classroom and school climate.* In D. Gabel (Ed.) *Handbook of research on science teaching and learning,* New York: Macmillan, 493–541.

Fraser, B.J., Fisher, D.L. and McRobbie, C.J. (1996, April). *Development, validation and use of personal and class forms of a new classroom environment instrument.* Paper presented at the annual meeting of the American Educational Research Association, New York.

Fraser, B.J., Giddings, G.J. & McRobbie, C.J. (1996). Development, and cross-national validation of a laboratory classroom environment instrument for senior high school science. *Science Education,* 77, 1–24.

Gardiner, W.L. (1989). *Forecasting, planning, and the future of the information society.* In P. Goumain, (Ed.), *High Technology Workplaces, Integrating technology, management, and design for productive work environments* (pp. 27–39). New York: Van Nostrand Reinhold.

Goumain, P. (1989). *Changing environments for high-technology workplaces.* In P. Goumain, (Ed.), *High Technology Workplaces, Integrating technology, management, and design for productive work environments* (pp. 1–23). New York: Van Nostrand Reinhold.

Khoo, H.S. & Fraser, B.J. (1997, April). The learning environments associated with computer application courses for adults in Singapore. Paper presented at the annual meeting of the American

Kroemer, K. & Grandjean, E. (1997). *Fitting the task to the human: A textbook of occupational ergonomics* (5th ed.). London: Taylor and Francis.

Maor, D. & Fraser, B.J. (1996). Use of classroom environment perceptions in evaluating inquiry-based computer assisted learning. *International Journal of Science Education,* 18, 401–421.

Teh, G. & Fraser, B.J. (1994). An evaluation of computer-assisted learning in terms of achievement, attitudes and classroom environment. Evaluation and Research in Education, 8, 147–161.

Walberg, H.J. (1991). *Educational productivity and talent development.* In B.J. Fraser & H.J. Walberg, (Eds.), *Educational environments: Evaluation, antecedents and consequences.* London: Pergamon, 93–109.

Zandvliet, D. & Fraser, B.J. (1998, April). The physical and psychosocial environment associated with classrooms using new information technologies. Paper presented at the annual meeting of the American Educational Research Association, San Diego, CA.

Zandvliet, D.B. & Straker, L. (2001, July). Physical and psychosocial ergonomic aspects of the learning environment in information technology rich classrooms. *Ergonomics.*

What is Happening in this Class
(while we are using computers)

Sample Items

Student Cohesiveness
Friendships are made among students in this class.
Students in this class know each other.

Involvement
Students discuss ideas in class.
Students give their opinions during class discussions.

Autonomy/Independence
Students have a say in how their class time is used.
Students have a say in deciding what activities they do.

Task Orientation
Students know what has to be done in this class.
Getting a certain amount of work done is important to this class.

Cooperation
Students cooperate with each other when doing assignment work.
Students share books and resources with each other when doing assignments.

Satisfaction (adapted from TOSRA)
I look forward to this class.
The lessons in this class are fun.

Sample case study

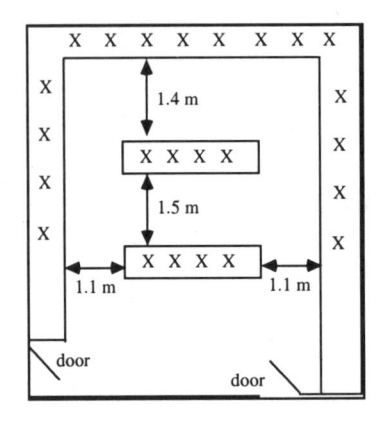

```
X X X X X X X X
X        ↑           X
         1.4 m
X                    X
     ┌─────────┐
     │ X X X X │
X    └─────────┘     X
         ↑
         1.5 m
X        ↓           X
     ┌─────────┐
     │ X X X X │
     └─────────┘
  ←─┤           ├─→
  1.1 m       1.1 m
  \ door
                door \
```

School 4 - Lab D3 (Peripheral lab)
School Location: Western Australia
School Type: Independent
<u>Physical and Environmental Measures</u>
Lighting: (475 -- 490 lux)
No. of Workstations: (24)
Carbon dioxide: (1000 ppm)
Mean Temperature: (22.4 C)
Relative humidity: (75 %)
<u>Ergonomic Inventory:</u>
(max. score = 5)
Workspace Environment   (1)
Computer Environment   (5)
Visual Environment   (5)
Spatial Environment   (4)
Overall Air Quality   (3)

Task Analysis Summary:

Teacher
Presenting or lecturing: (13.0 mins.)
Moving about room: (25.0 mins.)
Interacting with others: (25.0 mins.)
Reading Print material: (1.0 mins.)
Browsing (computer):   (8.0 mins.)
Entering data (computer):   (26.0 mins.)
Miscellaneous (off task):   (2.0 mins.)
Students
Listening to teacher: (10.0 mins.)
Moving about room: (5.0 mins.)
Interacting with others: (7.0 mins.)
Reading Print material: (6.6 mins.)
Browsing (computer):   (32.6 mins.)
Entering data (computer):   (34.8 mins.)
Miscellaneous (off task):   (4.0 mins.)

Questionnaire Responses:
(max. score =5):
Social Cohesion   (3.7)
Involvement   (3.3)
Autonomy / Independence   (1.9)
Task Orientation   (3.8)
Cooperation   (3.2)
Satisfaction   (3.6)

Interview comments:

Student IT Tasks

Students described their tasks as finishing off their current projects and assignments. One of these projects was the design of a personal home page. The teacher described that the intent of the project was for students to learn how to use another application (eg. Netscape). Students are rewarded for completing their projects with further work on the Internet.

Psychosocial environment

The teacher characterised the class as having a good psychosocial climate. Students said that they often work together (by choice) on their assigned projects.

Physical environment

Students believed that the class room layout was great, although they thought that the position of the projection panel should be changed. The teacher also liked the physical layout of the room because students' screens could easily be seen while they were working. Students and teachers both agreed that it would be better to have a climate controlled setting in the classroom.

Chapter 4

TEACHER EXPERIENCE AND THE TEACHER–STUDENT RELATIONSHIP IN THE CLASSROOM ENVIRONMENT

Mieke Brekelmans
Theo Wubbels
Perry den Brok

Utrecht University
The Netherlands

In the classroom environment, the interpersonal relationship between teacher and students is an important element contributing to the learning process of students. In this chapter, we explore the significance of the experience of the teacher in realising relationships with students, appropriate from the perspective of student outcomes. We use data from a cross-sectional and a longitudinal study to analyse differences between teachers in degree of dominant and co-operative behaviour in different stages of their professional career.

The results show that teachers' ideals of the teacher–student relationship are rather stable during the teaching career; they consistently strive for a high degree of dominance and co-operativeness. The actual teacher–student relationship however changes during the career. On average, there is a significant increase in dominant behaviour of teachers during the first decade of their career: a movement towards the ideal teacher–student relationship. After this period, dominance stabilises. On average, there is no change in co-operative behaviour. There is no shift towards the ideal as experience grows. Implications of these findings for professional development of teachers in view of improving the classroom learning environment include training of dominant behavioural patterns and differentiation of accompanying cognitions and attitudes for pre- and in-service beginning teachers. During the career, the cognitive component to training and staff development may be more important in order to support teachers to select appropriate skills in particular situations.

1. Introduction

In the classroom environment, the interpersonal relationship between teacher and students is an important element contributing to the learning process of students. Earlier studies investigating the associations between interpersonal relationships and student outcomes have shown that particular teacher–student relationships are more effective for student achievement and attitudes than others.

In this chapter, we explore the significance of the experience of the teacher in realising appropriate relationships with students. Knowledge of how teachers change during their professional career can help teacher educators understand the needs and abilities of teachers at different points in their careers. It can serve as the basis for customizing pre- or in-service programs: planning interventions, arranging instructional content and sequence; and so on. This can contribute to general improvement of the learning environment. Appropriate teacher–student relationships is an important means for preventing discipline problems and fostering professional development (Rosenholtz, Bassler & Hoover-Dempsey, 1986).

First, we present the theoretical framework we use to study the teacher–student relationship. Next, we characterise an appropriate relationship between a teacher and his or her students, based on results of studies investigating the associations between the teacher–student relationship and student outcomes. To explore the significance of the experience of the teacher in realising appropriate interpersonal relationships with students, we use data from a cross-sectional and a longitudinal study to analyse differences between teachers in different stages of their professional career. We end with a discussion of our findings for professional development of teachers in view of improving the classroom learning environment.

2. Theoretical Framework for Studying the Teacher–Student Relationship

To investigate the teacher–student relationship in the classroom environment, we study teaching from an interpersonal perspective. In our conceptualisation of the interpersonal perspective on teaching, some concepts of the so-called systems approach to communication (Watzlawick, Beavin & Jackson, 1967) are important.

In line with the systems approach to communication, we conceive classroom groups as ongoing systems. For ongoing systems, a certain stability is important for their continued existence. When students meet a teacher in a new class, they will be relatively open to any impression the teacher can make. The students are relatively open because the context of the classroom will raise certain (stereotypical) expectations for the role of the teacher. After the first lesson, the students will have ideas about the pattern of relationship with this particular teacher, based on experiences during the first lesson. For the second lesson, the teacher may behave differently and students may consequently adjust their ideas about the teacher. After a few lessons in a new class, tentative ideas about the teacher will have stabilised and students can tell what kind of teacher someone "is". This stability of perceptions equally applies to the teacher's ideas about the students. Once the tone is set, it is difficult to modify. Both students and teachers resist against changes (see also Blumenfeld & Meece, 1985; Doyle, 1986). To describe these kinds of processes, the systems approach to communication distinguishes different levels of communication. The lowest level consists of messages, one question, assignment, response, gesture, etc. The intermediate level is that of interactions, chains of several messages. When the interactions show recurrent patterns and some form of regularity, one has arrived at the pattern level. It is this pattern level that is important in describing the rather stable interpersonal relationships that determine the working atmosphere of classrooms.

In the systems approach to communication, the focus is on the effect of communication on the persons involved (pragmatic aspect). This pragmatic orientation shows up in our conceptualisation of the interpersonal perspective in the importance of the perception of students of the behaviour of their teacher. To be able to describe the perceptions students have of the behaviour of their teacher, Wubbels, Créton and Hooymayers (1985, see Wubbels & Levy, 1993) developed a model. They applied a general model for interpersonal relationships designed by Leary (1957) to the context of education. The Leary model has been extensively investigated in clinical psychology and psychotherapeutic settings (Strack, 1996). It has proven to be a rather complete model to describe interpersonal relationships (see e.g. Foa, 1961; Lonner 1980). In the Leary model, two dimensions are important. Leary called these the Dominance–Submission axis and the Hostility–Affection axis. While the two dimensions have occasionally been given other names — Brown

(1965) used Status and Solidarity, Dunkin and Biddle (1974) Warmth and Directivity — they have generally been accepted as universal descriptors of human interaction. The two dimensions have also been easily transferred to education. Slater (1962) used them to describe pedagogical relationships, and Dunkin and Biddle (1974) demonstrated their importance in the teachers' efforts to influence classroom events.

Adapting the Leary model to the context of education, Wubbels *et al.* (1985) used the two dimensions, which they called Influence (Dominance –Submission) and Proximity (Opposition – Co-operation) to structure the perception of leadership, helpful/friendly behaviour, understanding behaviour, giving students freedom and responsibility, uncertain, dissatisfied, admonishing and strict behaviour. Figure 1 presents a graphic representation of the model of Wubbels *et al.*, the Model for Interpersonal Teacher Behaviour.

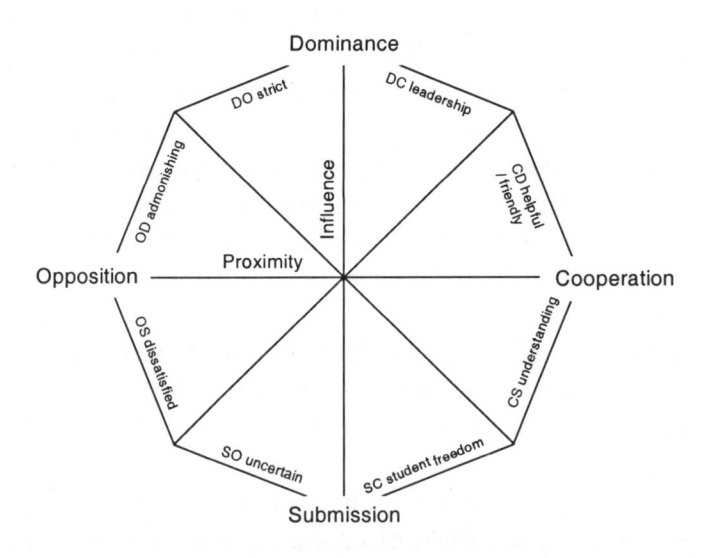

Fig. 1. The model for interpersonal teacher behaviour.

The sections are labelled DC, CD, etc. according to their position in the co-ordinate system (much like the directions in a compass). For example, the two sectors 'leadership' and 'helpful/friendly' are both characterised by Dominance and Co-operation. In the DC sector, the Dominance aspect prevails over the Co-operation aspect. A teacher displaying DC behaviour might be seen by students as enthusiastic, motivating, and the like. The adjacent CD sector, however, includes behaviours of a more co-operative and less dominant type; the teacher might be seen as helpful, friendly, considerate.

The model can be used to describe teaching at the message, interaction and pattern level. When describing patterns in interpersonal relationships in classrooms, eight different types of relatively stable patterns (interpersonal profiles) could be distinguished in both Dutch and American classes (Brekelmans, 1989; Brekelmans, Levy & Rodriguez, 1993), named Directive, Authoritative, Tolerant/ Authoritative, Tolerant, Uncertain/Tolerant, Uncertain /Aggressive, Drudging, and Repressive. These patterns can be characterised in terms of the two dimensions in the Model for Interpersonal Teacher Behaviour. In Fig. 2, we summarise each of the eight types by means of a main point indicated by the first letters of their names in the co-ordinate system of the two dimensions.

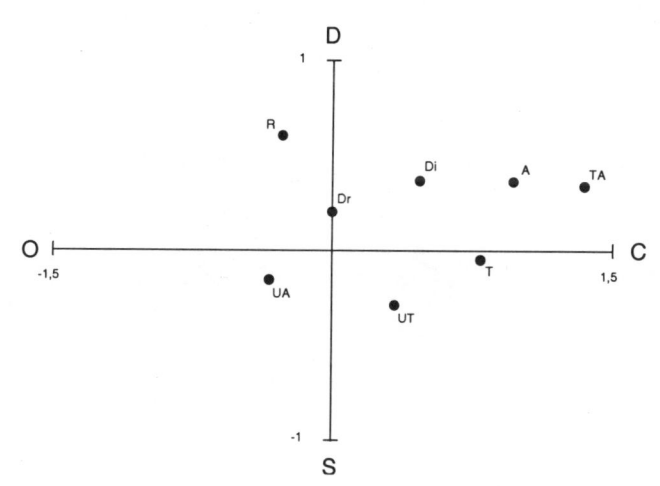

A=Authoritative, Di=Directive, Dr=Drudging ,T=Tolerant, R=Repressive, TA= Tolerant/Authoritative, UA=Uncertain/Aggressive, UT=Uncertain/Tolerant

Fig. 2. Main points of the eight types of patterns of interpersonal relationships.

The Authoritative, the Tolerant/Authoritative and the Tolerant type are patterns in which students perceive their teachers being relatively high on the Proximity dimension, with the Tolerant type lowest on the Influence dimension. Less co-operative than the three previous types are the Directive type, the Uncertain/Tolerant and the Drudging type, with the Uncertain/Tolerant type lowest on the Influence dimension. The least co-operative pattern of interpersonal relationships have Repressive and Uncertain/Aggressive type classes. In Repressive type classes, teachers are the most dominant of all eight types.

In Fig. 3, the types are also characterised by means of graphic representations using the eight sections of the Model of Interpersonal Teacher Behaviour. The greater the shaded part in each section, the more the pattern of interpersonal relationships characterised by this sector[1] (see Fig. 1).

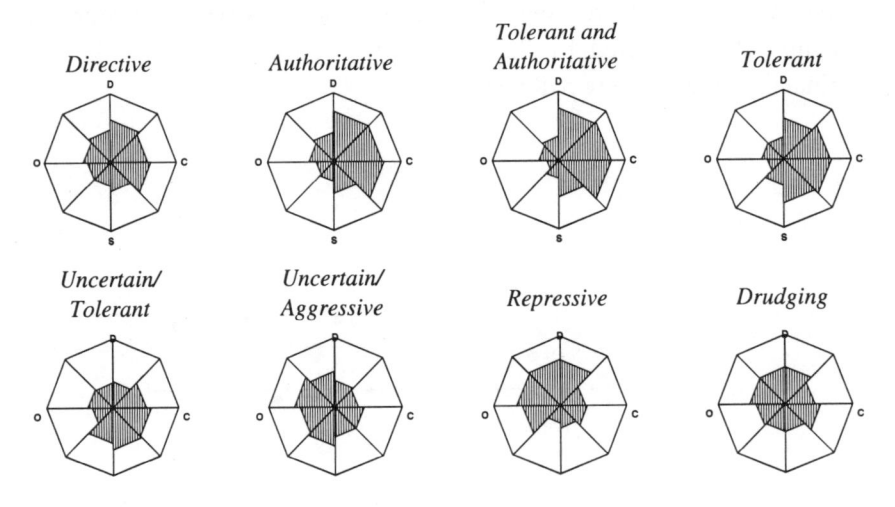

Fig. 3. Graphic representations of the eight types of patterns of interpersonal relationships.

---

[1] These graphic representations are achieved by shading in each sector of the model of interpersonal teacher behaviour. The ratio of the length of the perpendicular bisector of the shaded part and the length of the perpendicular bisector of the total sector equal the ratio of the observed score and the maximum score for that sector.

3. Teacher-Student Relationship and Student Outcomes

Classroom environment studies that have included the interpersonal perspective on teaching usually indicate a strong and positive relationship between perceptions of Influence and Proximity or their related subscales and cognitive student outcomes. In a study by Brekelmans (1989) for example, student perceptions of teacher Influence were related to cognitive outcomes. The higher a teacher was perceived on the Influence dimension, the higher the outcomes of students on a Physics test. In her study, teacher Influence was the most important variable at the class level. Other studies found positive correlations or regression coefficients for the leadership scale and cognitive student outcomes (Goh, 1994; Henderson, 1995).

Similar relationships have also been found for the Proximity dimension and Proximity related scales such as helpful/friendly and understanding, and to a lesser degree student responsibility/freedom (Goh, 1994; Henderson, 1995; Evans, 1998). The more teachers were perceived as co-operative, the higher students' scores on cognitive tests. Other evidence for the importance of Proximity on cognitive outcomes has been provided by studies on teacher Immediacy, an important concept in communication research. Immediacy is defined as 'that communication which enhances closeness to one another' (Mehrabian, 1981, Sanders & Wiseman, 1990) and includes behaviours that indicate approachability, signal availability for communication and increase sensory stimulation and interpersonal warmth and closeness (Sanders & Wiseman, 1990). Several studies both in secondary and higher education indicate the existence of a positive effect of Immediacy on cognitive student outcomes (Gorham & Zakahi, 1990; Sanders & Wiseman, 1990; Neuliep, 1995). However, relationships between Proximity (including Immediacy) and cognitive outcomes are not always straightforward. Sometimes it can only be proven that opposition, or uncertainty, dissatisfaction and admonishing behaviour lead to lower performance, but not that leadership, friendliness and understanding behaviour lead to higher performance (Rawnsley, 1997). In other studies, the relationship between Proximity/Immediacy and cognitive outcomes appears not linear but curvilinear (i.e. lower perceptions of proximity lead to lower outcomes, but intermediate and higher values lead to higher performance until a certain ceiling of optimal Proximity has been reached). Indirect effects have been found via variables such as attention and motivation (Gorham & Zakahi, 1990; Comstock, Rowell & Bowers, 1995). If report card grades have been used as outcome measures, relationships with interpersonal behaviour are inconclusive (Levy, Wubbels & Brekelmans, 1992; Van Amelsvoort, Bergen, Lamberigts & Setz, 1993; Van Amelsvoort, 1993; 1999).

Studies investigating associations between the teacher–student relationship and affective outcomes display a much more consistent pattern than studies investigating the relationship with cognitive outcomes. All studies find a positive effect of both Influence and Proximity on affective outcome measures, usually measured in terms of subject-specific motivation. Generally, effects of Proximity are somewhat stronger than effects of Influence. In a study with Physics teachers and their students, Brekelmans (1989) found a clear relationship between Proximity and student motivation for Physics. The higher the perception of Proximity, the higher the motivation of the students. This result has been supported by studies on Immediacy, which indicate a strong, direct and positive relationship between Immediacy and affective student outcomes (Gorham & Zakahi, 1990; Sanders & Wiseman, 1990; Powell & Harville, 1990; Comstock *et al.*, 1995; Neuliep, 1995; McCroskey, Richmond, Sallinen, Fayer & Barraclough, 1995). With more specific measures of students' subject-specific motivation, other studies found positive relationships for helpful/friendly and understanding behaviour with pleasure, confidence, effort and relevance of students (Derksen, 1994; Van Amelsvoort *et al.*, 1993; Setz, Bergen, Van Amelsvoort, & Lamberigts, 1993; Van Amelsvoort, 1993; 1999).

Strong and positive associations have also been demonstrated between several interpersonal sectors or scales, such as leadership and helpful/friendly, and affective outcomes, while negative relationships have been found with admonishing, dissatisfied, and, in most cases, strictness (Goh, 1994; Henderson, 1995; Rawnsley, 1997; Evans, 1998; Van Amelsvoort *et al.*, 1993; Setz *et al.*, 1993; Van Amelsvoort, 1993). The weakest associations have been found between interpersonal behaviour and confidence (Derksen, 1994; Van Amelsvoort *et al.*, 1993; Setz *et al.*, 1993; Van Amelsvoort, 1993). Van Amelsvoort (1999) demonstrated that the effect of interpersonal teacher behaviour on students' subject-specific motivation is both direct as well as indirect via student motivation and regulation processes.

In a recent study on EFL-teachers, Den Brok (2001) found that the interpersonal perspective on teaching was mainly relevant for the affective student outcomes. For all of the affective student outcome variables — pleasure, relevance, confidence and effort — a positive and strong effect was found for teacher Proximity. For some of the affective variables — pleasure, relevance and effort — Influence also had a positive effect.

In general, we conclude from the above mentioned studies that with respect to student outcomes, appropriate teacher–student relationships are characterised by a rather high degree of teacher Influence and Proximity towards students.

Studies (e.g. Créton & Wubbels, 1984) investigating how students and teachers themselves perceive appropriate teacher–student relationships showed that both teachers and students agree with the results of studies investigating the associations of teacher–student relationship with student outcomes.

4. Design of the Study

In the study reported in this chapter, we explore the significance of the experience of the teacher in realising appropriate relationships with students. We compare teacher–student relationship in different stages of the teaching career.

While there is a lot of research on the teacher-relationship, very little addresses change during the professional career. Since the 1970s, the number of studies on the teaching career has been growing. Most studies rely on (retrospective) self-reports of teachers and concentrate on the general commitment to the job rather than daily-classroom practice (e.g. Floden & Huberman, 1989; Huberman, 1993; Kelchtermans, 1993). In this study, we describe natural changes that occur during the teaching career, and concentrate on daily-classroom practice, studied by students' (and teacher) perceptions. To explore the associations between experience and teacher–student relationship, we use both cross-sectional and longitudinal data.

4.1. Sample

For the longitudinal part of the study, we collected data on a group of teachers (n = 51) once every year throughout the first decade of their professional careers. The teachers are from about 40 different secondary schools located throughout the Netherlands. They represent all kinds of subject areas. 14 of them (27%) are female teachers. 826 classes (more than 19,000 students) participated in our study. The number of classes participating in gathering annual data varied from 2–14 per year per teacher, with a mean of 3.7.

For 8 teachers we have data on the first 8 years of their career, for 12 about the first 7, for 19 teachers about the first 6 years, for 26 about the first 5, for 41 about the first 4 and for all teachers about the first 3 years of their career.

To get an idea of changes during the remaining part of the career, we use cross-sectional data from 573 teachers and more than 25,000 students located in about 100 different secondary schools throughout The Netherlands. The teachers represent all different subject areas. Normally, two or more classes for each teacher participated. For the analyses, we divided the teachers into the following six groups:

1. student teachers (217),
2. teachers with 1 – 5 years of experience (159),
3. 6 – 10 ten years (53),
4. 11 – 15 years (81),
5. 16 – 20 years (42), and
6. more than 20 years (21).

4.2. Instrumentation

Data about the perceptions of students and teachers of the teacher–student relationship have been gathered by means of the Questionnaire on Teacher Interaction (QTI).

The Dutch version[2] of the QTI consists of 77 items which are answered on a five-point Likert scale. These items are divided into eight scales which conform to the eight sectors of the model. Table 1 presents a typical item and the number of items for each scale.

Table 1. Number of items and a typical item for the QTI scales.

Scale	Number of items	Typical item
DC Leadership	10	S/he is a good leader
CD Helpful/friendly	10	S/he is someone we can depend on
CS Understanding	10	If we have something to say s/he will listen
SC Student responsibility/freedom	9	S/he gives us a lot of free time in class
SO Uncertain	9	S/he seems uncertain
OS Dissatisfied	11	S/he is suspicious
OD Admonishing	9	S/he gets angry
DO Strict	9	S/he is strict

Several studies have been conducted on the reliability and validity of the QTI. They have included Dutch (e.g. Brekelmans, Wubbels & Créton, 1990, Brekelmans, 1989, Den Brok, 2001; Créton & Wubbels, 1984; Wubbels, Créton & Hooymayers 1985; Wubbels, Brekelmans & Hermans, 1987), American (Wubbels & Levy, 1991) and Australian (Fisher, Fraser & Wubbels, 1992) samples. Both reliability and validity were satisfying.[3]

---

[2] Versions exist in different languages, among others: Dutch, English, German, Hebrew, Russian, Slovenian, Swedish, Finnish and Chinese (Singapore) (Wubbels, Brekelmans, Van Tartwijk & Admiraal, 1997).

[3] The homogeneity of each of the eight groups of items was considerable. The internal consistencies (Cronbach's α) at class level are generally above .80. The agreement between the scores of students in a single class met the general requirements for agreement between observer scores. The mean of the internal consistencies was 0.92 (Cronbach's α; students' scores in one class were considered as repeated measures). From a generalisability study (Shavelson, Webb & Burstein, 1986), it was concluded (Brekelmans 1989) that the QTI should be administered to at least 10 students in a class for the data to be reliable. The QTI does not need to be administered more than once per year, since interpersonal style remains relatively stable. A minimum of 2 classes should

Each completed questionnaire yields a set of eight scale scores. Scale scores equal the sum of all item scores and are reported in a range between 0 and 1. When the QTI was administered to students, scale scores of students from the same class are combined to a class mean.

In the study presented in this chapter, we analyse the teacher–student relationship on the basis of dimension scores. To summarize the scale scores by means of dimension scores, we use linear combinations of the scale scores.[4] We designate the two linear combinations of the eight scores as an Influence (DS) score and a Proximity (CO) score. The higher these scores are, the more dominance (DS) or cooperation (CO) is perceived in the behaviour of a teacher. In addition to dimension scores, we use graphic representations of the eight scale scores ("interpersonal profiles") to report on the teacher–student relationship (see Fig. 3).

We have collected data on perceptions of students of the teacher–student relationship and data on perceptions of teachers. Data about the perceptions of the students of a particular teacher were for most teachers gathered in two or more of his or her classes, from at least 10 students from each class. The perceptions of teachers concern their own actual behaviour (self-perception) and the behaviour they would like to display (ideal perception). Data on the perception of the actual behaviour were collected in the same classes where data about students' perceptions were gathered. These data have been averaged to one self-perception score for every teacher. The interpretations of teachers and students of the behaviour of a teacher are considered separate and distinct variables, each with their own significance.

---

complete the questionnaire for each teacher to achieve a reliable measure of overall style. Factor analyses on class means and LISREL analyses (Wubbels, Créton, Brekelmans & Hooymayers, 1987; Brekelmans, 1989; Den Brok 2001) determined that the two-factor structure did indeed support the 8 scales. Brekelmans (1989) demonstrated that both factors explain 80 per cent of the variance on all the scales of the Dutch QTI. Similar results were obtained for the American version (Wubbels & Levy, 1991).

[4] To this end the eight scores are represented as vectors in a two dimensional space, each dividing a section of the model of interpersonal behaviour in two and with a length corresponding to the height of the scale score. We then compute the two coordinates of the resultant of these eight vectors.

Data about the experience of the teachers were gathered by asking them how many years (including the year in which the QTI data were gathered) they had been working as a teacher in education.

We use multilevel models to analyse the data (Bryk & Raudenbush 1992). We will present qualitative descriptions of classroom learning environments based on data collected in a study by Créton and Wubbels (1984).

5. Results of the Study

5.1. Changes in the Influence Dimension During The Teaching Career

First we analysed if the degree of Influence of teachers changed in the first eight years of their teaching career. Multilevel analyses showed different trends for ideal, self, and students' perceptions. There are differences between teachers at the start of the career and differences in the way perceptions change during the first eight years. Figure 4 gives a graphical representation of the results.

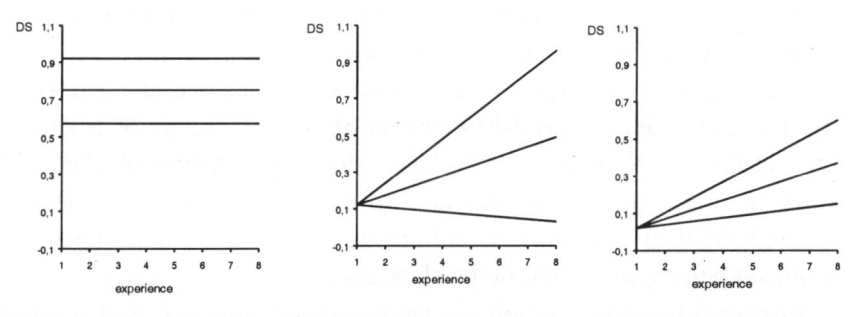

Ideal perceptions of teachers   *Self-perceptions of teachers*   *Students' perceptions*

Fig. 4. Estimated growth curves for Influence scores in the first eight years of their career (students' perceptions, and ideal and self-perceptions of teachers).

The middle lines in Fig. 4 present the estimated mean growth curves: the growth rates for an "average" teacher. The two outside lines present the estimated linear curves for teachers whose growth rate is one standard deviation above or below average. They represent the range for the development of two-thirds of the teachers. For the ideal perceptions, the outside lines surround the (constant) scores of two-thirds of the teachers. For self and students' perceptions, the three lines start from the estimated mean DS-score in the first-year of the teaching career. For self-perceptions, differences between teachers at the start are larger ($s.d. = 0.35$) than for students' perceptions ($s.d. = 0.24$).

Figure 4 shows that ideal perceptions of teachers are rather stable during the first decade of their career. In teachers' self-perceptions and students' perceptions, dominant behaviour grows with most teachers constantly every year in the first eight years of their careers. There is a linear upward trend in the changing behaviour towards the ideal perception. The mean growth rate is about the same for teachers' and students' perceptions. Perceptions of teachers are more dispersed, however, than those of students. With students' perceptions, the lower of the three lines still has an upward trend. According to teachers, their Influence-score is on average higher at the start of their career than according to students

To get an idea of possible changes in the remaining part of the teaching career, we compared the Influence scores of six groups of teachers with different amounts of experience.

Figure 5 plots the means of the Influence (DS) scores for students' and teachers' ideal and self-perceptions of the six groups of teachers. The results of an analysis of variance show that the mean scores of teachers' ideal perceptions do not differ significantly (5 % level). Throughout their careers, teachers apparently agree on the amount of dominant behaviour desired in the classroom.

Based on the results of Fig. 5, we can expect that of teachers will remain rather stable after the first decade of their teaching career.

Students' and teachers' perceptions of actual behaviour, however, noticeably vary for teachers across experience levels. Students' perceptions of dominant behaviour of student teachers and teachers with 1–5 years' experience differ significantly from the other groups. An increase in dominant behaviour can be seen from the student–teacher period through 6–10 years. After this point, there is a relative constancy. Teachers' self-perceptions show the same pattern. The upward trend in students' and teachers' self-perceptions found in the longitudinal part of our study possibly ends after the first decade.

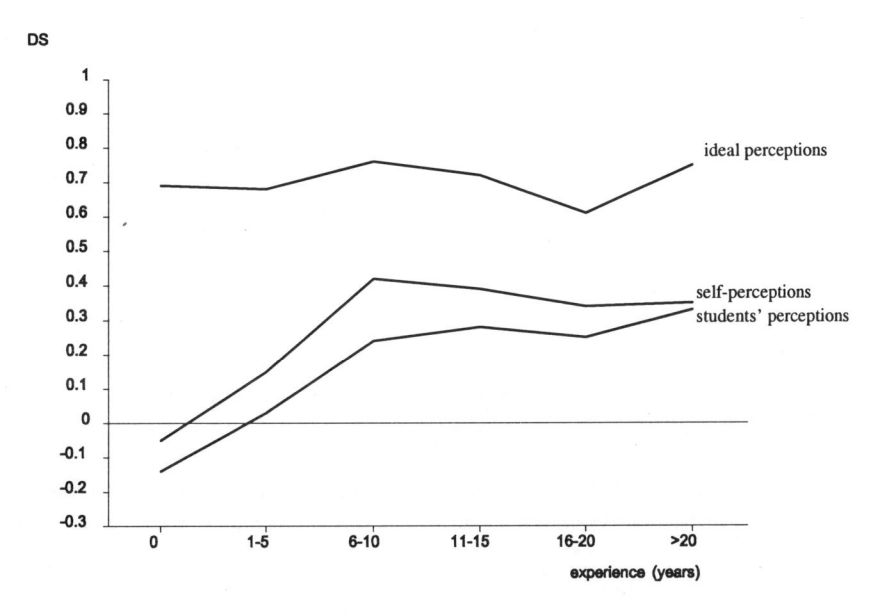

Fig. 5. Mean Influence (DS) scores by experience level.

5.2. Changes in the Proximity Dimension During The Teaching Career

As with the DS (Influence) scores, we used multilevel models to describe changes in the CO (Proximity) scores of teachers in the first eight years of their teaching career.

Figure 6 gives a graphical representation of the results. In line with Fig. 5, we present in Fig. 6 for ideal, self and students' perceptions the estimated mean growth curves, surrounded by two lines representing the range of two-thirds of the teachers. The mean growth curves of Fig. 6 show that during the first eight years of their professional career, there is on average no upward or downward trend in ideal, self-perceptions and perceptions of students of co-operative behaviour of teachers. There are however differences between teachers at the start of the career (ideal ($s.d.$ = 0.26), self ($s.d.$ = 0.27) and students' perceptions ($s.d.$ = 0.42) and the way self and students' perceptions change during the first eight years. As with the Influence dimension, Proximity scores are according to teachers on average higher at the start of the career than according to students.

Ideal perceptions of teachers   *Self-perceptions of teachers*   *Students' perceptions of teachers*

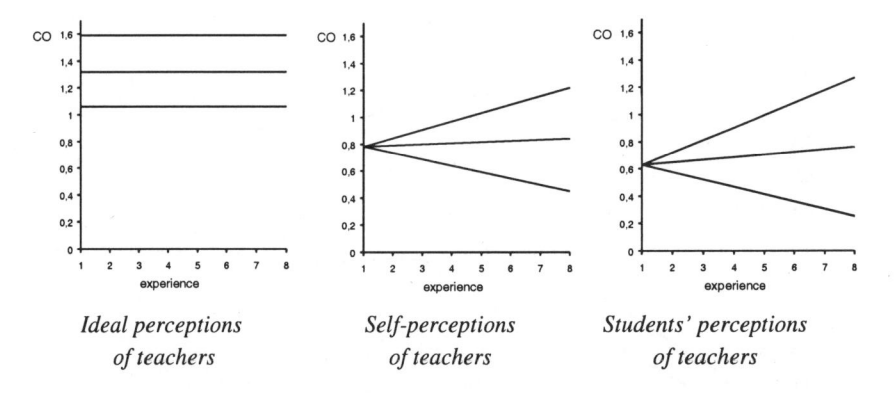

Fig. 6. Estimated growth curves for Proximity scores in the first eight years of the teaching career (students' perceptions, and ideal and self-perceptions of teachers).

To get an idea of possible changes in the remaining part of the teaching career, we compared the Proximity scores of six groups of teachers with different amounts of experience (see Fig. 7).

As with the longitudinal part of our study, teachers' perceptions of ideal behaviour do not significantly change throughout their careers. Regardless of experience level, teachers basically agree on the amount of co-operative behaviour they desire in the classroom.

As with the Influence dimension, the mean Proximity scores for the students' and teachers' perceptions differ significantly across groups. The differences in the Proximity dimension, however, are much smaller than on the Influence dimension and only a few are significant. According to students, student teachers behave more co-operatively than 1–5 and 11–15 year teachers. For teachers' self-perceptions, only the difference between student–teachers and teachers with 11–15 years of experience are significant. This indicates a moderate decline in Proximity scores throughout the career.

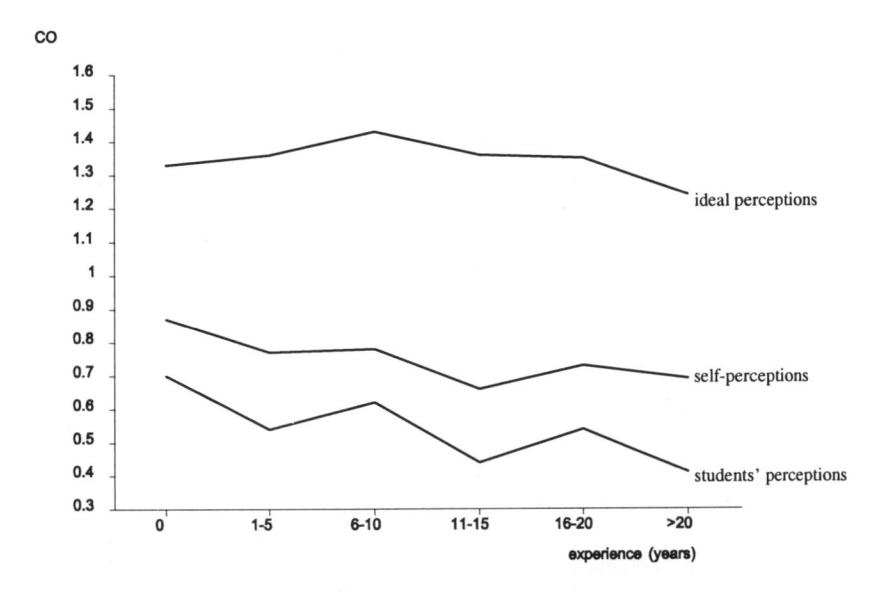

Fig. 7. Mean Influence (DS) scores by experience level.

5.3. Interpersonal Profiles During the Teaching Career

Table 2 presents for each of the eight years of experience the most common types of interpersonal profiles.

Of all ideal perceptions of the teacher–student relationship, three-fourths (73%) was most similar to the Tolerant and Authoritative profile, while 25% was most similar to the Authoritative type. At all experience levels, more than 90% of the teachers preferred one of these two relatively similar interpersonal profiles. Characteristic for the classroom environment of the Authoritative teacher is that the atmosphere is well-structured, pleasant and task-oriented. Rules and procedures are clear and students do not need to be reminded. The Authoritative teacher is enthusiastic and open to students' needs. S/he takes a personal interest in them, and this comes through in the lessons. While his/her favourite method is the lecture, the authoritative teacher frequently uses other techniques. The lessons are well planned and logically structured. Characteristic for the classroom environment of Tolerant and Authoritative teachers is that they maintain a structure which supports student responsibility and freedom. They use a variety of methods, to which students respond well. They frequently organise their lessons around small group work. While the class environment resembles that of the Authoritative teacher, the Tolerant and Authoritative teacher develops closer relationships with students. They enjoy the class and are highly involved in most lessons. Both students and teacher can occasionally be seen laughing, and there is very little need to enforce the rules. The teacher ignores minor disruptions, choosing instead to concentrate on the lesson. Students work to reach their own and the teacher's instructional goals with little or no complaints.

Table 2. Percentages of the most common types of interpersonal profiles for different experience levels[5] (ideal-, self- and students' perceptions).

Experience (years)	Ideal perceptions TA	AU	Self-perceptions TO	TA	AU	DI	Students' perceptions UT	TO	TA	AU	DI
1	73	25	26	20	19	15	19	27	17	9	11
2	64	29	13	20	23	22	8	23	18	25	16
3	79	12	19	29	25	13	10	23	15	21	18
4	73	26	16	21	30	18	10	15	16	26	21
5	80	17	18	8	49	16	8	12	12	38	27
6	79	15	11	22	39	13	12	16	12	41	9
7	93	3	0	35	47	18	9	11	14	36	25
8	91	0	24	43	24	0	11	22	19	30	15

DI = Directive; AU = Authoritative; TA = Tolerant and Authoritative; TO = Tolerant;
UT = Uncertain/Tolerant; UA = Uncertain/Aggressive.

The results for students' perceptions in Table 2 show that the major profiles in the first-year of the teaching career are the Tolerant and the Uncertain/Tolerant profile. For the Tolerant teacher, the atmosphere is pleasant and supportive and students enjoy attending class. They have

---

[5] We used data of all classes in the sample. Because the number of classes is not the same for all teachers, we repeated the analyses with a reduced data file with only 2 classes selected at random for each teacher. In every year, data were gathered. The same trends emerged from the data.

more freedom with Tolerant teachers than with Authoritative or Tolerant and Authoritative teachers, and have some real power to influence curriculum and instruction. Students appreciate the teacher's personal involvement and his/her ability to match the subject matter with their learning styles. They often work at their own pace and the class atmosphere sometimes may be a little confused as a result. The teacher often begins the lesson with an explanation and then sends the students off to complete an assignment individually. While the teacher is interested in the students' personal lives, his/her academic expectations for them are not evident. Characteristic for the classroom environment of Uncertain/Tolerant teachers is that they are highly co-operative but do not show much leadership in class. Their lessons are poorly structured, are not introduced completely and do not have much follow-through. They generally tolerate disorder, and students are not task-oriented. The Uncertain/Tolerant teacher is quite concerned about the class, and is willing to explain things repeatedly to students who have not been listening. The atmosphere is so unstructured, however, that only the students in front are attentive while the others play games, do homework, and the like. They are not provocative, however, and the teacher manages to ignore them while loudly and quickly covering the subject. The Uncertain/Tolerant teacher's rules of behaviour are arbitrary, and students do not know what to expect when infractions occur. The teacher's few efforts to stop the misbehaviour are delivered without emphasis and have little effect on the class. Sometimes the teacher reacts quickly, and at other times completely ignores inattentiveness. Class performance expectations are minimal and mostly immediate rather than long-range. The overall effect is of an unproductive equilibrium in which teacher and students seem to go their own way. In a study of physics teachers, the Tolerant and Uncertain/Tolerant profiles reflected average affective outcomes (student attitudes). The Uncertain/Tolerant profile had lower cognitive outcomes (student achievement) than almost all other interpersonal types (Brekelmans, 1989).

When teachers get more experienced, a larger proportion of interpersonal profiles fit the more structured and task-oriented

Authoritative and Directive profiles according to their students. The Directive teacher is organised efficiently and normally completes all lessons on time. S/he dominates class discussion, but generally holds students' interest. The teacher usually isn't really close to the students, though s/he is occasionally friendly and understanding. S/he has high standards and is seen as demanding. While things seem businesslike, the teacher continually has to work at it. S/he gets angry at times and has to remind the class that they are there to work. S/he likes to call on students who misbehave and are inattentive. This normally straightens them up quickly. According to teachers, more structured and task-oriented profiles are realised earlier during the professional career and with a larger proportion of teachers than according to students.

To get an idea of possible changes in the remaining part of the teaching career, we compared the interpersonal profile scores of the six groups of teachers with different amount of experience.

As to the ideal perceptions, the results show the same pattern as the first decade of the teaching career. More than 90 percent in all groups prefer the Tolerant and Authoritative profile or the Authoritative type.

Table 3 presents the number of different types for students' perceptions. The table shows that according to their students, more student–teachers than first-year teachers conform to the Tolerant and Uncertain/Tolerant type. The contribution of these profiles decreases as teachers get more experienced. During the first decade of the teaching career, the number of Authoritative profiles increases, after about five years of experience the Directive type gets on top. Towards the end of the teaching career, the number of teachers with a Repressive profile goes up. Characteristic of the learning environment of these teachers is that students are uninvolved and extremely docile. They follow the rules and are afraid of the teacher's angry outbursts. S/he seems to overreact to small transgressions, frequently making sarcastic remarks or giving failing grades. The Repressive teacher is the epitome of complementary rigidity. The Repressive teacher's lessons are structured, but not well-organized. While directions and background information are provided, few questions are allowed or encouraged. Occasionally, students will work on individual assignments, for which they receive precious little help from the teacher. The atmosphere is guarded and unpleasant, and the students are apprehensive and fearful. Since the Repressive teacher's expectations are competition-oriented and inflated, students worry a lot about their exams. The teacher seems to repress student initiative, preferring to lecture while the students sit still. They perceive the teacher as unhappy and impatient and their silence seems like the calm before the storm. In comparison with the other types, students of Repressive Physics teachers achieved the most, though their affective needs were left unsatisfied (Brekelmans, 1989). The Repressive profile was less apparent in teachers with fewer years of experience. For example, no student teachers and only 4 % of the 6–10 year teachers were categorized in this manner.

Table 3. Percentages of students' perceptions (interpersonal profiles) for six groups of teachers with different experience levels.

Type	0*	1–5	6–10	11–15	16–20	>20
Directive	6	12	30	37	29	28
Authoritative	7	19	21	19	16	17
Tolerant and Authoritative	11	8	6	4	11	6
Tolerant	42	19	21	11	13	6
Uncertain/Tolerant	27	20	6	4	3	11
Uncertain/Aggressive	4	8	2	6	8	11
Repressive	0	1	4	8	11	17
Drudging	3	13	9	11	11	6
Total	100	100	99	100	102	102

(Experience (years))

* student teachers

6. Some Interpretations

In all, the results of our study show that the ideal perceptions of teachers are rather stable during their teaching careers. The actual teacher–student relationship however changes during the career according to the students and the teachers themselves. When averaging the individual growth curves, there is a significant linear upward trend in dominant behaviour. With most teachers, this behaviour intensifies during the first eight years of their teaching career towards teachers' perceptions of the ideal interpersonal style: a shift from more 'uncertain' behaviour and 'giving students freedom' towards more leadership and strict behaviour. When averaging the individual growth curves, there is no linear trend in co-operative behaviour. On average, teachers do not become more friendly and understanding. On average, there is no shift towards the ideal as experience grows.

We think the following could provide an explanation for these results. At the start of their careers, most teachers are about twenty to twenty-five years old and have not, to any large degree, as yet provided leadership to other people. From this point of view, the professional role does not coincide perfectly with their stage of personal development. Beginning teachers are often confronted with a lack of behavioural repertoire and inadequate cognitions in this area. This often results in students' perceptions of their interpersonal style as Uncertain/Tolerant and Tolerant. This urges teachers to do something about it. This need for change is reinforced by the ideal perception of beginning teachers, mainly a classroom situation with the teacher in control. Through daily classroom practice, dominance patterns are developed. This interpretation of the upward trend in dominant behaviour somewhat resembles Huberman's description of modal sequences in the professional engagement of teachers during their career. The sequence survival and discovery-stabilisation-experimentation/diversification can be recognized (Huberman, 1993).

According to the above interpretation, beginning teachers mainly attribute (consciously or unconsciously) problems in interacting with students to the Influence area. The ability to empathise with students (recent peers) and to show co-operative behaviours is considered a less problematic area by them. The greater attention to the dominant behaviour is probably reflected in the fact that there is more dispersion with teachers' perceptions of the Influence dimension than with students' perceptions, while students perceive larger differences between teachers on the Proximity dimension (e.g. Den Brok, 2001). With the greater attention to dominant behaviour practice and experimentation related to the Proximity dimension of interpersonal behaviour fade somewhat into the background.

The above interpretation of the differences in changes in dominant and co-operative behaviour is relevant when teachers show an increase in dominant behaviour (as most teachers do) and rather stable or decreasing co-operative behaviour. There are however teachers with an increase in co-operative behaviour in the first-years of their teaching career. This may be due to an increasing behavioural repertoire and/or a better understanding of classroom processes.

Let us assume that it can be considered a desirable development when teachers' actual behaviour evolves towards the ideal perception of teachers. On the basis of the above interpretation of the results of our study, it can then be concluded that the development of dominant behavioural patterns and differentiation of accompanying cognitions and attitudes is fruitful for pre- and in-service programs for beginning teachers. Training of strict and leadership behavioural skills accompanied by more adequate cognitions may be most effective in developing the Influence dimension. Adequate differentiation between 'leadership' and 'strict' behaviour and between 'freedom and responsibility' and 'uncertain' behaviour (the transition from the co-operative to the opposite sectors of the model of interpersonal behaviour) is complex. We think this kind of training should be a more prominent part of pre-service and teacher induction programs (in The Netherlands) than is the case at present.

We think the Proximity dimension may require procedures and interventions in teacher education that are somewhat different from the Influence dimension. On the Proximity dimension, the cognitive component to training and staff development may be more important, in order to help teachers to use their skills more adequately and to help them select the appropriate skills in particular situations. Giving teachers insight into the circular processes of communication and the impossibility to solve the problem by just blaming the other party may help them to activate interpersonal behaviour that was already part of their behavioural repertoire.

References

Blumenfeld, P.C. & Meece, J.L. (1985). Life in classrooms revisited. *Theory into Practice, 24,* 50–56

Brekelmans, M. (1989). *Interpersonal teacher behavior in the classroom.* In Dutch: Interpersoonlijk gedrag van docenten in de klas. Utrecht: W.C.C.

Brekelmans, M., Levy, J. & Rodriguez, R. (1993). A typology of teacher communication style. In Wubbels, Th. & Levy, J. (Eds.) *Do you know what you look like?* London: The Falmer Press, 46–55.

Brekelmans, M., Wubbels, Th. & Créton, H.A. (1990). A study of student perceptions of physics teacher behavior, *Journal of Research in Science Teaching, 27,* 335–350.

Brown, R. (1965). *Social psychology.* London: Collier-McMillan.

Bryk, A.S. & Raudenbush, W. (1992). *Hierarchical linear models.* Newbury Park: Sage.

Comstock, J., Rowell, E. & Bowers, J.W. (1995). Food for thought: teacher nonverbal immediacy, student learning and curvilinearity. Communication Education, 44, 251–266.

Créton, H.A. & Wubbels, Th. (1984). *Discipline problems with beginning teachers.* In Dutch: Ordeproblemen bij beginnende leraren. Utrecht: W.C.C.

Den Brok, P. (2001). *Teaching and student outcomes. A study on teachers' thoughts and actions from an interpersonal and a learning activities perspective.* Utrecht: W.C.C.

Derksen, K. (1994). *Between taking over and activating instruction.* In Dutch: Tussen sturen en activeren. Masters thesis. Nijmegen: Vakgroep Onderwijskunde.

Doyle, W. (1986). Classroom organization and management. In M.C. Wittrock (Ed.), *Handbook of research on teaching (third edition)* (pp. 392–431). New York: Macmillan.

Dunkin, M. & Biddle, B. (1974). *The study of teaching.* New York: Holt, Rinehart & Winston.

Evans, H. (1998). *A study on students' cultural background and teacher-student interpersonal behaviour in Secondary Science classrooms in Australia.* Unpublished doctoral dissertation. Perth: Curtin University of Technology.

Fisher, D.L., Fraser, B.J. & Wubbels, Th. (1992) *Teacher communication style and school environment,* Paper presented at the 1992 ECER conference, Enschede.

Floden, R.E. & Huberman, M. (1989). Teachers' professional lives: the state of the art. *International Journal of Educational Research, 13,* 455–466.

Foa, U.G. (1961). Convergence in the analysis of the structure of interpersonal behavior. *Psychological Review, 68,* 341–353.

Goh, S.C. (1994). *Interpersonal teacher behaviour, classroom climate and student outcomes in Primary Mathematics classes in Singapore.* Unpublished doctoral dissertation. Perth: Curtin University of Technology.

Gorham, J. & Zakahi, W.R. (1990). A comparison of teacher and student perceptions of immediacy and learning: monitoring process and product. *Communication Education, 39,* 354–379.

Henderson, D.G. (1995). *A study of the classroom and laboratory environments and student attitude and achievement in senior Secondary Biology classes.* Unpublished doctoral dissertation. Perth: Curtin University of Technology.

Huberman, M. (1993). Steps toward a developmental model of the teaching career. In L. Kremer-Hayon, H.C. Vonk & R. Fessler (Eds), *Teacher professional development: a multiple perspective approach* (pp. 93–118). Amsterdam: Swets & Zeitlinger.

Kelchtermans, G. (1993). Teachers and their career story. A biographical perspective on professional development. In C. Day, J. Calderhead & P. Denicolo (Eds.), *Research on teacher thinking: towards understanding professional development* (pp. 198–220). London: The Falmer Press.

Leary, T. (1957). *An interpersonal diagnosis of personality.* New York: Ronald Press Company.

Levy, J., Wubbels, Th. & Brekelmans, M. (1992). Student and teacher characteristics and perceptions of teacher communication style. *Journal of Classroom Interaction, 27,* 23–29.

Lonner, W.J. (1980). The search for psychological universals. In H.C. Triandis & W.W. Lambert (Eds.), *Handbook of cross cultural psychology* (vol.1) (pp. 143–204). Boston: Allyn and Bacon.

McCroskey, J.C., Richmond, V.P., Sallinen, A., Fayer, J.M. & Barraclough, R.A. (1995). A cross-cultural and multi-behavioral analysis of the relationship between nonverbal immediacy and teacher evaluation. *Communication Education, 44,* 281–291.

Mehrabian, A. (1981). *Silent messages: implicit communication of emotions and attitudes.* Belmont: Wadsworth Publishing company.

Neuliep, J.W. (1995). A comparison of teacher immediacy in African-American and Euro-American college classrooms. *Communication Education, 44,* 267–280.

Powell, R.G. & Harville, B. (1990). The effects of teacher immediacy and clarity on instructional outcomes: an intercultural assessment. *Communication Education, 39,* 369–379.

Rawnsley, D.G. (1997). *Associations between classroom learning environments, teacher interpersonal behaviour and student outcomes in Secondary Mathematics classrooms*. Unpublished doctoral dissertation. Perth: Curtin University of Technology.

Rosenholtz, S.J., Bassler, O. & Hoover-Dempsey, K. (1986). Organizational conditions of teacher learning. *Teaching and Teacher Education, 2*, 91–104.

Sanders, J.A. & Wiseman, R.L. (1990). The effects of verbal and nonverbal teacher immediacy on perceived cognitive, affective and behavioral learning in the multicultural classroom. *Communication Education, 39*, 341–353.

Setz, W., Bergen, Th., Van Amelsvoort, J. & Lamberigts, R. (1993). *Perceived and observed behaviour of teachers*. In Dutch: Gepercipieerd en geobserveerd lesgedrag van docenten. Research report. Nijmegen: Katholieke Universiteit Nijmegen/ITS.

Shavelson, R.J., Webb, N.W. & Burstein, L. (1986). Measurement of teaching. In M.C. Wittrock (Ed.), Handbook of research on teaching, third edition (pp. 50–91). New York: Mc.Millan.

Slater, P.E. (1962). Parental behavior and the personality of the child. *Journal of Genetical Psychology, 101*, 53–68.

Strack, S. (1996). Special series: Interpersonal theory and the interpersonal circumplex: Timothy Leary's Legacy, *Journal of Personality Assessment, 66*, 211–307.

Van Amelsvoort, J. (1993). Teachers' behaviour during the lesson as perceived by students. In Th. Bergen, J. Van Amelsvoort, K. Derksen, R. Lamberigts, W. Setz & P. Sleegers (Eds.), *Between taking over and activating instruction* (research report). Nijmegen: VON/ITS.

Van Amelsvoort, J. (1999). *Perspective on instruction, motivation and self-regulation*. In Dutch: Perspectief op instructie, motivatie en zelfregulatie. Nijmegen: Katholieke Universiteit Nijmegen.

Van Amelsvoort, J., Bergen, Th., Lamberigts, R. & Setz, W. (1993). *Teacher behaviour, student motivation and school outcomes*. In Dutch: Docentgedrag, leerlingmotivatie en schoolprestaties. Research report. Nijmegen: Katholieke Universiteit Nijmegen/ITS.

Watzlawick, P., Beavin, J.H. & Jackson, D. (1967). *The pragmatics of human communication*, New York, Norton.

Wubbels, Th., Brekelmans, M. & Hermans, J. (1987). Teacher behavior an important aspect of the learning environment, in Fraser, B.J. (Ed.) *The study of learning environments*, (volume 3), Perth, Curtin University, 10–25.

Wubbels, Th., Brekelmans, M., Van Tartwijk, J. & Admiraal, W. (1997). Interpersonal relationships between teachers and students in the classroom.

In H. C. Waxman & H. J. Walberg (eds.), *New directions for teaching practice and research* (pp. 151–170). Berkely: McCutchan Publishing Company.

Wubbels, Th., Créton, H.A., Brekelmans, M. & Hooymayers, H.P. (1987). Perceptions of the teacher-student relationship (in Dutch) *Tijdschrift voor Onderwijsresearch, 12*, 1, 3–16.

Wubbels, Th., Créton, H.A. & Hooymayers, H.P. (1985). Discipline problems of beginning teachers, interactional teacher behavior mapped out, Paper presented at the AERA Annual meeting, Chicago. Abstracted in Resources in Education, 20, 12, p. 153, ERIC document 260040.

Wubbels, Th. & Levy, J. (1991). A comparison of interpersonal behavior of Dutch and American teachers, *International Journal of Intercultural Relationships, 15*, 1–18.

Wubbels, Th. & Levy, J. (Eds.), (1993). Do you know what you look like? Interpersonal relationships in education. London: The Falmer Press.

Chapter 5

LEARNING ENVIRONMENTS IN URBAN SCIENCE CLASSROOMS: CONTRADICTIONS, CONFLICT AND REPRODUCTION OF SOCIAL INEQUALITY

Kenneth Tobin
Rowhea Elmesky
Cristobal Carambo

Graduate School of Education
University of Pennsylvania
United States of America

Learning environments are dynamic and interactive sociocultural entities that are shaped by the agency of individuals interacting with human and material resources in ways that afford their agency while constraining what they can accomplish. All activity is mediated by history and social and cultural phenomena. The chapter illustrates how teaching in urban science classrooms can only sustain productive environments with the collective acceptance of all members of a learning community and a conscious awareness of the intersection of cultural fields and a necessity to build science literacy on the capital from those fields while actively suppressing strategies of action from those same fields that would otherwise inhibit learning.

1. The Urban Context

To a startling extent, the nature of high schools in the United States often reflects their social locations. Because of the way education is funded in most states and local communities the buildings, fiscal infrastructure, teachers, and students vary drastically from one school district to another. In large inner city school districts, like Philadelphia, high schools may lack diversity in terms of ethnicity and the socioeconomic characteristics of the homes of students. For example, at City High School, 97 percent of the students are African American and 87 percent are from families with an income that is below the nation's poverty line. This is a significant issue because, according to the U.S. Census Bureau (2001), nearly 80 percent of the U.S. population resides in urban communities. Similar trends are occurring in the developing world with the population of the cities increasing at three times the rate of rural areas, more than half of the population of the developing world living in mega-cities, and globally 7 out of the 10 largest cities are in the developing world. Furthermore, a growing proportion of the world's population lives in cities; by the middle of the 1990s three billion people, almost half of the world's population lived in large cities (Barton & Tobin, 2001).

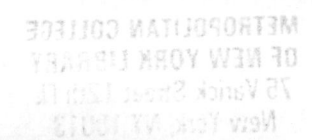

For the past five years, we have been conducting research on the teaching and learning of science in urban high schools, especially City High School, a neighbourhood school consisting of more than 2,000 students, most of whom are African American. What struck us immediately is that most of what we had learned from research undertaken in suburban schools did not seem to apply to our experiences in urban schools (Tobin, Seiler & Smith, 1999). Not only that, there was a dearth of research to guide us on how to plan and enact curricula in urban settings, particularly in those schools where poverty was a factor and most students were culturally different than their teachers. Initially, we felt that teachers may have been to blame for the state of affairs in urban high school science classes and, in an effort to learn more about the salient issues, Tobin decided to teach science at City High School (Tobin, 2000; Tobin, Seiler & Walls, 1999). He found that his dispositions to teach science in particular ways were breached continuously and he had to re-learn to teach in urban settings, and learn how to earn the respect of his students while showing them respect. He had difficulty communicating with his students, building rapport with them, and especially having them regard him as their teacher (i.e., earning the right to teach them). Most of what he took for granted as a science teacher could not be assumed in urban high schools in the U.S. Events tended to unfold at a furious pace and he had difficulty anticipating what was happening next and what he should do to teach appropriately. The eventful nature of teaching in an urban high school was overwhelming to him and it was apparent that there needed to be fresh ways to think about the teaching and learning of science in urban high schools and associated different approaches to research classroom learning environments.

There have been many studies in urban schools in the U.S. that have identified poverty as a salient factor in shaping enacted curricula (e.g., Anyon, 1997, 1981). Haberman (1993) described a pedagogy of poverty in urban schools in which teachers enacted curricula in ways that afforded their control over students. Urban classroom learning environments were often characterised by activities in which students were required to complete worksheets and copy notes from the board. Tobin's experiences were similar. When he felt a desperate need to get back in control of the students and buy some time for reflection, he would require the students to copy notes into their books. The transformation was almost miraculous. The students knew what to do and they usually were compliant and began to copy the notes (if they had brought their notebooks to school). There were tendencies for them to accept roles that were highly structured by the teacher and not to participate as expected, in open-ended laboratory activities for example. Significantly, Toussaint (1997), in his study of teaching African American youth in Philadelphian high schools, observed that urban high schools tend to have more oppressive environments than their suburban counterparts. More specifically, Seiler (2002) explored the relevance of enacted high school science curricula in a small learning community at City High in terms of the interests of students and the extent to which their studies of science prepared them for improved social lives. She concluded that the curricula enacted in science were potentially oppressive to students and did little more than fuel cycles of reproduction. Students, many of whom are involved in the research reported in this chapter, were uncooperative in their science class and made it difficult for teachers and other learners to focus on the enactment of a curriculum that was conducive to learning. Certainly, in our ongoing studies there appears to be a press toward the sorts of activity described by Haberman as a pedagogy of poverty, possibly associated with impoverished students, insufficient finances to fully equip and maintain building, equipment and supplies, and a huge cultural divide between most teachers and their students.

Traditional research showed large and persistent gaps in science achievement of urban students and their suburban peers and the achievement of African Americans lagged considerably behind the achievement of Whites (Seiler, 2002). The science achievement scores on the Stanford Achievement Test (version 9) for students in grade 11 at the highest performing magnet school (Magnet High) were all in the highest three performance levels (advanced, 22 percent; proficient 38 percent; and basic 35 percent). Only five percent were below basic, most of these in the 'highest' below basic level. In a stunning contrast, City High has only six percent at basic level or above. Ninety four percent of the students are below basic with 33 percent at the lowest performance level. Notably, these science achievement scores are highly correlated with reading scores. At Magnet High 87 percent of the students are above the fiftieth percentile whereas at City High only seven percent are above the fiftieth percentile, none in the top quartile and 81 percent in the bottom quartile. Not surprisingly, few students from neighbourhood high schools gain entrance to college (Whitman, 2000).

Such wide achievement gaps significantly coincide with educational tracking, and Oakes and Wells (1998) discuss the deleterious effects for students assigned to the lower tracks. This is especially a problem in Philadelphia where there are several levels of tracking in the system. To begin with, there is the tiered system identified by Kozol (1991) that is characteristic of schools in U.S. cities like Philadelphia; suburban, magnet schools for high performing students, and neighbourhood schools for the remainder. Within City High School, there also is a tracking system because of a movement to create small learning communities (SLCs), or schools within schools. At City High there are presently nine SLCs, each containing 200-300 students and about 7 teachers. Two of the small learning communities have the goal of preparing students for college, one is math and science oriented and the other is oriented toward the humanities. Six of the remaining SLCs are vocationally oriented (e.g., Health, Business, and EcoTech) and Incentive is for students who have difficulty settling into high school or remaining in high school due to academic and/or emotional problems. Most of our research has been undertaken in one of the vocational SLCs associated with Science, Education and Technology (SET) and to a lesser extent in Health and

Incentive. The three SLCs we have been involved with tend to be among the lowest-performing in a school that is among the lowest-performing in a large, low-performing, urban school system.

The multi-tiered system of schools within the city and then the SLC structure within schools also has the potential to track resources in insidious ways and thereby to greatly shape the resources available to support learning (Martin, 2002). For example, Martin described how there were fewer equipment and supplies to support enacted curricula at neighbourhood schools than at Magnet High. There also is evidence to suggest that at neighbourhood high schools, many teachers teach out of field for a great proportion of their time. In fact, the SLC structure makes it more likely that this will happen in science. Since all high school students are required to take four science courses and most SLCs have only one science teacher, many teachers will be out of field in their teaching of three of the four science courses. For example, Carambo, the teacher in this study is certified to teach general science and chemistry. When he teaches physics and biology, he is technically out of field. Ingersoll (2001, 1997) has identified critically high levels of teaching out of field in U.S. high schools, especially in urban school districts and in science. We regard the teacher and her competence to teach science as a critical component of learning environments. Moreover, we cannot envision credible research in the U.S. that ignores the role of the teacher in mediating the learning of students. Even the same teacher will have vastly different roles when teaching science in and out of field.

2. Perspectives on Learning Environments

Upon considering science classrooms in an urban neighbourhood school like City High, the very idea of a classroom learning environment is a paradox. There are so many ways to think about learning and the places at which learning occurs, yet for well over a quarter of a century, researchers have used much the same psychosocial framework to explore learning environments. Most studies employed a methodology that was ontologically realist in nature such that learning environments were regarded as 'out there' to be experienced by learners, teachers and researchers and to support learning or not, depending on its nature.

Learning depended upon the extent to which particular learners availed themselves of opportunities to participate and learn. Teachers were thought to be able to manipulate their classroom learning environments, to make them more conducive to learning, especially by increasing the fit of the preferred and actual environments experienced by students. Furthermore, such studies suggested that when there was a fit between the preferred and actual learning environments, the students achieved at a higher level and were favourably disposed toward science (Fraser, 1998). Despite what we consider to be conceptual difficulties in this way of characterising learning environments, the measurement and manipulation appeared to benefit learners, teachers, and teacher educators.

Assumptions of a linear relationship between the constructs measured in learning environment research and learning were oversimplified. For example, learning opportunities were considered as maximised when the perceptions were scored as 5 or 1 on a Likert scale. It was not assumed that learning was optimised at a level of 2, 3, or 4. Nor was it possible to indicate in the completion of a questionnaire that ratings for particular items were contingent on factors not addressed in the questionnaire. Hence, although scholars in this field implied that those environments were not real, but were constructed in an interaction of a learner with human and non-human resources, there still was a tendency to glean insights into the nature of these environments through the use of such questionnaires. Moreover, even with qualitative data resources such as interviews being utilised in conjunction with quantitative measures, learning environments were still regarded in terms of what participants could talk or write about, phenomena that could be accessed by language. Scant attention was directed to those practices associated with learning and knowing that were learned by being in a cultural and social setting over time; habits developed to support practices that were in some instances essential if particular outcomes, such as the learning of science, were to be attained in a particular setting.

Despite the influence of a constructivist theoretical frame, our perception is that for too long the mainstream approach to research on learning environments has been shrouded in a cloak of methods that are essentially positivist in character. More recently, scholars like Wolff-Michael Roth have advocated the use of a broader array of social and cultural theories that include phenomenology, communities of practice, critical psychology, and activity theory (Roth, 2000, Roth, Tobin & Zimmermann, 2002). In a similar vein, this paper seeks to add to the expansive field of research on learning environments through the use of a theoretical framework that synthesises cultural sociology (Sewell, 1992, 1999; Swidler, 1986) with activity theory (Engeström, 1999, 1987).

3. Classrooms as Cultural Fields

A field is a setting that is characterised by the enactment of particular culture (Swartz, 1997). Fields can be overlapping and are not necessarily bounded spatially. In this chapter, the field is the science classroom at City High School. Although bounded by walls, roof and floor and contained within a four story building, at different times during the day, the field we refer to as the science classroom does not exist in any real sense. For example, before and after school hours or during lunch recess, the classroom does not exist as a cultural field. Thus, a field consists of more than a physical space; rather, it includes social and cultural structures, participants, and a history of existence. Elmesky (2001) undertook a case study involving five City High students, selected for participation in her study because of their at risk status. Notable in Elmesky's study is that the boundaries between the different fields in which the students live their lives are shown to be porous. As students participate in activities designed to mediate their learning of science, they enact strategies that originate in their youth subcultures (Clarke, Hall, Jefferson & Roberts, 1976), or as we refer to it here, in the streets (Anderson, 1999). Elmesky clearly showed that these cultural strategies, or strategies of action (Swidler, 1986), are enacted without conscious awareness and sometimes afford learning but as often as not disrupt the learning of most students in the field. Because so many teachers have different cultural backgrounds than their students, we regard the extent to which they understand the culture of their students as a critical factor in shaping the quality of the learning environments of students. Hence, in considering the learning environments experienced by students in a science classroom, it is necessary to know more than what students know and can do, value and feel about science and school, and the extent to which they are influenced by peers. A vital part of any research on learning environments is the identification of the relevant community, where relevance is considered in relation to the nature of the activity being undertaken in the field of concern. For example, if the object of an activity is becoming literate about chemistry and its relations to the lifeworlds of students, then it is critical to identify those in the community that potentially can shape the attainment of those outcomes.

3.1. Cultural Enactment and Production within a Classroom

If science is a form of culture, then the doing of science can be considered as cultural enactment and learning science as cultural production. According to Sewell (1999), culture can be regarded as a dialectical relationship between a system of referents used to make sense of social life within a field and associated practices of the participants of that field. Within a cultural field, culture is enacted heterogeneously at sites of intensive cultural practice, referred to as nodes and distributed temporally and spatially throughout the field (Sewell, 1999). If the field of concern is a science classroom, such as Carambo's, in an urban high school, a node might involve a place in the classroom, such as the chalkboard, the back row of desks, or the sink. More often than not, it is essential that the time be specified. Hence, the doorway is a site for cultural enactment of a particular type during a lesson whereas, at the beginning and end of class, as students enter and exit the classroom, the practices that are enacted might be different. Also, what happens at a node will likely reflect the type of activity that is planned. For example, laboratory activities occur in groups but usually involve different tools than small group activities with a discussion orientation.

Salient to culture is that it can be enacted at nodes both consciously or unconsciously and its effects can be intended and unintended. It is not possible for persons to say with certainty what they did in entirety or why they did what they did with any certainty. Individuals can, in good faith, endeavour to provide a full account of their actions and construct likely reasons for why they acted in particular ways Bourdieu, 1977; Sewell, 1992; Swartz, 1997). From a research perspective though, there can be no guarantees that these accounts are either complete or valid as the unconscious practices within a cultural field always will be beyond the complete description of language and much of what happens routinely will happen without deliberation (Swidler, 1986). However, as shown by Lavan and Martin (2002), within a classroom, the identification of nodes and the practices associated at each can provide a dimension to learning environment studies previously ignored.

3.2. Resistance within the Field

When culture is enacted, there is likely to be resistance since some participants within the classroom will experience what is enacted as more appropriate for other nodes and, perhaps, as belonging to other cultural fields (Elmesky, 2001). For example, in a science laboratory activity in Carambo's class, some students may want to do the activity prescribed by the teacher and, in the same group, peers may want to take advantage of a relative lack of teacher control to impress particular peers so as to earn their respect. This is a relatively common occurrence that can lead to a lack of focus and associated tension between the teacher and students and also between students in a small group. Similarly, the use of a scientific register (Lemke, 1995) by the teacher or some students might be resisted by others because they are unable to make good sense of what is being said and done. Resistance to the culture enacted by others is a characteristic of life in a field, and such resistance can manifest in struggles of various types and in the presence of contradictions to what is expected and experienced (Sewell, 1999). However, resistance is only one source of contradictions. It is important to realise that, in a field, cultural production and enactment produce patterns of practice and sense-making that have coherence that is thinned by the continual presence of ways of making sense and practicing that do not fit the pattern. These contradictions are not necessarily examples of foreign culture but can be idiosyncratic of a minority of participants. Indeed, these examples of culture might reflect deeper learning or more advanced forms of practice. Or they might reflect the agency of individuals or groups of individuals that become seeds for change within the field. Hence, from a learning environment research perspective, it is paramount that an effort to understand cultural production and enactment extend, beyond a search for patterns, to include the identification of contradictions and an effort to understand their salience within a field.

3.3. The Role of Cultural & Social Capital

Bourdieu (1986) theorised about different forms of capital. The lifeworlds of most teachers in urban schools differ significantly from those of their students in one or more of these forms of capital. For instance, cultural capital often takes centrality within an urban classroom as 'cultural otherness' and is identified as a problem by many urban teachers. Cultural differences extend beyond ethnicity and it is necessary for teachers to consider the social and economic capital available to support student learning. Unless a teacher knows the culture of her students, it is unlikely that she will be a successful teacher, irrespective of what she knows about science. Also, critical to the functioning of a learning environment is social capital. Our research in urban schools has highlighted the centrality of respect in interactions with urban youth (Elmesky, 2001; Seiler, 2002; Tobin, Seiler, & Walls, 1999). Anderson (1999) noted that respect is the currency of the streets and urban youth from cities like Philadelphia earn respect in the streets by being able to handle themselves physically and being sexually attractive to others. The campaign for respect among urban youth is relentless, and one of the ways that youth can earn the respect of peers is by showing disrespect for those in authority. The campaign does not stop at the doorway to the classroom and at some nodes in an urban science classroom, students might act in ways to earn the respect of peers. In the U.S., especially in inner city schools, it is unlikely that the status of being a teacher will carry the symbolic capital needed to earn the respect of students. Hence, it becomes imperative for learning environment research to consider how teachers build social capital with students, establish patterns of rapport that are respectful and thereby earn the right to be respected and to be regarded by students as their teacher. Moreover, while there is this need to understand how the learning environment accommodates different culture, it is also important to study how a culture of science is created within the field of the urban science classroom. Thus, understanding a learning environment requires understanding how the classroom community evolves to be more science-like as students and the teacher build on the culture they have already have, to build new culture that is accepted as science.

4. Cultural Nodes in Carambo's Classroom

The cultural enactment at different nodes can complement that which is enacted at other nodes or it can be quite discrete. There are many nodes in a science class and, as an illustration of how the learning environments can vary at each of them, we provide here a description of the different sorts of cultural enactment that occur at different nodes in Carambo's science class. In the following sections and subsections, we explore the following nodes from the perspective of research on learning environments; the chalkboard, space away from the chalkboard but in its vicinity, laboratory activities, use of the World Wide Web, transitions, and one-on-one interactions.

4.1. Chalkboard

At the chalkboard, Carambo coordinates the use of his voice with notes that summarise the key points he is making, diagrams and sketches, gestures, body movements and intonation, amplitude and register of his voice. He has two main foci as he teaches; to gain the attention of most of the students in the class and to mediate their learning of science. When he teaches from the front of the class, Carambo wants the students to learn at a deep level about procedures or the subject matter of science. Activities at the chalkboard are mainly teacher-centred and Carambo uses his voice to minimise multi-party talk and to maintain a focus on what he is saying and doing. Frequently activities at the chalkboard are interrupted by students who do not sustain their focus, at which time Carambo enacts strategies to refocus the class (these are discussed in a subsection called regaining order in the next section).

During a discussion (5 minutes and 32 seconds) of a laboratory activity the class had just completed, Carambo commenced with a review of the definition of a cathode and what it meant to say it was positively charged (CPR). He reviewed the metals that had been cathodes in the laboratory (copper, iron), and then, when zinc was mentioned, he stressed that zinc would be the negative electrode in each of their activities. Deconstruction of the meaning of CPR (cathode, positive, reduction) led to a discussion of reduction. As Carambo explained the chemistry that occurred in the cell, he wrote key words and phrases onto the chalkboard and referred to a diagram of an electrochemical cell that he had drawn on the left hand side ("Zinc is pretty much always going to be the negative one," he said as he wrote Zn on the chalkboard and connected a line from the symbol to the anode of the diagram of the cell). Carambo spoke clearly and emphatically, and his presentation was only occasionally interspersed with Staccato styled comments intended to refocus student attention ("You had copper as the cathode right? Heh!"). He also wanted students to do more than watch and listen, and he reminded them from time to time to look at their notes and "get this down." Carambo wanted students to learn the value of taking good notes in lectures such as this one ("Please just get this down. This really is very central").

The lecture using the board was interactive with Carambo asking many questions, getting answers from the students, and writing their responses onto the chalkboard as key words. His focus here was on having students understand the discourse of science, and he interacted with them and used tools to mediate learning from the laboratory activity. The tools used in this activity included written notes, diagrams, and oral language, including explanations, questions, evaluative remarks, and gestures. Carambo paced from the chalkboard to a front desk where there was a copy of the worksheet for the laboratory activity. Students were to use the inscriptions on the chalkboard together with Carambo's gestures and words to recall what they had done in the laboratory and connect it with what they knew of chemistry (e.g., what reduction is and how it occurs at a cathode). The primary tools they had available to them were associated with Carambo's practices, their recollections of the laboratory activity (just completed), their notebooks, and their knowledge of chemistry.

Elmesky voiceover: During the time spent in Carambo's class, I found the node of the chalkboard most interesting. In a school where many teachers receive little attention or respect at the front of the classroom, it always amazed me to find Carambo's students largely attentive and participating through note-taking and by providing answers to questions or making comments. What commonly occurs at the chalkboard node in an urban science class like Carambo's is often described as resistance, although usually students are enacting culture that belongs in a different field (either consciously or unconsciously). What allowed Carambo to be successful in engaging student learning around chemistry concepts such as electrochemical cells, oxidation and reduction, was particularly related to his strategies for breaching the (unwanted) habitus of the student. At the chalkboard, Carambo has a near zero tolerance for students with heads down on the desks, those without notebooks open, or violations of the dress code.

4.2. Away from the Chalkboard

When Carambo teaches away from the board, he uses fewer tools to mediate the learning of his students. Language is the essential tool at this node and it includes the words he utters, his intonations and gestures, bodily movements, frowns and smiles, and a multitude of ways in which he interacts with students. This section contains different types of activity that occur at this node and reflect in part, the different types of analyses we undertook as we searched for the conscious and unconscious enactment of culture. The subsections discussed here are mini-lectures, demonstrations, good-natured exchanges, regaining order, and maestro Carambo (which involves analyses of non-verbal practices).

4.2.1. Mini-lectures

The class had been talking about heating metal objects and why they do not continue to get hotter and hotter as more energy is added from a flame. Because he does not use the chalkboard, Carambo is much more reliant on gestures and voice inflection. Also, he uses the register of the students rather than the register of science and he endeavours to connect to topics of interest to them; especially the boys in the class. Carambo explains about welding in an effort to connect with the students' interests and their knowledge of phenomena outside of the classroom. The following 46 second interaction occurs with Carambo standing at the front left corner of the class and addressing his remarks to the whole class.

12:39:33	Carambo	Have you ever noticed the people that use the tanks, the tanks to do welding? They've got like two knobs on it. When they first turn it on it's like yellow, a yellow colour ... and they start playing with the air and it goes whshshsh... and they start changing. Right. The length of the light is controlled by air and thing and stuff. Well that's how you make it really really hot. You don't have it on your stove. Your stove is...
12:39:56	Boy	What fire is the hottest fire? Blue ...Yellow ... Blue ...
12:39:59	Carambo	Blue. Blue. Blue-white. Remember when we did the candle?
12:40:02	Boy	Yes.
12:40:03	Carambo	When we did the candle the blue-white part of the candle ... blue-white is the hottest colour, is the hottest temperature than red or yellow. Right? It goes red ...red-yellow ... red-yellow white and then blue-white. That's like the hottest flame.

During this short interaction with the class, Carambo uses language, principally a coordination of spoken words and gestures to remind students about oxy-acetylene tanks being used in welding. Initially, his gestures are an indication of how the knobs on each tank are turned to control the flow of gas and characteristics of the flame. He also uses his voice to simulate the sound of the gas and the flame (whshshsh). When he responds to the question asked of him, he uses his hands to emphasise the words he is speaking. In this interaction, Carambo is limited in the tools available to him and uses voice intonation and changes in volume to capture the attention of the class. Although there was one question asked and it was highly relevant to the explanation, the resources available to students were their ears. They were required to listen to and learn from what might be characterised as a mini lecture.

4.2.2. Demonstrations

Carambo does demonstrations for numerous reasons that include providing concrete examples of otherwise abstract phenomena, motivating his students, and providing a visual example of science being done.

Carambo	1:07:54	See the copper on the nails? See the nails were silver when they came in, weren't they? I can see that. Russ, can you see it? Can you see it? Can you see it? Can you see it?	Looking at test tube while he shows it to the class. He moves the test tube so that students in the class can see and brings it down close to Russ who is in the front seat.
Student	1:08:01	Yeah.	A student from the class responds.
		So what's happening here? When here's what's for. Does anyone notice what I snuck in here? Does anyone notice what I snuck in this one?	He coordinates his questions with pointing and gestures that draw attention to different parts of the test tube.
Student	1:08:08	Polish?	Indicative of a guess based on everyday experience.
Carambo	1:08:09	I put some salt in there right?	Responds to his own questions

In this short demonstration, Carambo is showing the students a simple chemical reaction in which copper ions are reduced and form a copper coating on steel nails. His bodily movement is energetic and his gestures direct the attention of students to various parts of the test tube. His words are from his everyday register and nothing is said that belongs to the register of chemistry. The students are attentive and focused on what he is saying and doing. Carambo pays no attention to the incorrect response from one child that the coat on the nail might be due to polish. His main goal in the short demonstration is to pique the scientific curiosity of the students and to have them see that interesting changes can occur during chemistry experiments. Also, by doing science in front of his students, they have a chance to see their teacher as scientist and learn from his practices.

4.2.3. *Good-natured exchanges*

At 12:30:10, Hakeem appears on the screen on the left hand side of the classroom. Hakeem has a history of being very difficult and although he is exceptionally bright, he rarely directs his academic talents to his schoolwork. He is streetwise and has a history of violence, including some involvement in selling drugs. He loves to rap and regards himself as a better than average rapper. Hakeem does a little dance using his right arm and bodily movement. He seems to be rapping as he moves closer to the front of the classroom. Over the course of a few seconds, the dance becomes more pronounced and his bodily movements quicken and are more exaggerated. When he is within five feet of Carambo, he raises his voice and gestures widely in mock anger at his teacher. For a moment, Hakeem is role playing a teacher and how he might respond to someone who is rapping. Carambo laughs with joy as Hakeem turns and returns quickly to his seat. As Hakeem moves away, Carambo moves decisively to the centre front to address the class. The brief moment of humour has passed and his demeanour is now business-like.

4.2.4. *Regaining order*

Carambo is well aware of the research that has been undertaken in his classroom and he has been a co-author on papers on his teaching of science and the identity of students in his class (e.g., Roth, Tobin, Elmesky, Carambo & McKnight). Earlier in the semester, he read parts of research undertaken by Seiler (2002) and Elmesky (2001) and knew of the need to attend to the habitus of students. We decided that it might be useful to breach their habitus when they enacted strategies from the street. The breach would bring their habitus to consciousness and, perhaps, over time they would develop strategies to eliminate those strategies in the field of the urban science classroom. In this activity, Carambo is cleaning the board energetically. There is considerable noise in the classroom with some male voices audible above a general background buzz of conversation. After 12 seconds, Carambo completes his cleaning of the chalkboard and turns to the class.

Learning Environments in Urban Science Classrooms 117

12:29:03	Carambo	Excuse me. Hey!
		EB (EeBe). Sit down.
		Jack! Jack!
12:29:10	Jack	Yes?
12:29:11	Carambo	Sit down.
12:29:12		Daniel! Come on (beckons with arm, hand and fingers)
12:29:13		Jack!
12:29:14		Here! (points to seat and moves chin emphatically)

Carambo then stands motionless as he surveys the class as they return to their seats and quiet down. After a period of relative silence, which extends for just over 10 seconds, Carambo initiates a transition to the next activity.

4.2.5. *Maestro Carambo*

Associated with maintaining management was Carambo's role in clarifying the rules for behaviour to his students. During the review lesson on electrochemical cells, Carambo realised that the students were not doing the task that had been assigned. He moved from the left hand side of the class and came to a central position at the front of the classroom, just at the end of the chalkboard but 5 feet in front of it. He squarely faced the class and called them to order. For two minutes, he then admonished the class for their juvenile behaviour and clearly reiterated what they should be doing and what they should not be doing (as in the above subsection, this is enactment of Carambo's call to order strategy). He connected the specific activity of tidying up their notes to an open book quiz to be administered on Friday and its relationship to the final examination. Microanalysis of the videotape reveals that Carambo used his body to emphasise various points but, and most of the two minutes he remained squarely facing the class. Analyses of the gestures, without the sound, reveal familiar patterns. Almost immediately Carambo raises his right arm, pointing forward with his hand, until the arm is parallel to the ground. He then raises it up to shoulder level and drops it to the ground in a rhythmic movement. The movement is repeated as he speaks and a rhythm is maintained. He twirls his hand and wrist at times and at one stage appears to spiral his arm downward. Without the sound, the arm movements are similar in appearance to those that might be seen as a maestro conducted an orchestra. We are not sure what to make of these non-verbal rhythms but report them here as a possible direction for research in learning environments. We feel that an absence of gesture would produce very different meaning than the coordination of gesture and words.

Carambo voiceover: I am a bit uneasy with this two minutes of admonishing the class. I find that I do that kind of activity when I'm at the end of my respectful limits. I don't feel that the students necessarily feel disrespected, but I find that this kind of activity on my part exemplifies a major contradiction in the classroom environment that this group presents. The fact that I can take only two minutes to refocus them is a vast improvement from their behaviour as ninth graders, but it is still not a good method of controlling the class. I feel that it does not engender the kind of internal control and awareness of appropriate strategies of action that I feel is so important to have. That activities tend to fall (or become less directed) apart when I am not near (not always, but often enough) is evidence of this contradiction.

4.3. Small Group Activities

Two nodes that were critical components of the learning environments in Carambo's class are presented in this section, laboratory activities and computer-focused activities. In each case, we explore the roles of the teacher and students and the distribution of power.

4.3.1. Laboratory activities

Laboratory activities typically extend from 30 minutes to one hour. Carambo makes behaviour-related interventions less often while working as a co-participant with his students in their laboratory groups. Students seem to almost be set free. They break out of the invisible boundaries surrounding their desks — for example, during a lab on chemical bonding, Elmesky's field notes stated that: jackets slide back on, hoods get flipped unconsciously back into a familiar position, and some students are heard to joke and laugh about sniffing household chemicals such as turpentine and moth balls as they work through the procedure associated with their lab. At this node, the porous boundaries of this field are most clearly visible and the associated learning environment reveals a rich mixture of cultural production and reproduction.

During an activity on electrochemistry the students were given 30 minutes to build an electrochemical cell and try out a number of different metals as electrodes. The way laboratory activities are enacted allows students to work at their own pace and also socialise with one another. Carambo moved from group to group, assisting students to get underway with the activity, such as by setting up apparatus so that the lab could be undertaken successfully. However, his role was not surveillance as he usually assumed a central role in the group; he was a central co-participant with a group of 3–4 students. When Carambo was with a group, they were focused and serious in their doing of science. Students in the group in which Carambo was working assisted him and some watched. In the other groups, there was a variety of activity as most students followed the directions to complete the laboratory activity. There was ample evidence of students being involved in the activity without the presence of Carambo.

During laboratory activities it is apparent that Carambo gets close to his students. Here, he is their teacher and he is able to connect between the doing of science and what each student knows and can do. He is prepared to allow students to work at their own paces and he allows a high level of noise (a working buzz). He is attentive in groups to what students ask and do and it is evident that laboratory activities are a central component of becoming scientifically literate in this class.

In some laboratory activities Carambo emphasised the following of directions and insisted that students know what they were to do in a pre-lab prior to being given permission to participate in the lab itself. There is a strong emphasis on doing and laboratory activities in this class provide ample opportunities for all students to develop a scientific habitus by doing science with others in a context of equipment and materials. Of course it is important that there is a diversity of competence in the community and through his practices, Carambo assumes the role of central participant and students can learn at his elbows. In addition, there is scope for students to learn science-related attitudes through their active involvement in laboratory activities as they are enacted in this classroom. Perhaps the development of dispositions and science related attitudes are precursors to building conceptual knowledge at a deep level.

4.3.2. *Computer*

The roles of the teacher and students at internet-connected computers were similar to those of a laboratory activity except for the tools used in this activity. Students worked together in groups of three to four and sat in chairs or stools around a computer that is connected to the internet. Networked computers are available in Carambo's office, in the front right of the class, and in the back-left corner of the room. Although students are able to use the internet-connected computers throughout the day, they serve a different function in a science activity. A principal role is for the students to use the World Wide Web as a resource to support their learning. For example, Carambo had instructed the groups to utilise the internet as a resource when Elmesky joined a group of students who were surfing the web. In a conversation with the students, Elmesky realised that they wanted to prepare a poster about vitamin C. They told her they wanted a picture of vitamin C. She wondered what they meant by a picture and ventured a guess, Oh, so you want a picture of an orange or something that has vitamin C in it? But that was not what they wanted. They wanted a picture of a pill or capsule and did not seem to be thinking about vitamins on a very complex level. Elmesky was relieved when Carambo joined the group and immediately assumed a central role, positioning himself directly in front of the computer and taking control of the mouse. His actions quickly put an end to the students' quest for a picture of pills. No! No! No! Remember when we looked at that website with diagrams of the chemical structures of vitamins? As Carambo spoke, he swiftly scanned through Favourites and chose a pre-selected bookmark. Within less than a minute, the chemical structure of vitamin C was displayed on the screen. The students had their picture of vitamin C even though it was not what they expected. Their facial expressions indicated that their mental image of vitamins was very different from the image on the screen. Carambo had assumed a central role in the group and had demonstrated how to use the computer to identify relevant information. The students were peripheral participants in the activity, but he had not completed the entire task. His role as a central participant demonstrated to the students at his elbows how to use a computer to identify relevant information about chemical structure. He provided structure without which the students would have been unable to make satisfactory progress. In so doing, he recognised that the students were peripheral participants and would have numerous opportunities in the weeks and years to come to become more expert in their use of the World Wide Web as a resource for their learning and activity in science.

Carambo voiceover: The work with this group is an example. By this time in the year, we had already done two inquiry trials and I had prepared the bookmarks for vitamins, this allowed me to get this group working quickly. As this was my first time doing this type of work, I made some structural mistakes early that I was able to improve during the course of the semester. The manner in which I interacted with the kids was similar to my lab persona that blends with the kids for awhile, gives some information and then moves on. This was a good instance. My concern with the computer node is that the activities were not structured well enough so that the kids could have a modicum of success. This would have aided their confidence, and their learning. I do think that my students needed some more teaching about the culture of working/researching at the computer and creating presentations. There were a few contradictions from my perspective. However as in the case of the computer issue, I feel that these contradictions (may or will) be resolved over time. I have the luxury of possibly being with these kids for several years.

4.4. Transitions

Transitions between activities allow the teacher and students to finish up one activity and get ready to commence the next. Traditionally, transitions in urban schools are slow. This can be of benefit to urban teachers who do not necessarily have the support of laboratory technicians to assist them in setting up and packing away equipment and materials. Students tend to engage in an "urban shuffle" as they walk slowly and delay being ready to commence the next activity. During transitions, the teacher will often be busy getting materials ready and preparing the materials and equipment for teaching and learning. Hence, it is convenient for transitions to take some time as long as they do not drag on for too long. Usually the students in Carambo's chemistry class will make the transitions last as long as they can. This tendency is consistent with at least one of the dispositions identified by Boykin (1986) for African Americans — communality, or a disposition to interact socially with peers. Hence, students use transitions to socialise and in so doing often will enact codes from other places such as the street or the basketball court. For example, as students interact during transitions, it is not unusual to hear profanity and loud verbal exchanges. Jousting is common and students will often engage in freestyle rapping (consistent with other dispositions identified by Boykin). During transitions, Carambo usually moves briskly about the class and may go to his office, the storeroom at the back of the room or re-arrange materials on the side bench. To end a transition, it is usually necessary for Carambo to enact strategies like those described above for regaining order (that is, his breaching strategies).

4.5. One-on-One Interactions

Carambo dedicated a great deal of his time in the early part of the year toward the building of social capital. Also, since he is now in his second year at the school, he has established a reputation of being cool. Most students we spoke to about Carambo responded, without a moment of thought: "Carambo? He cool." The students like to be with him while he is at school and throughout the class, there are many times when students can be heard calling out his name, "Carambo! Carambo!" Because of his popularity, Carambo spends a great deal of his time in one-on-one interactions with students (in and out of class time and also in and out of the building). Typically they want to talk to him about their activities and seek him out. Also, since he runs an open classroom, students will come to the classroom to hang out and in so doing, use the computers and perhaps get involved in some science. Perhaps they want to discuss part of an investigation, show him something they have written or read, or just enjoy some light-hearted humour. Significantly, Carambo is willing to engage in the full variety of activities with students and shows great interest and empathy in what they say and do. Through his one-on-one interactions with numerous students, Carambo shows that he is interested in them, their work, and their lives outside of school. He demonstrates his care and in so doing earns their respect. What is salient is that it is these one-on-one interactions with students that set the stage for their active participation in a great variety of activities. One-on-one interactions happen throughout the classroom and are spread across time. Because of the potential for Carambo and his students to build social capital in one-on-one interactions. we see these as having transformative potential as Carambo and his students endeavour to remove some of the contradictions that continue to exist in terms of creating and sustaining productive learning environments for all students. Despite serious efforts from Carambo and his students, there are still those who Carambo just cannot reach, whose practices are not consistent with those needed to become scientifically literate. Further research may show how Carambo and these students are able to remove these contradictions and create learning environments that afford increased scientific literacy.

5. Issues

Whereas researchers on learning environments have traditionally relied on reports from students, teachers and other participants within a field, we believe that studying learning environments through different theoretical lenses illuminates the dark corners and hidden dimensions previously overlooked in classrooms. As we have shown here, the interdependence of the nodes in Carambo's classroom and the significance of the spatial and temporal distribution of enacted culture served as useful foci for understanding what was occurring in the learning environment. Although, within a field, different forms of culture are enacted at different nodes, as is apparent in Carambo's classroom, nodes are not isolated islands where practices occur independently of what is happening at other nodes at a given time, what has happened historically, or what is likely to happen in the future. Time is a factor that shapes practices; and events, as they are reconstructed, experienced and imagined, are resources for cultural enactment at any node. Cultural enactment at any node within a field produces practices, conceptual objects and artefacts that are resources for present and future cultural production and enactment throughout a field. For example, a diagram left on a chalkboard can be a resource for small group discussions at some later time and remarks made by a teacher about rules that must be followed can serve as a challenge to a student several days later (e.g., "don't wear those hoods in class"). In particular, Sewell's theory of culture was an invitation to us to look carefully for examples of culture from other fields seeping through porous boundaries to be enacted at nodes within urban science classrooms. Sewell also predicted that nodes would be sites for resistance to cultural enactment. Both of these trends were evident in our research as contradictions to patterns in the practices of participants that constituted a thin coherence. We find the patterns of thin coherence to be of significance to the task of affording the learning of science. Accordingly, we regard as central to research on learning environments the concepts of field, boundaries and nodes.

Through introducing a sociocultural theoretical frame to learning environment discussions, what it means to learn science becomes a central issue to consider. More specifically, here we illustrate that our cultural approach suggests that lessons about electrochemical cells (which required knowledge not only of new terms but also of processes such as oxidation and reduction), as enacted in Carambo's review lesson, can have a key role in expanding the scientific identity and literacy of his urban science students.

Carambo voiceover: I worry that my student's do not possess sufficient science knowledge, nor have they learned the value of, or how to get that knowledge. I don't want the knowledge for its own sake; rather I feel that an important element of science literacy is knowing the language of science. Even if we inculcate the attitudes and dispositions of the community in the students, the language/discourse methods of the community need be present. We don't imply that having a positive disposition toward science or being engaged while doing interesting science activities is enough.

In fact, a key issue for practitioners and researchers is the value of teaching the discourse of science and moving on when students do not understand the concepts in a deep way. Is there value in doing this? Is it just inevitable that this will happen, or is it actually a necessary part of learning in a deep way? We regard these as issues associated with learning environment studies in urban high schools. Many teachers have reified verbal forms of learning, and an assumption usually is made that instruction should not proceed unless students thoroughly know the prerequisite knowledge. This may be a legacy of adhering for so long to models of learning that assumed learning hierarchies consisting of sets of linear chains arranged vertically. From a cultural perspective, it seems reasonable for peripheral participants to experience culture in all of its forms and to build new culture by experiencing it through co-participation at the elbows of more central participants. It is possible that the resources for building deep meaning reside in additional experiences with science content that are usually presented later in a hierarchy.

Bourdieu's seminal thinking on habitus, or dispositions to act in particular ways in given circumstances, has high significance for our thinking about scientific literacy (Swartz, 1997). As part of culture, habitus or strategies of action, afford the everyday practices of participants within a field. Being able to act without consciousness and intention is a significant aspect of life in any community. It is clear to us that any consideration of becoming scientifically literate must attend to those parts of literacy that are beyond what can be described with language. As we have seen here, participants will practice in ways that have salience to knowing science but remain unaware of their knowledge and are unable to explain why they do what they do. Thus, focusing on the development of strategies of action is an area of research on learning environments that is critical. Moreover, if researchers are to undertake such studies, it is important to ground the methodology and substantive questions in theories that relate to strategies of action. These theories depart from the psychosocial frame of Moos (1991) and invite fresh questions and approaches to resolving them. We exhort our colleagues to go beyond the identification of patterns of coherence and also to search for those contradictions that might be evidence of the importation of habitus from other fields, resistance to enacted culture, and agency of individuals and groups of individuals. The question of how contradictions are dealt with in research has critical significance in advancing the field of research on learning environments.

Whereas there has been a strong concern with cultural reproduction in schools — learning science as it is known and practiced by scientists — an exploration of science learning as cultural production invites questions about agency and structure. If learners exercise agency with respect to the structures of the urban science classroom, it is important to ask not only how the identities and cultural capital of the learners change, but also, how the actions of learners transform the field itself. Should we expect students only to be passive recipients of culture? It strikes us as odd that we expect scientists to change the face of science through their practices as scientists in their laboratories, yet, when urban youth practice science there is no expectation that their cultural production and enactment will transform science. We exhort our colleagues to consider the roles of all participants in urban science education in transforming the culture of science. What culture should count as science? This is not entirely an empirical question, nor is it entirely theoretical. From the perspective of cultural sociology, there is a strong claim for considering science in terms of shifting boundaries, especially when it is produced and enacted by urban youth who bring to their practices histories and cultural capital that differ greatly from those who traditionally have practiced science. From this perspective, it does not appear useful to consider learning and enactment independently of the learners and the communities in which they live. Accordingly, when learning environments are considered in relation to whether what is learned has transformative potential, it is imperative that our studies extend beyond just the field of the urban science classroom, and, for that matter, the fields of the school and surrounding streets. Questions of transformation relate to all culture in a cultural toolkit and the building of an understanding of just how culture produced in the field of an urban science classroom is enacted in other fields and contributes to the agency of students as they move through life.

Acknowledgement

The research in this chapter is supported by the National Science Foundation under Grant No. REC-0107022. Any opinions, findings, and conclusions or recommendations expressed in this chapter are those of the author and do not necessarily reflect the views of the National Science Foundation.

References

Anderson, E. (1999). *Code of the street: decency, violence, and the moral life of the inner city.* New York, NY: W.W. Norton.

Anyon, J. (1997). *Ghetto schooling: A political economy and urban educational reform.* NY: Teachers College Press.

Anyon, J. (1981). Social class and school knowledge. *Curriculum Inquiry, 11*, 3–42.

Barton, A.C. & Tobin, K. (2001). Preface: Urban science education. *Journal of Research in Science Teaching, 38,* 843–846.

Bourdieu, P. (1986). The forms of capital. In J.G. Richardson (Ed.) *Handbook of theory and research for the sociology of education* (pp. 241–258). New York, NY: Greenwood Press.

Bourdieu, P. (1977). Cultural reproduction and social reproduction. In J. Karabel & A. H. Halsey (Eds.) *Power and ideology in education* (pp. 487–511). New York, NY: Oxford University Press.

Boykin, A.W. (1986). The triple quandary and the schooling of Afro-American Children. In U. Neisser (Ed.), *The school achievement of minority children: New perspectives* (pp. 57–92). Hillsdale, NJ: Erlbaum.

Clarke, J., Hall, S., Jefferson, T. & Roberts, B. (1976). Sub cultures, cultures and class (pp. 9–69). In S. Hall & T. Jefferson (Eds), *Resistance through rituals: Youth sub cultures in post-war Britain.* London: Hutchinson.

Elmesky, R. (2001). *Struggles of agency and structure as cultural worlds collide as urban African American youth learn physics.* Doctoral dissertation, The Florida State University.

Engeström, Y. (1999). Activity theory and individual and social transformation. In Y. Engeström, R. Miettinen & R.-L. Punamäki (eds.), *Perspectives on activity theory* (pp. 19–38). Cambridge, England: Cambridge University Press.

Engeström, Y. (1987). Learning by expanding: An activity-theoretical approach to developmental research. Helsinki, Finland: Orienta-Konsultit.

Fraser, B.J. (1998). Science learning environments: Assessment, effects and determinants. In B.J. Fraser and K. Tobin (Eds). *International handbook of science education* (pp. 527–564). Dordrecht, The Netherlands: Kluwer.

Haberman, M. (1993). The pedagogy of poverty versus good teaching. *Phi Delta Kappan, 73*, 290–294.

Ingersoll, R.M. (2001). The realities of out-of-field teaching. *Educational Leadership, 58*(8), 42–45.

Ingersoll, R.M. (1997). Teacher turnover and teacher quality: The recurring myth of teacher shortages. *Teachers College Record, 99*, 41–44.

Kozol, J. (1991). Savage inequalities: children in America's schools. New York: Crown.

Lavan, S.-K. & Martin, S. (2002, March). *Social structure of high schools and enacted science curricula.* Paper presented at the 23rd Annual Ethnography in Education Research Forum, University of Pennsylvania, Philadelphia, PA.

Lemke, J.L. (1995). *Textual politics: Discourse and social dynamics.* London: Taylor & Francis.

Loman, L. (2002). *My cultural awakening in the classroom.* Paper presented at the 23rd Annual Ethnography in Education Research Forum, University of Pennsylvania, Philadelphia, PA.

Martin, S. (2002, March). *Not so strange in a strange land: An autobiographical approach to becoming a science teacher in an urban high school.* Paper presented at the 23rd Annual Ethnography in Education Research Forum, University of Pennsylvania, Philadelphia, PA.

Moos, R.H. (1991). Connections between school, work and family settings. In B.J. Fraser & H.J. Walberg (eds.), Educational environments: Evaluation, antecedents and consequences (pp. 29–53). London: Pergamon

Oakes, J. & Wells, A.S. (1998). Detracking for high student achievement. *Educational Leadership, 55*(6), 38–41.

Roth, W.-M. (2000). Learning environments research, lifeworld analysis, and solidarity in practice. *Learning Environments Research, 2*, 225–247.

Roth, W.-M. & Tobin, K. (2002). *At the elbow of another: Learning to teach by coteaching.* New York: Peter Lang.

Roth, W.-M., Tobin, K., Elmesky, R., Carambo, C. & McKnight, Y. (in press). Re/making identities in the praxis of urban schooling: A cultural historical perspective. *Mind, Culture and Activity.*

Roth, W.-M., Tobin, K. & Zimmermann, A. (2002). Coteaching/cogenerative dialoguing: Learning environments research as classroom praxis. *Learning Environments Research.*

Seiler, G. (2002). *A critical look at teaching, learning, and learning to teach science in an inner city, neighborhood high school.* Doctoral dissertation, University of Pennsylvania.

Sewell, W.H. (1992). A theory of structure: Duality, agency, and transformation. *American Journal of Sociology, 98*, 1–29.

Sewell, W.H. (1999). The concept(s) of culture. In V.E. Bonnell & L. Hunt (Eds.), B*eyond the cultural turn* (pp. 35–61). Berkeley: University of California Press.

Swartz, D. (1997). *Culture & power: The sociology of Pierre Bourdieu.* Chicago, IL: University of Chicago Press.

Swidler, A. (1986). Culture in action: Symbols and strategies. *American Sociological Review, 51*, 273–286.

Tobin, K. (2000). Becoming an urban science educator. *Research in Science Education, 30*(1), 89–106.

Tobin, K., Seiler, G. & Smith, M.W. (1999). Educating science teachers for the sociocultural diversity of urban schools. *Research in Science Education, 29*, 68–88.

Tobin, K., Seiler, G. & Walls, E. (1999). Reproduction of social class in the teaching and learning of science in urban high schools. *Research in Science Education, 29*, 171–187.

Toussaint, K.C. (1997). *Domination, power and racial stereotypes: Towards an alternative explanation of black male school resistance.* UMI Microform No. 9738009. Ann Arbor, MI: UMI Dissertation Services.

U.S. Census Bureau. (2001). *Population change and distribution: Census 2000 brief.* Washington, DC: U.S. Census Bureau Public Information Office.

Whitman, G. (2000). Neighborhood schools prepare few for college. *Philadelphia Public School Notebook, 7*, 1 & 9.

Chapter 6

STUDY OF LEARNING ENVIRONMENT FOR IMPROVING SCIENCE EDUCATION IN BRUNEI

Myint Swe Khine
Nanyang Technological University
Singapore

Many countries around the world realise that there must be an adequate provision made for science education in order to face challenges in the new millennium. In recent years, the Government in Brunei has given due emphasis to science education by making available adequate resources for the teaching of science in all schools. In general, studies made on the learning of science revealed that there was a trend towards a decrease in the number of students in the science stream. Although government schools are well equipped and provided with the necessary resources, there are indications that examination results have been unsatisfactory. In order to improve the teaching and learning context, it is important to look into the learning environment created by teachers, the interactions and interrelationships among teachers and students. This chapter describes the recent attempts to study various aspects of educational learning environment in Brunei with the aim of improving science education in primary and secondary schools. This chapter also discusses the issues and future directions of investigations in different science classrooms.

1. Introduction

With rapid development in the science and technology fields, many countries around the world realise that there must be an adequate provision made for science education in order to face challenges in the new millennium. In recent years, the Government in Brunei has given due emphasis to science education by making available adequate resources for the teaching of science in all schools.

There is a general consensus amongst policy makers and administrators that Science, Mathematics and Technology (SMT) education is important for national development. Government departments are urged to collaborate to achieve SMT for the economic, technological, educational, and social development of the nation. Teachers, educators, scientists, engineers, and technologists have been encouraged to publish their work and help to disseminate interesting research and development findings (Ismail, 1998). As a result, a sizeable number of research studies which examine various issues related to science education has been conducted in Brunei over the past few years. This paper describes some of this research and its findings.

2. The Context

Brunei Darussalam is one of 35 countries in the world which has a population of less than half a million and is categorised as a micro-state. The country is situated on the north-west coast of the island of Borneo with an area of approximately 5700 sq.km. According to the 1999 census, the population of Brunei stands at 331,000 and has an annual growth rate of 3.1%. The majority of the population is Malay (67%) while Chinese (15%) and other indigenous groups (6%) are represented as minorities. The rest of the population is made up of Asian and European expatriate workers. According to the Brunei Yearbook, 1999, more than one third of the population is under 15 years of age.

The education policy of Brunei in its present form aims to establish an effective, efficient, and equitable system of education that is in agreement with the national philosophy of a Malay Islamic Monarchy. The education system therefore aims to provide opportunities for all Bruneians to realise their full potential. It is believed that an educated workforce will contribute to the development of a progressive and peaceful nation, where the Malay language and culture, Islamic faith and values, and loyalty and allegiance to the Monarch and the State are emphasised (Hamid, 2000).

Brunei Darussalam gained independence in 1984, and the British left a legacy of influence in legal, administrative, public service, and education systems. With the growing population and expansion of economy and infrastructure, high priority is now given to the education sector with an allocation amounting from 15% to 20% of the total government expenditure. The Government's investment in education is seen not only as a response to population growth, but is basic and central to the development of a trained local work force and to the people of Brunei as a whole (Jumat, 1992).

3. Overview of the Current Education System in Brunei

In 1954, Brunei embarked on a five-year development plan for education. The plan created the infrastructure for what eventually formed the Ministry of Education. New schools were planned, and large numbers of teachers, mostly expatriates, were employed in the schools.

The formal school system in Brunei has adopted a 7-3-2-2 pattern. This pattern represents primary, lower secondary, upper secondary, and pre-tertiary levels, respectively. In 1997, one year of pre-school education was introduced. The Department of Schools coordinates the implementation of educational programs, projects and activities of the Ministry. According to the 2000 statistics, there are 175 primary schools, 39 secondary schools and 70 non-government or private schools.

Within the broad aims of the Brunei education system, one of the important features is to enable the students to develop fluency in the native tongue of Bahasa Melayu, and at the same time the learning and use of English as a second language is encouraged. As such, a bilingual system of education was introduced. The bilingual system of education implemented in 1985 aimed to establish a policy for the language of instruction used in schools and also to consolidate the national system of education for the newly independent nation. Bilingual means the languages used as mediums of instruction are both English and Malay in all subjects. English Language, Mathematics, Science, History, Geography, Economic are taught in English, while Malay language and Literature, Islamic Religious Knowledge and Physical Education are taught in the native Malay language.

Students after successfully completing the six years of schooling in the primary level, join the lower secondary level. The duration at the lower secondary level is three years. At the end of their third form, students sit for lower secondary assessment (Penilaian Menengah Bawah — PMB) examinations. Those students who pass the examinations can then join the upper secondary education leading to the Brunei Cambridge General Certificate of Education.

Placement of students into science and humanities streams in upper secondary education is based on the results of the lower secondary level. The intention is to provide students with opportunities to continue in full-time education after sitting the PMB. The duration of the schooling at this level is either two or three years.

Education at the upper secondary level is general in nature with some provision for specialisation in science, arts and technical fields. At the end of second year, high academic achievers may sit for the General Certificate of Education Ordinary Level (GCE 'O') examinations.

The Brunei Cambridge GCE 'O' Level examination is conducted at the end of the second year of upper secondary education or Form 5. Subjects covered in this examination include English, Malay, Mathematics and pure science subjects such as Physics, Chemistry and Biology, Double Sciences (Chemistry and Physics, Biology and Physics, Chemistry and Biology) or Combined Science.

4. Science Education and Science Teachers

The Ministry of Education believes that the goal of scientific literacy for all can be achieved through a balanced curriculum in which science is taught with four broad aims. These aims address science for the informed citizen, for further and life-long education, for the world of work, and for personal development. Jumat (1998) elaborated these aims in the following way:

Science for the informed citizen

> In the age of technology, the aim of science education must be amongst the most important. If members of our society fail to understand the interaction of science, technology and society, they lose control of the most important forces shaping their world. With this in mind, momentum towards a science education that incorporates science-technology-society has become firmly established in Brunei science education.

Science for further and life-long education

One of the major functions of schooling in Brunei Darussalam has been to prepare students to enter post-secondary educational institutions. Science education is a preparation and encouragement for students to learn about science throughout their lives. Science programmes with this goal will prepare students for a lifetime of learning and enable them to examine their own knowledge critically.

Science for the world of work

Brunei Darussalam needs trained workers and individuals need employment. Because science, mathematics and technology will be a factor in the careers of many of the students, they must learn how technology will influence the nature of work and career opportunities in the future.

Science for personal development

Science and technology education can contribute to the development of rationality and ability to think critically. As a discipline that uses rational argument and critical thinking, science can be the means by which students developed such skills as observing, classifying and hypothesising. (p. 13)

With these broad aims, science education is structured to help students acquire high quality science knowledge and skills at all levels. At the primary level, science is a compulsory subject taught from the beginning of the fourth year. Science continues as integrated science at the lower secondary level and the current syllabus is adapted from the Scottish Integrated Science course. The main aims and objectives of the science curriculum are to ensure that the students gain some knowledge of the world, the vocabulary and grammar of science, the ability to observe objectively, solve problems and think scientifically, and be aware of the implications and effects of science on society.

At the upper secondary level, students are required to take at least one type of science subject. Based on their abilities and interests, students can choose pure science subjects, combined science or other science-based subjects. Examples of pure science subjects are Physics, Chemistry or Biology or double science (Physics & Chemistry; Chemistry & Biology or Biology & Physics). Combined Science covers combination of all science subjects such as Physics, Chemistry and Biology). Other science-based subjects are Human and Social Biology and Agricultural Science. Usually science stream students will take pure science courses and other students will study one of the double sciences or combined science or human and social biology or agricultural science. All the science courses emphasise understanding and application of scientific concepts and principles.

To ensure the smooth implementation of the curriculum, at the primary level the schools are provided with locally developed textbooks and workbooks. For secondary level, science textbooks are imported. However, at the lower secondary level, additional textbooks and teachers guides are developed locally. Secondary schools have well-equipped science laboratories and the School Department provides an annual budget to cover expenses for the purchase of consumables.

Science laboratories in secondary schools are normally maintained by laboratory assistants and technicians. They prepare apparatus, chemicals, and other materials required for the science practical lessons. Schools also appoint one of the teachers as the specialist science teacher to supervise the teaching and learning of science. At the secondary level, science theory classes are given six periods per week of thirty-five minutes per period. For practical classes, laboratory time is given between one to two hours per week.

Generally, school science and mathematics curricula in Brunei are adopted from the British model. Attracting students to study science and mathematics in Brunei has been a problem in the past. Issues on how to make science and mathematics more interesting and relevant in order to attract more students who want to pursue careers related to science and mathematics need to be addressed (Bakar, 1997).

According to 1998 statistics, there are approximately 2,087 teachers employed in government secondary schools in Brunei. Secondary school teachers are recruited locally as well as from overseas since there is still a shortage of qualified teachers in the country. This has been a practice for many years since the inception of secondary education. These expatriate teachers come from Sri Lanka, India, Singapore, Malaysia, Philippines, the United Kingdom, and Australia. In recent years, teachers from New Zealand and Canada have also been recruited. Sharifah (1997) noted that recruitment of science teachers from other countries has been a feature of the schools in Brunei Darussalam.

The SHBIE Institute of Education at the Universiti Brunei Darussalam is the sole teacher training institution in Brunei. The Institute offers a four-year Bachelor of Science (BSc Education) degree program, a Postgraduate Certificate in Secondary Science education, and a Bachelor of Education (BEd General Science). The education studies component in each of the degree programmes accounts for approximately one-third of the programme. The education courses are designed to provide students with an understanding of such matters as the patterns of human growth and learning and the relevance and application of modern technology to teaching and learning. The remainder of the courses are comprised of content and specialised subject matter which teachers will be required to teach in secondary schools. The Institute also regularly conducts in-service courses to introduce new teaching methods to teachers.

In 1994, the Government established the National Committee on Science and Technology which was charged with the responsibility of promoting and encouraging the development of science and technology in the interest of national development. The main areas of focus in the Science and Technology Plan are to promote science and technology awareness among students and to focus on the science and technology based human resource development. The policy laid down in the Plan has considerable implications for the school system and science education in Brunei Darussalam (Sharifah, 1997).

With the rapid development in the science and technology fields, many countries around the world realise that there must be an adequate provision made for science education for the younger generation. It is generally agreed that such an attempt is crucial for the modernisation and growth of economic and social systems for a country. Brunei Darussalam is one of the countries which has given priority to improvement in science education in the school system in order to face the challenges in the next millennium.

In recent years, science education has been given due emphasis by the Government in Brunei and adequate provision of resources are made available in all schools. When there is a shortage of science teachers, expatriate teachers from Western countries are recruited for the jobs. In general, there is a belief in Brunei that students are not interested in learning science subjects in schools. Studies of the participation of students in science revealed that there is a decreasing trend in the number of students enrolling in the science stream. There are also indications that although government schools are well equipped and provided with necessary resources, the results of the examinations are unsatisfactory (Sharifah, 1997).

In order to improve the teaching and learning situation in context, it is important to look into the learning environment created by the teachers and interactions and interrelationships among teachers and students. Educational environment can be considered as the socio-psychological context or determinant of learning, and providing favourable and conducive environments can maximise learning outcomes (Fraser & Walberg, 1991). Classroom environment assessments may provide a means of monitoring and evaluating the teaching of science subjects.

5. Past Research on Learning Environment

A number of attempts have been made in the past to find out the science classroom environment in Brunei by educational researchers. An examination of the relationships between personal attribute variables (consisting of district, school type, age, sex and personal aspirations), home background variables (consisting of family size, family income, parental occupations and parental aspirations), and intermediate variables (consisting of involvement in science activities, classroom atmosphere and practices and attitudes toward science) and cognitive achievement test scores in Mathematics, English, Malay and General Paper in Brunei was undertaken by Alvarez (1989).

In her study, attitudinal measures were made by using an 8-item classroom atmosphere and practice, 10-item involvement in science activities, and 10-item attitude toward science questionnaires. Four hundred and twenty two primary six students were randomly selected through stratified proportional sampling techniques from four school districts. The results showed that the relationships between the three sets of independent variables and the dependent measures in the four subject areas, personal attribute variables (specifically school district, school type, age and personal aspirations) correlated positively with cognitive achievement in Mathematics, English and General Paper. Involvement in science activities and students' perceived classroom atmosphere and practices did not correlate with cognitive achievement in any of the four subject areas.

The results also indicated the interrelated nature of the students' involvement in science activities, the extent to which they perceive their classroom to be interesting and enjoyable, and their attitudes towards science as a subject in their curriculum. It is inferred that involvement in science activities like science subjects, science hobbies and reading books about science and scientists influenced in part their interest and positive attitude towards science.

In another study, Alvarez (1988) examined the self-perceived difficulties of teaching skills, needs assessment of teaching skills, science teaching resources and attitudes towards teaching science of primary and secondary science teachers. In her study, 171 science teachers were involved. Of this sample, 56 science teachers were Bruneian and 115 teachers were expatriates. The study suggested the need for more research into the science classroom behaviours of both students and teachers in Brunei. It was concluded that the analysis of a teacher's actual behaviour in the science classroom is critical to determine if behaviours are those intended by the science curriculum or are just the teacher's ideal or perceived classroom behaviour.

Asghar (1994) reported the findings from a study to assess Form 3 pupils' perceptions of their science classroom environment and to explore the relationships between these perceptions and the students' science achievement. A random sample of 120 Form 3 students from primary schools in Brunei were the subject of the study and the ICEQ was used. The study found that three dimensions of the science classroom environment were found to be correlated with science achievement. The highest positive correlation with science achievement was with the Participation scale and the lowest with the Investigation scale. Science achievement was also negatively correlated with the Differentiation scale of the instrument.

Poh (1995) evaluated O-Level Biology laboratory teaching across government secondary schools in Brunei with regards to process skills and learning environment. The study was designed to evaluate the quality of O-level biology laboratory work in Brunei schools from the perspectives of the students' process skills development, and their perceptions of the learning environment. A total of 220 Form 5 science stream students who were enrolled for the GCE O-Level examination in nine government secondary schools were the subjects of the study. The study involved content analysis of laboratory instruction using the *Laboratory Assessment Inventory* (LAI) (Fuhrman, Lunetta, Novick, & Tamir, 1978) to assess the tasks required for a number of process skills, and assessment of students' perceptions of their laboratory classroom learning environment using the SLEI. The study found that laboratory activities given to students in this context gave little opportunity for practice in higher order process skills and the laboratory activities were often close-ended.

The study also found that female students perceived their laboratory learning environment more favourably than did their male counterparts. The findings of this study provided valuable information regarding the nature of O-level biology laboratory learning environment in government schools in Brunei. The differences in the perceptions of laboratory learning environment between female and male students suggested that different treatment, attention or guidance by the teachers was necessary (Poh, 1996). There were higher levels of students' preferences for certain laboratory learning environments, meaning that students would like a more favourable environment, particularly on the dimensions of Student Cohesiveness, Rule Clarity and Material Environment. The study suggested that science teachers in Brunei should make classroom practice more participative, more investigative, and less differentiated to improve the science achievement of students.

Hunus (1998) investigated the learning environment and its associations with student outcomes in Chemistry in Brunei's secondary schools. The study involved 644 chemistry students from 23 government secondary schools. Students' perceptions of the classroom environment of chemistry theory classes were examined by using modified versions of the WIHIC questionnaire and the QTI. An adapted version of the SLEI was used to assess the students' perceptions of the chemistry laboratory classroom environment. It was found that students perceived their chemistry classroom learning environment as favourable and gender differences were detected. The girls perceived the chemistry classroom learning environment more favourably than did the boys. It was also found that students' perceptions of chemistry classroom environments were associated with students' cognitive learning outcomes. The WIHIC scales, Teacher Support, Involvement, and Task Orientation and the QTI scale, Understanding, were positively associated with attitudinal and cognitive outcomes.

It was also reported that Investigation, Autonomy/Independence and Open-Endedness were positively associated with students' attitudinal outcomes but negatively associated with students' achievement in Chemistry. The study suggested that teachers should be cautious when introducing innovative teaching approaches, such as giving students autonomy and independence in their learning tasks, allowing students to do their own investigations, working cooperatively in theory classes, and giving open-ended practicals in laboratory classes.

To investigate students' perceptions of their science teachers' interpersonal behaviours and their enjoyment of science lessons in government primary schools in Brunei, Scott and Fisher (2000) translated an elementary version of the QTI into Standard Malay. The study involved 3104 Year 6 students from 136 classrooms in 23 primary schools. The Questionnaire on Teacher Interaction (Elementary) [QTIE] has 48 items in 7 scales. Similarly they have translated the Enjoyment of Science Lessons (ENJ) from the Test of Science Related Attitudes (TOSRA). During the process of translation, attempts were being made to ensure that original meanings was maintained. The process also involved back-translation and the final translation was checked by bilingual native Malay speaking adults and a group of secondary students.

Scale means show that students perceived their teacher mostly as good leaders, seldom uncertain or dissatisfied and seldom admonishing. It was also found that students' enjoyment of their science lessons correlated with each of the QTI scales. Further analysis revealed that the QTI scale impacted most on students' enjoyment of their science lessons was teachers' helping/friendly behaviour. Associations between a small sub-sample of students' perceptions of their teachers' interpersonal behaviour and their end-of-year result on an external examination in science were investigated. It was found that students' perceptions of more cooperative behaviour were positively correlated, while perceptions of submissive behaviour were negatively correlated with their cognitive achievement. The study utilises a large data-base from students in co-educational primary schools and suggests that providing valuable feedback from students to primary teachers and other educators in Brunei allows to reflect upon their practice.

An attempt to validate the QTI in a specific cultural context was made in Brunei. Out of 48 statements contained in the Australian version of QTI, 20 statements were re-worded and re-phrased in order to suit the local context (Khine, Larwood & Fisher, 2000). The revised questionnaire was administered to 276 Form 5 students in 14 classrooms and it was found that the reliabilities ranged from 0.60 to 0.76 with the individual student as the unit of analysis. It was suggested that when a learning environment research tool such as the QTI is used, the first consideration needs to be ensuring that many of the language difficulties are overcome. Even if the problems with cognition of vocabulary and genuine understanding of true intent of the statements in the QTI are worked through and the version of the QTI is proven to be statistically reliable, the results cannot be always taken at face value due to the fact that there could be cultural differences inherent in the students' responses.

Majeed, Fraser and Aldridge (2001) reported a study of lower secondary mathematics classroom learning environments in Brunei and their associations with students' satisfaction with learning mathematics among a sample of 1565 students from 81 classes in 15 government secondary schools. Students' perceptions of the classroom learning environments were assessed with a version of My Class Inventory (MCI) that had been modified for the Brunei context. A measure of student satisfaction also was included in the study to permit investigation of satisfaction-environment associations.

The study found that internal consistency reliability (Cronbach Alpha Coefficient) for the scales in MCI, Cohesiveness, Difficulty and Competition ranges from 0.61 to 0.81 when the class means were used. The study also found the significant associations between Satisfaction and all three MCI scales. While positive associations were found between Satisfaction and Cohesiveness, negative associations were detected between Satisfaction and Difficulty and Competition respectively.

In terms of gender differences in Mathematics classrooms, the study reported that boys perceived significantly more Cohesiveness and significantly less Competition than did girls. However, gender differences were negligible for Difficulty scale. Overall, the results suggest that the mathematics classroom environment was perceived more favourably by boys than by girls.

Despite the above-mentioned research studies in science education and classroom environment in Brunei, there is still a need for more investigations which could help to improve the teaching of science. It is evident that recent research has contributed to a better understanding of science classroom climate in Brunei, but that these studies are confined to a few science subject only. A study which investigates the classroom climate covering all science subjects with a bigger sample size is necessary to provide a broader picture of the overall situation of science learning environments. Among the questionnaires used to assess the educational environments, the MCI, SLEI, QTI and the WIHIC are known to give reliable, valid and important information about classroom climate.

6. Science Educational Learning Environment

The most recent study on the science classroom environment was conducted by Khine (2001). The study examines the science classroom environment by using QTI, WIHIC questionnaires and 2 sub-scales of the TOSRA. The study involved 1188 students from 54 classrooms in 10 government secondary schools. The sample represents 50% of the total Form 5 student population in Brunei schools.

Validation of Instruments

In the process of validation, the Cronbach alpha reliability coefficients for QTI scales were found to be 0.49 to 0.88 when using the individual student as the unit of analysis, and from 0.49 to 0.94 when using the class mean as the unit of analysis. The lowest reliability coefficient was seen in the scale Strict. It is likely that students in this context, due to cultural reasons, may not respond to such questions genuinely and openly. This factor could have contributed to the low reliability coefficient to this particular scale (Khine & Fisher, in press).

The Cronbach alpha reliabilities ranged from 0.78 to 0.87 were found in the WIHIC questionnaire when the individual student scores were used as the unit of analysis. When the class means were used as the unit of analysis, the reliability coefficient ranged from 0.81 to 0.94.

Two sub-scales of TOSRA, Enjoyment of Science Lessons and Attitude towards Scientific Inquiry, were used as outcome measures. The Cronbach alpha reliability coefficient for the Enjoyment of Science scale was found to be 0.83 when individual scores were used as the unit of analysis and 0.93 when class means were used. On the other hand, the Cronbach alpha reliability coefficient for the Attitude towards Scientific Inquiry sub-scale was found to be 0.57 when individual scores were used as the unit of analysis and 0.65 when class means were used as unit of analysis.

Gender Differences in Teacher Interpersonal Behaviour

Universally, gender equity has been a major concern in science education . Harding (1996) noted that in most countries of the world, girls continue to show little interest in studies and careers related to science and technology. Some research studies on gender equity have noted that girls are at disadvantage compared with boys in terms of learning opportunities in science (Parker, Rennie, & Fraser, 1996). Other studies indicating the disparities in the science achievement of girls and boys showed differences in achievement favouring boys in many science subjects (Fisher & Rickards, 1997; Henderson, Fisher, & Fraser, 2000). In the past, classroom interactions were dominated by boys, thus putting girls at a disadvantage (Kahle & Meece, 1994). One of the objectives of the study was to investigate whether female students were given equal learning opportunities with male students in science classes.

Gender differences in students' perceptions of teacher interpersonal behaviour were measured by the eight scales of the QTI. The results show that there are significant differences in six out of the eight QTI scales. In particular, significant differences were noted in the Leadership, Understanding, Uncertain, Admonishing, Helping/Friendly and Dissatisfied scales.

Gender Differences in Classroom Learning Environment

Similarly, with the WIHIC, male and female secondary school students perceived differences in their classroom learning environments. Female students perceived their classroom learning environment more favourably than did the male students in the same class. Female students perceived significantly higher levels of task orientation, cooperation and equity than did male students. Because female and male students perceived different science learning environments, it suggests that students may not have equal learning opportunities in their classes.

Warrington and Younger (1996) reported that girls are submissive and have docile behaviours towards authority and that teachers seem to establish better rapport with girls. Teachers tended to give more attention to girls than boys in terms of helping and friendliness. It was also common that boys showed disrespectful behaviours and challenge teachers authority. In many cases, teachers were critical of boys and gave less help and encouragement to them.

The existence of gender differences in the students' perceptions of classroom environment warrants further research in order to establish causation of the gender differences in the students' perceptions of science learning environment. Details of the results can be found in Khine (2001).

In terms of gender differences in enjoyment of science and attitude towards scientific inquiry, it was found that male and female students equally enjoy their science lessons, male students seem to have a more positive attitude towards scientific inquiry.

7. Implications for Improving Science Education in Brunei

It is evident that findings from above mentioned studies have some implications for improving science education in Brunei. These implications are mainly concerned with teachers and teacher education.

The findings of associations between students' perceptions of interpersonal teacher behaviour and science-related attitudes show that there is a significant link between QTI scales and the students' enjoyment of science lessons. The results show that students enjoy science lessons more when their teachers display greater leadership, understanding, and are helping and friendly. On the other hand, teachers' uncertain, admonishing and dissatisfied behaviours are negatively associated with students' enjoyment of science lessons.

It is remarkable to note here that all the WIHIC scales are significantly associated with the enjoyment of science lessons. In creating a conducive and productive science learning environment, the findings suggests that teachers should strive for greater student cohesiveness, teacher support, involvement, investigation, task orientation, cooperation and equity in their classes. This also indicates that all the WIHIC scales are important factors and determine the students' enjoyment of science lessons both at individual and class levels.

The results also show significant associations between all of the WIHIC scales and students' attitude to scientific inquiry. This means that an individual student's attitude towards scientific inquiry is greatly influenced by their classroom environment. The evidence generated from this study indicates that student cohesiveness, teacher support, involvement, investigation, task orientations and equity are all positively associated with a student's attitude to scientific inquiry.

The various findings from this study have some implications for teacher education. The findings suggest that teachers need to improve their interpersonal relationships and classroom learning environment. Teachers should be aware of means of monitoring and assessing classroom environment and some practical strategies for improving learning environment should be considered. Incorporating learning environment ideas into teacher education programs would be highly desirable (Fisher & Fraser, 1991).

8. Future Directions

The studies mentioned in this chapter opens up a host of possibilities for exploring many areas of the learning environment in Brunei. Although there have been a few previous studies in Brunei, the concept of learning environment research is still in its infancy. These research could be replicated for specific science subjects and at different grade levels in both government and non-government schools. The subjects for the present studies are drawn from urban schools so the research could also be extended to cover students from rural schools. The information obtained from these extended studies will provide a more comprehensive view of science classroom environments in Brunei and make the drawing of conclusions more legitimate.

To support the quantitative data derived from the questionnaires, qualitative analysis through focused interviews with students and teachers are also desirable. The qualitative information could be used to counter check the validity of the questionnaire responses and how students arrive at specific answers. This could further explain the relationships found in the quantitative data. Some studies were designed to explore the relationships between learning environments and attitudinal outcomes. Other studies investigate the associations between the learning environment and students' cognitive outcomes and achievement. Further research are needed to address the issues in the areas of evaluation of educational innovations, studies of the transition from primary and secondary schooling, teacher education and teacher-as-researcher in an attempt to improve the classroom learning environments in general and science education in particular.

References

Aldridge, J.M., Fraser, B.J. & Huang, T. (1999). Investigating classroom environments in Taiwan and Australia with multiple research methods. *Journal of Educational Research, 93*, 48–57.

Alexander, R. (2000). *Culture and pedagogy*. Oxford: Blackwell Publishers.

Alvarez, A.A. (1988). *A study of primary and secondary science teachers in Negara Brunei Darussalam: Their professional orientation, perceived difficulties, needs assessment and attitudes towards teaching science*. Brunei Darussalam: Faculty of Education, Universiti Brunei Darussalam.

Alvarez, A.A. (1989). *Correlation of personal, home background and intermediate variables with cognitive achievement in Mathematics, English, Malay and General paper of primary six Bruneian students*. Brunei Darussalam: Faculty of Education, Universiti Brunei Darussalam.

Asghar, M. (1994). Science education in Brunei: A study of the relationship between classroom environment and student achievement. *Unicorn, 20* (3), 62–66.

Atwater, M.M. (1994). Research on cultural diversity in the classroom. In D.L. Gabel. (Ed.), *Handbook of research on science teaching and learning* (pp. 558–576). New York: Macmillan Publishing Co.

Bakar, A. (1997). Opening speech. In M. Quigley & P.K. Vello. (Eds.), *Proceedings of the Seminar on Innovations in science and mathematics curricula* (pp. i–ii). Brunei: Universiti Brunei Darussalam.

Baker, D.A. & Taylor, P.C.S. (1995). The effect of culture on the learning of science in non-western countries: The results of an integrated research review. *International Journal of Science education, 17*, 695–704.

Ballard, B. & J. Clanchy, J. (1991). *Teaching students from overseas*. Melbourne: Longman.

Cobern, W.W. & Aikenhead, G.S. (1998). Cultural aspects of learning science. In B.J. Fraser & K.G. Tobin. (Eds.) *International handbook of science education*, Part 1 (pp. 39–52). Dordrecht, The Netherlands: Kluwer.

Conlan, F. (1996). Can the different learning expectations of Australian and Asian students be reconciled in one teaching strategy? In J. Abbott & L.

Willcoxson (Eds.), *Teaching and learning within and across disciplines. Proceedings of the 5th annual teaching learning forum* (pp. 41–45). Perth: Murdoch University.

Fisher, D.L. & Fraser, B.J. (1991, April). *Incorporating learning environment ideas into teacher education: An Australian perspective.* Paper presented at the annual conference of American Educational Research Association, Chicago. USA.

Fisher, D.L. & Rickards, T. (1997). Cultural and gender differences in teacher-student interpersonal behaviour in science classrooms. In D. Fisher & T. Rickards. (Eds.), *Science, Mathematics and Technology Education and National Development. Vietnam Conference Proceedings* (pp. 1–9). Hanoi: Vietnam.

Fisher, D.L. & Waldrip, B.G. (1999). Cultural factors of science classroom learning environments, teacher-student interaction and student outcomes. *Research in Science and Technology Education, 17*(1), 83–96.

Fraser, B.J. & Walberg, H.J. (Eds.)(1991). *Educational environments: Evaluation, antecedents and consequences.* Oxford: Pergamon Press.

Hamid, R. (2000). Education in Brunei Darussalam. *Journal of Southeast Asian Education,* 1(1). 21–52.

Harding, J. (1996). Girls' achievement in science and technology. Implications for pedagogy. In P.F. Murphy & C.V. Gipps (Eds.), *Equity in classroom* (pp. 111–123). London: Falmer Press.

Hunus, R. (1998). *Learning environment and its association with student outcomes in chemistry in Brunei Darussalam's secondary schools.* Unpublished Doctoral Thesis. Perth: Curtin University of Technology.

Hunus, R. & Fraser, B.J. (1999). Secondary school students' perceptions of learning environment: Gender differences. In M.A. Clements & L.Y. Pak (Eds.), *Cultural and language aspects of science, mathematics and technical education* (pp. 95–102). Brunei: Universiti Brunei Darussalam.

Jumat, H.H.A. (1992). Dwibahasa (Bilingual) system of education in Brunei Darussalam. *Journal Pendidikan, 2*, 9–33.

Jumat, H.H.A. (1998). Science, mathematics and technology education for human resource development: A Brunei Darussalam perspective. In L.Y. Pak, L. Ferrer & M. Quigley. (Eds.), *Science, mathematics and technical education for national development* (pp. 21–34). Brunei: Universiti Brunei Darussalam.

Henderson, D., Fisher, D.L. & Fraser, B.J. (2000). Interpersonal behaviour, laboratory learning environments, and student outcomes in senior biology classes. *Journal of Research in Science Teaching, 37* (1), 26–43.

Kahle, J. & Meece, J. (1994). Research on gender issues in the classroom. In D. Gabel (Ed.), *Handbook of research on science teaching and learning* (pp. 542–557). New York: Macmillan Publishing.

Khine, M.S. (2001). *Associations between teacher interpersonal behaviour and aspects of classroom environment in an Asian context.* Unpublished Doctoral Thesis. Perth: Curtin University of Technology.

Khine, M. & Fisher, D. (2001, December). *Classroom Environment and Teachers' Cultural Background in Secondary Science Classes in an Asian Context.* Paper presented at Annual Conference of Australian Association of Research in Education (AARE). Fremenlle: Australia.

Khine, M. & Fisher, D. (2002, April). *Classroom Environments, Student Attitudes and Cultural Background of Teachers in Brunei.* Paper presented at Annual Conference of American Educational Research Association (AERA). New Orleans, USA.

Khine, M., Fisher, D. & Nair, S. (2002, April). *Analysing Interpersonal Behaviour in Science Classrooms: Associations Between Students' Perceptions and Teacher's Cultural Background.* Paper presented at Annual Conference of the National Association of Research in Science and Technology (NARST). New Orleans, USA.

Khine, M. & Fisher, D. (in press). Teacher-Student interactions in science classrooms in Brunei. *Journal of Classroom Interaction.*

Khine, M., Larwood, G. & Fisher, D. (2000). Cross-cultural validation of a learning environment instrument. In K.Y. Wong, H. Tairab & M.A. Clements. (Eds.). *Science, mathematics and technical education in the 20th and 21st centuries.* (pp. 369–376). Brunei: Universiti Brunei Darussalam.

Majeed, A., Fraser, B. & Aldridge, J. (2001, April). *Learning environments and student satisfaction among junior secondary mathematics students in Brunei Darussalam.* Paper presented at the Annual Meeting of the American Educational Research Association (AERA). Seattle, Washington, USA.

Moore, A. (2000) *Teaching and learning: Pedagogy, curriculum and culture.* London: Routledge-Falmer.

Parker, L.H., Rennie, L.J. & Fraser, B.J. (1996). *Gender, science and mathematics.* Dordrecht, The Netherlands: Kluwer.

Phelan, P., Davidson, A. & Cao, H. (1991). Students' multiple worlds: negotiating the boundaries of family, peer, and school cultures. *Anthropology and Education Quarterly, 22,* 224–250.

Poh, S.H. (1995). *An evaluation of O-Level biology laboratory teaching across government secondary schools in Brunei Darussalam: Process skills and learning environment.* Unpublished Master Thesis. Perth: Curtin University of Technology.

Poh, S.H. (1996). A study of biology laboratory learning environment in Brunei Darussalam. In M. Quigley, P.K. Veloo & W.K. Yoong. (Eds.), *Assessment and evaluation in science and mathematics education: Innovative approaches* (pp. 272–281). Brunei: Universiti Brunei Darussalam.

Rickards, T. & Fisher, D.L. (1999). Teacher-student classroom interactions among science students of different sex and cultural background. *Research in Science education, 29*(4), 445–455.

Scott, R. & Fisher, D. (2000). Validation and use of a Malay translation of a learning environment questionnaire. In K.Y. Wong, H. Tairab & M.A. Clements (Eds.) *Science, mathematics and technical education in the 20th and 21st centuries.* (pp. 389–398). Brunei: University of Brunei.

Sharifah, M.S.Z. (1997). *Science education provision in secondary schools in Brunei Darussalam.* Paris: International Institute for Educational Planning.

Warrington, M. & Younger, M. (1996). Goals, expectations and motivation: Gender differences in achievement in GSE. *Curriculum, 17,* 80–93.

Chapter 7

LEARNING ENVIRONMENT RESEARCH IN INDONESIA

Eko S. Margianti
Gunadarma University
Indonesia

Learning environment as an integral part of the learning process has received considerable attention from educational researchers in the past decades. Studies in learning environment in Indonesia had been conducted in the late 1970s and early 1980s in Padang (West Sumatra) and East Java. In 2000, learning environment studies began to make its appearance again in Indonesia. These recent studies were carried out mainly in computer science classes at the tertiary level and they focused on the influence of the learning environment on students' cognitive and affective outcomes. Students' perceptions of the classroom environment were measured using adapted and translated versions of the What Is Happening In This Class? (WIHIC) Questionnaire. Results of the research are highlighted in the chapter. It is hoped that this information will help readers understand the current status of research in educational learning environments in Indonesia.

1. Introduction

Learning environment as a significant and integral part of the learning process has received considerable attention from educational researchers in the past decades. In recent years, the learning environment has been considered increasingly as one of the crucial factors associated with students' affective and cognitive learning outcomes. It is therefore important to be more aware of its role in educational developments in Indonesia, particularly more so in the midst of changing social and political climates. This chapter attempts to provide an overview of learning environment research in Indonesia and to discuss future directions in this context.

In the first section, an overview of the geographical situation and the education system in Indonesia are presented to serve as background information. In the second section, initial learning environment research in Indonesia is described. The third section is devoted to recent learning environment research conducted in Indonesia. In the fourth section, some suggestions of future learning environment research within the context of educational developments are presented. This section aims to address the issue of future research and classroom practices for education stakeholders.

2. The Geography

Indonesia consists of some 1300 islands which varies greatly in size. The islands of Java, Sumatra, Kalimantan, Sulawesi and Irian Jaya are the largest in terms of both size and population, while the remaining islands are relatively small. The population of Indonesia is approximately 200 million and the people live mostly in the larger islands, especially in Java (about 30% of the population). Farming and fishing are the common occupations of the people.

3. Education System in Indonesia

Schooling in Indonesia begins with playgroups, an informal education for children from two to four years old. The next stage is preprimary schooling until the age of five. The playgroups and preprimary school are optional education for children while compulsory education begins with the primary school for children from six to 12 years old. At the age of 13, students attend junior high school for three years. At the age of 16 to 18, students are at the senior high school level. Generally, students spend another three years to obtain qualifications at tertiary level colleges. Those who choose to attend universities will spend another four to five years studying. At each level of education, students attend either public or private educational facilities, although tuition fees at private institutions are generally higher than that of public institutions.

At the senior secondary level, students can opt for a general secondary school or a special secondary school providing an education in technical studies, pharmacy, nursing, hospitality, tourism, etc. It is important to note that the number of private universities is significantly higher than that of public universities and hence the number of students is also proportionally higher in the private universities. It is very difficult to establish a public university since the funds have to come from the government. But for private universities, funding comes from the private sector. As a result of this situation, the public universities only receive a certain quantity of students as allocated by the government according to the funds for subsidising tuition fees, while the private universities, where most funds come from tuition, try to increase student intake in order to increase their income.

As the world moves towards globalisation and the information technology decade, all aspects of life are enriched and affected by computers and telecommunication technologies. Indonesia has also been influenced by the rapid changes taking place in the midst of such phenomena. Computer sciences and information technology are new topics in Indonesia that are rapidly gaining in popularity in the educational sector. Between 1978 and 1999, approximately 150 private institutions were registered in tertiary education with approximately 75,000 student enrollment. In Jakarta alone, there are about 30,000 students learning computer studies in 49 private tertiary institutions. How these students learn and the learning environments in which they learn provide the background for research in learning environments in Indonesia.

4. Initial Efforts in Learning Environment Research in Indonesia

The influence of the learning environment on the process of education has received a great deal of attention from educational researchers during the last three decades (Fraser, 1994; 1998). Early studies that established the validity of classroom environment instruments translated into other languages had been conducted in India (Walberg, Singh & Rasher, 1977) and Indonesia (Schibeci, Rideng & Fraser, 1987). The studies replicated associations between students' outcomes and classroom environment perceptions. Fraser, Pearse and Azmi (1982) and Fraser (1985) reported a study in Indonesia involving an Indonesian translation of a modified version of the *Individual Classroom Environment Questionnaire* (ICEQ) and four of the *Classroom Environment Scale* (CES). The sample consisted of grades 8 and 9 students in 18 co-educational social studies classes in Padang, West Sumatra. This study used student's satisfaction and anxiety as the learning outcomes. The findings indicated that student satisfaction was greater in classes perceived as having less independence and greater involvement, while anxiety was reduced in classes perceived as having greater differentiation, involvement and affiliation.

In another study of elementary classrooms in Indonesia, Paige (1978; 1979) translated and modified an instrument based on the *Classroom Environmental Scale* (CES), and three *Learning Environment Instrument* (LEI) Scales. The sample was a stratified random group of 1621 sixth grade students in 30 rural and 30 urban schools in East Java, using the revised and translated instrument. Paige examined relationships between perceptions of the classroom learning environment and the two outcomes of cognitive achievement and individual modernity. Specific findings included the trend that individual modernity was enhanced in classrooms perceived as having greater task orientation, competition and difficulty and less order and organisation, while achievement was enhanced in classes higher in speed and lower in order and organisation.

It is obvious that research in learning environment in Indonesia first emerged in the 1970s and 1980s. For example, the studies conducted by Paige (1978; 1979), Fraser, Pearse & Azmi (1982) and Fraser (1985). However, there was no further documented research in this area until 2000. This is fully understandable for during the period, Indonesia was in the middle of physical development, where almost all potential efforts and resources were directed to support national development programs.

5. Recent Research in Learning Environment in Indonesia

In 2000, research in learning environment began to make its appearance again. Recent studies of learning environment in Indonesia emphasise on the influence of the classroom learning environment on students' cognitive and affective outcomes. Soeryaningsih & Fraser (2000) developed a questionnaire consisting of four scales adapted from the *What is Happening in this Class* (WIHIC) combined with one scale of College and University Classroom Environment Inventory (CUCEI) developed by Fraser & Treagust (1986). This was in line with the development of a new questionnaire designed to measure students' attitudes towards their computer-related studies at the tertiary level, namely *Test of Computer Related Attitudes* (TOCRA) based on the *Test of Science Related Attitudes* (TOSRA, Fraser, 1981). This study, conducted at the tertiary level, also used two of the seven scales, namely leisure interest in computers and attitudes towards computers as its starting point. In addition, a satisfaction scale was also added. The response format was modified to make use of the Semantic Differential Technique in which seven pairs of polarised adjectives were used in conjunction with a five-point scale. The study revealed that the association between students' perceptions of the learning environment and their course achievement score is statistically not significant, while association with their Grade Point Average (GPA) score and their satisfaction is statistically significant.

Another recent study (Margianti, Fraser & Aldridge, 2001) was conducted also at the tertiary level. This study involved the investigation of factors that could influence students' outcomes (achievement and attitudes) in private computer institutions in Indonesia, including students' perceptions of the learning environment and their mathematical ability at the secondary and tertiary levels.

The sample consisted of almost 2,500 students who were enrolled to study Computer Science in one of the private universities in Indonesia. In this particular study, students' perceptions of the classroom environment were measured using an Indonesian version of the *What Is Happening In This Class?* (WIHIC) Questionnaire. To assess students' affective outcomes, a scale derived from the *Test of Science Related Attitudes* was adapted for use in higher education computing classes and translated into Indonesian. Students' final scores in their mathematics course (either linear algebra or statistics) were used as a measure of cognitive achievement. The secondary aims of this study were to examine whether differences exist between (a) students' perceptions of the actual and preferred classroom learning environment, (b) males' and females' perceptions of the actual classroom environment and (c) students' perceptions of the learning environment in linear algebra and statistics courses. Altogether four Indonesian versions of the WIHIC were developed for use in the study. These were the versions of Student

Actual and Student Preferred, and Teacher Actual and Teacher Preferred. The Indonesian version of the WIHIC Student Actual is attached for your reference in the Appendix at the end of the chapter.

This study made an attempt to address the problems faced by the students in their transition from secondary to tertiary education. It was gathered in this study that many students experienced problems during the transition from secondary to tertiary education. It was observed that while some students managed to overcome the problems associated with the transition, others never learned to cope. The results of this study contributed towards explaining why students achieve less than desirable scores in their computing courses and provide information regarding the process of achieving the goals of the course. The study provides valuable information to instructors and administrators that can be used to improve the learning environment in ways that are likely to enhance student achievement and attitudes. The present study also provides insights into the field of learning environments in Indonesia where few such studies have been undertaken.

The results of the research could help to identify numerous variables that could affect the achievement and attitudes of Indonesian students in private computer studies institutions. Clearly, the study is of practical importance to private institutions because it is likely to provide evidence that can assist with the identification of problems (especially during the transition from secondary to tertiary education) and to guide the improvement of students' outcomes.

The development of an actual and preferred form of a learning environment questionnaire in the Indonesian language provides valuable information regarding students' perceptions at the tertiary level. Careful translation and extensive validation of the instruments ensure its suitability at the tertiary level. At the university level in Indonesia, information can be used to help identify the types of learning environment in which student are more likely to achieve. The details of this study are reported in Margianti, Fraser & Aldridge (2002).

The results of the study provided practical benefits to the students, teachers, the Vice-Chancellor, and administrative staff of the institution in which the data were collected. Feedback from the study provides information regarding the teaching and learning processes within the institution, in addition to identifying the need for staff development programs that could be beneficial to staff and students at the institution.

The study found that the scale reliability estimates of the Indonesian version of WIHIC range from 0.65 to 0.87 for the individual as the unit of analysis and from 0.68 to 0.92 for the class mean as the unit of analysis. These internal consistency indices are comparable to those obtained when the WIHIC was used with an Australian sample (Fraser, McRobbie & Fisher, 1996), which ranged from 0.67 to 0.88. The internal consistency reliability (Cronbach alpha coefficient) for the attitude scale is 0.77 with the individual and 0.87 with the class mean as the unit of analysis.

As a further indication of the validity of the Indonesian version of the learning environment instrument, a one-way ANOVA was used to indicate whether the questionnaire was able to differentiate significantly between the perceptions of students in different classes. The results suggest that only the Teacher Support and Task Orientation scales were able to do so. The eta^2 statistic (an estimate of the strength of association between class membership and the dependent variable) ranged from 0.02 to 0.05. On the whole, these figures are lower than those for the original WIHIC (Fraser, McRobbie & Fisher, 1996), which ranged from 0.18 to 0.35. This could be due to the nature of university classrooms, which could be more uniform than high school classrooms.

To determine whether students' perceptions of their learning environment were related to their achievement and their attitudes towards their lectures, the data were analysed using simple and multiple correlation analyses. The results for the simple correlation analysis for achievement indicate a statistically significant association between the seven learning environment scales and student achievement at both the individual and class mean levels of analysis. The results for the multiple regression analysis using the individual as the unit of analysis indicate that six of the seven learning environment scales uniquely account for a statistically significant amount of variance in students' achievement beyond that attributable to other environment scales. The results tentatively suggest that lecturers wishing to improve student achievement should include lessons that allow for more Student Cohesiveness,

Teacher Support, Task Orientation, Equity, Involvement and Order and Organisation.

For student attitudes, the results of the simple correlation analysis suggest that, at the individual level of analysis, all seven learning environment scales are positively and significantly correlated to student attitudes and that, at the class mean level of analysis, all learning environment scales except Student Cohesiveness and positively and significantly correlated to attitudes. The multiple correlation was significant at both the individual and class mean levels of analysis. The results tentatively suggest that lecturers wishing to improve students' attitudes should include lessons that allow for more of each dimension of the WIHIC.

To determine whether differences exist between students' perceptions of actual and preferred learning environments, t tests for paired samples were calculated. Statistically significant differences between students' perceptions of their actual learning environment and the one that they would prefer were found for all seven learning environment scales. The results indicate that students would prefer more of each WIHIC dimension than is currently perceived in their classes.

To examine whether students of different gender perceive the learning environment differently, t tests for matched pairs were used. The within-class gender mean provided a matched pair of means — one for males and one for females. Female students perceived more Student Cohesiveness, Order and Organisation, Task Orientation and Cooperation than did male students, whereas male students perceived more Teacher Support, Involvement and Equity than did female students.

The other results revealed statistically significant differences for five of the seven learning environment scales, with students in the linear algebra classes perceiving significantly more Teacher Support, Involvement, Task Orientation, Cooperation and Equity. More details of the results are reported in Margianti, Fraser & Aldridge (2001).

6. Future Direction of Research

Studies in classroom learning environments in Indonesia are still in its infancy. More such studies can be done in many areas of educational practice. It seems that past research merely repeat, clarify and confirm the results of other countries. However, it does not involve larger samples to cover nation-wide studies and cover various subject disciplines. It will be worthwhile to widen the scope of studies to other parts of the country and examine the state of the learning environment in different areas, urban as well as rural. In order to obtain comprehensive data, studies could be extended to different types of schools, subjects and levels across the educational system in Indonesia.

Since the original learning environment questionnaires were developed in western countries, it is necessary to find out the cultural adaptability of the questionnaires. In fact, the studies conducted in Indonesia so far have been dependent on the translated and adapted versions of available questionnaires, which might not convey succinctly the cultural nuances in Indonesia. It is also important that some qualitative data be incorporated into future studies. This will provide in-depth information about learning environments in Indonesia.

References

Fraser, B.J. (1981). *Test of Science Related Attitudes.* Melbourne: Australian Council for Educational Research.

Fraser, B.J. (1985). Differences between preferred and actual classroom environment as perceived by primary students and teachers. *British Journal of Educational Psychology, 54,* 336–339.

Fraser, B.J. (1994). Research on classroom and school climate. In D. Gabel (Ed.), *Handbook of research on science teaching and learning* (pp. 493–541). New York: Macmillan.

Fraser, B.J. (1998). Science learning environments: Assessment, effects and determinants. In B.J. Fraser & K.G. Tobin (Eds.), *The international handbook of science education* (pp. 527–564). Dordrecht, The Netherlands: Kluwer Academic Publishers.

Fraser, B.J., McRobbie, C.J. & Fisher, D.L. (1996, April). *Development, validation and use of personal and class forms of a new classroom environment instrument.* Paper presented at the annual meeting of the American Educational Research Association, New York.

Fraser, B.J., Pearse, R. & Azmi. (1982). A study of Indonesian students' perceptions of classroom psychosocial environment. *International Review of Education, 28,* 337–355.

Fraser, B.J. & Treagust, D.F. (1986). Validity and use of an instrument for assessing classroom psychosocial environment in higher education. *Higher Education, 15*, 37–57.

Margianti, E.S., Fraser, B.J. & Aldridge, J.M. (2002, April). *Learning environment, attitudes and achievement: Assessing the perceptions of Indonesian university students.* Paper presented at the annual meeting of the American Educational Research Association, New Orleans, MS.

Margianti, E., Fraser, B.J. & Aldridge. J.M. (2001, December). *Investigating the learning environment and students' outcomes in university level computing courses in Indonesia.* Paper presented at the International Educational Research Conference, Australian Association for Educational Research (AARE), Fremantle, Western Australia.

Paige, R.M. (1978). *The impact of classroom learning environment on academic achievement and individual modernity in East Java, Indonesia.* Unpublished doctoral dissertation. Stanford University.

Paige, R.M. (1979). The learning of modern culture: Formal education and psychosocial modernity in East Java. *International Journal of Intercultural Relations, 3*, 333–364

Schibeci, R.A., Rideng, I.M. & Fraser, B.J. (1987). Effects of classroom environments on sciences attitudes: A cross-cultural replication in Indonesia. *International Journal of Science Education, 9,* 169–186.

Soeryaningsih, W.Th. & Fraser, B.J. (2000). *Association between student outcomes and learning environment among computing students in an Indonesian university.* Paper presented at the Second International Conference on Science, Mathematics and Technology Education, Taipei, Taiwan.

Walberg, H.J., Singh, R. & Rasher, S.P. (1977). Predictive validity of students' perceptions: A cross-cultural replication. *American Educational Research Journal, 14*, 45–49.

APPENDIX

GUNADARMA UNIVERSITY
JAKARTA - INDONESIA

WHAT IS HAPPENING IN THIS STATISTIC CLASS
STUDENT ACTUAL FORM

PETUNJUK

Ini bukan sebuah test.

Pernyataan- pernyataan berikut ini membahas mengenai *'kenyataan'* pada pelaksanaan mata kuliah *Statistik* yang telah anda ikuti.

Tidak ada jawaban *'benar'* atau Salah . Yang diharapkan adalah *'Pendapat'* anda.

Pertimbangkanlah baik-baik pernyataan-pernyataan berikut ini dan bandingkan seberapa jauh kenyataan yang ada dikelas anda sehari-hari sebagai *'seorang mahasiswa'*.

Lingkarilah angka-angka sebagai berikut:

1. Apabila pada kenyataan   Hampir tidak pernah
2. Apabila pada kenyataan   Jarang
3. Apabila pada kenyataan   Kadang-kadang
4. Apabila pada kenyataan   Sering
5. Apabila pada kenyataan   Hampir selalu

Jangan menjadi ragu apabila ada beberapa pernyataan yang hampir sama.

Berikan pendapat anda pada semua pernyataan yang ada.

Apabila anda berubah pendapat, berilah *'tanda silang'* pada angka yang dibatalkan dan ' ***lingkarilah*** ' angka pengganti yang anda pilih.
CONTOH

Pernyataan: Anggauta kelas ini saling tolong-menolong.

Yang perlu anda lakukan adalah mempertimbangkan apakah para mahasiswa yang ada dikelas anda saling tolong menolong satu sama lain   *'Hampir tidak pernah'* ,
'Jarang' ,   *'Kadang-kadang'*,   *'Sering'*,   *'Hampir selalu'*.

Apabila anda berpendapat hal itu Sering terjadi, maka lingkarilah angka 4 pada kuestioner yang anda isi.

Nama: Kelas: Npm: L/P (jenis kel):

Terimakasih atas kerjasamanya, selamat bekerja

Ingatlah bahwa anda sedang memberi pendapat mengenai kelas Statistik anda

SC		Hampir tidak pernah	Jarang	Kadang-kadang	Sering	Hampir selalu
1	Saya berkawan dengan semua mahasiswa di kelas.	1	2	3	4	5
2	Saya tahu semua mahasiswa di kelas ini.	1	2	3	4	5
3	Saya merasa familiar dengan anggauta kelas ini.	1	2	3	4	5
4	Semua anggauta kelas ini adalah teman saya.	1	2	3	4	5
5	Saya bekerjasama dengan baik dengan anggauta kelas ini.	1	2	3	4	5
6	Saya menolong anggauta kelas saya (kawan2 saya) apabila mereka mempunyai kesulitan dalam pekerjaan mereka.	1	2	3	4	5
7	Semua mahasiswa dikelas ini menyukai saya.	1	2	3	4	5
8	Dikelas ini saya dapat mendapat bantuan / pertolongan dari mahasiswa lainnya.	1	2	3	4	5
TS						
9	Dosen dapat menarik perhatian saya secara khusus.	1	2	3	4	5
10	Dosen menolong saya secara khusus.	1	2	3	4	5
11	Dosen menghargai perasaan saya.	1	2	3	4	5
12	Dosen menolong / membantu saya ketika saya mendapat kesulitan dalam menyelesaikan pekerjaan saya.	1	2	3	4	5
13	Dosen berbicara kepada saya	1	2	3	4	5
14	Dosen menaruh perhatian / tertarik terhadap masalah saya.	1	2	3	4	5
15	Dosen mengatur / merubah kelas agar dapat berbicara kepada saya	1	2	3	4	5
16	Pertanyaan dosen membantu saya untuk mengerti.	1	2	3	4	5

I						
17	Saya mendiskusikan ide2 / gagasan2 dikelas.	1	2	3	4	5
18	Saya memberikan pendapat saya selama diskusi dikelas berlangsung.	1	2	3	4	5
19	Dosen bertanya kepada saya.	1	2	3	4	5
20	Ide dan saran saya dipakai selama diskusi berlangsung.	1	2	3	4	5
21	Saya menanyakan pertanyaan kepada Dosen.	1	2	3	4	5
22	Saya menerangkan ide saya kepada mahasiswa lainnya.	1	2	3	4	5
23	Para mahasiswa (kawan2) berdiskusi dengan saya tentang cara menyelesaikan masalah.	1	2	3	4	5
24	Saya diminta untuk menerangkan tentang cara menyelesaikan masalah.	1	2	3	4	5
OO						
25	Kelas ini tertib dan teratur dengan baik.	1	2	3	4	5
26	Kelas ini sangat ribut.	1	2	3	4	5
27	Saya diberi tahu apa yang akan terjadi apabila saya tidak menurut pada aturan.	1	2	3	4	5
28	Saya mengetahui semua aturan dikelas ini.	1	2	3	4	5
29	Mahasiswa yang melanggar aturan akan mendapat kesulitan.	1	2	3	4	5
30	Mahasiswa yang menyelesaikan tugasnya lebih cepat dari yang lain, segera dilanjutkan dengan topik selanjutnya.	1	2	3	4	5
31	Dosen menentukan siapa-siapa yang akan bekerja dalam satu grup.	1	2	3	4	5
32	Para mahasiswa akan dihukum apabila berperilaku buruk dikelas.	1	2	3	4	5

TO						
33	Dapat menyelesaikan suatu tugas adalah suatu hal yang penting bagi saya.	1	2	3	4	5
34	Saya bekerja sebanyak yang sudah saya tentukan untuk dikerjakan.	1	2	3	4	5
35	Saya tahu tujuan dari pada pelajaran / topik ini.	1	2	3	4	5
36	Saya siap untuk memulai pelajaran / topik ini tepat pada waktunya.	1	2	3	4	5
37	Saya tahu apa yang harus saya capai dalam pelajaran /topik ini.	1	2	3	4	5
38	Saya menaruh perhatian sepanjang pelajaran / topik ini.	1	2	3	4	5
39	Saya berusaha untuk mengerti pekerjaan/ tugas di kelas / pelajaran ini.	1	2	3	4	5
40	Saya tahu berapa besar / banyak tugas yang saya harus lakukan.	1	2	3	4	5
CO						
41	Saya bekerjasama dengan mahasiswa lain ketika mengerjakan tugas dan pekerjaan saya.	1	2	3	4	5
42	Saya memakai bersama-sama buku dan fasilitas lainnya dengan mahasiswa lainnya ketika mengerjakan tugas.	1	2	3	4	5
43	Ketika bekerja didalam grup, terdapat kerjasama yang baik.	1	2	3	4	5
44	Saya bekerja dengan mahasiswa lainnya dalam proyek di kelas ini.	1	2	3	4	5
45	Saya belajar dari mahasiswa lain dalam kelas ini.	1	2	3	4	5
46	Saya bekerja dengan mahaiswa lainnya di kelas ini.	1	2	3	4	5
47	Saya bekerjasama dengan mahasiswa lainnya dalam kegiatan kelas.	1	2	3	4	5
48	Saya bekerja dengan para mahasiswa lainnya untuk mencapai tujuan dari kelas ini.	1	2	3	4	5

EQ						
49	Dosen memberi perhatian yang sama terhadap pertanyaan saya seperti kepada mahasiswa lainnya.	1	2	3	4	5
50	Saya mendapat bantuan yang sama dari Dosen seperti mahasiswa lainnya.	1	2	3	4	5
51	Saya mendapat kesempatan bicara yang sama dengan mahasiswa lainnya dikelas.	1	2	3	4	5
52	Saya mendapat perlakuan yang sama seperti mahasiswa lainnya dikelas.	1	2	3	4	5
53	Saya mendapat dorongan yang sama seperti mahasiswa lainnya.	1	2	3	4	5
54	Saya mendapat kesempatan untuk berpartisipasi dalam diskusi kelas seperti mahasiswa lainnya.	1	2	3	4	5
55	Pekerjaan saya mendapat penghargaan seperti mahaiswa lainnya.	1	2	3	4	5
56	Saya mendapat kesempatan yang sama untuk menjawab pertanyaan seperti mahasiswa lainnya.	1	2	3	4	5
ATT						
57	Saya menyukai bidang saya.	1	2	3	4	5
58	Setelah lulus saya akan mudah mendapat pekerjaan.	1	2	3	4	5
59	Menurut saya bidang saya bagus dan bergengsi.	1	2	3	4	5
60	Pelajaran statistik menarik.	1	2	3	4	5
61	Karir dibidang statistik akan baik dimasa datang.	1	2	3	4	5
62	Saya menyukai penerbitan statistik di Universitas.	1	2	3	4	5
63	Saya menyukai programa statistik di TV.	1	2	3	4	5
64	Menurut saya statistik bukanlah bidang yang sulit.	1	2	3	4	5

Chapter 8

CURRICULUM DEVELOPMENT AND LEARNING ENVIRONMENT RESEARCH IN KOREA

Seon Uk Lee
Curtin University of Technology
Australia

Heui Baik Kim
Seoul National University
Korea

The research on Korean classroom environment was initiated by a graduate student in 1994 on psychosocial environment in science laboratory classes. Since then, researchers have undertaken several studies on learning environment within diverse contexts, namely, primary, junior high and senior high, theory lessons and laboratory lessons, with adapted questionnaires. Among those researchers, Heui Baik Kim especially has shown continuous effort in research on learning environment, which involved various levels of stakeholders and diverse contexts, by being aware of usability of recent instruments. She also suggested that more qualitative investigations are needed to explain the quantitative results and to understand the real socio-psychological environments of science classrooms in detail so that they can be improved in Korea. With guidance of previous researchers' effort, Sunny Lee undertook more in-depth study, involving high school students from three different streams. She employed combination of quantitative and qualitative methodology and also used multiple instruments in her single study. Recently, researchers have conducted several studies, reflecting on current curriculum reform movement. Learning Environment study is a growing field in Korea, with huge potential in terms of depth and width. Authors expect this chapter to be able to encourage researchers in Korea to look at with wider and deeper perspectives and contribute to improve current educational situation in Korea.

1. Introduction

Initially, learning environment was studied within the context of laboratory classroom in secondary schools by Yoon (1993). Recently, the learning environment has been dealt with as one of the crucial factors associated with implementing curriculum in Korea. In the first section, the recent curriculum changes are described as background information. In the second section, learning environment research in Korea will be shed light on with curriculum evaluation. In the third section, the learning environment involved in teaching and learning (classroom) situation will be discussed. In the fourth section, the learning environment research embedded in the paradigm of alternative evaluation or assessment will be described. Final two sections will be dedicated to the issue of methodologies in Korean learning environment research and suggestions for future research and classroom practices for diverse stakeholders.

2. Preliminary Effort in Learning Environment Study

The research on classroom environment in Korea was initiated by Yoon's pioneering study (1993) on psychosocial environment in science laboratory classes. Since then, researchers have undertaken several studies on learning environment within diverse contexts (primary, junior high and senior high, theory lessons, laboratory lessons). In the case of Noh and Kang's study (1997), the new instrument was constructed by selecting a few scales from several existing instruments (Individualised Classroom Environment Questionnaire, Science Laboratory Environment Inventory, Classroom Environment Survey) in order to explore specific aspects proposed in their study. They aimed at investigating the impact of newly proposed curriculum on students' perceptions about their science classroom environment. Since the new curriculum was organized and has been implemented only for year 10 students, the researchers compared two groups of students (year 10 students, year 11 students) in terms of their perceptions about their science classroom environments. They found that the new curriculum contributed to improve students' perception about their science classroom environments.

Noh and Choi (1996) investigated the theory classroom environment, by involving students from three different levels (primary, junior high and senior high) with the translated CES (Classroom Environment Survey). They constructed the instrument by selecting several items from the originally developed version of CES and modified so that it could be suitable for Korean schools' contexts. They reported that students' perceptions about their science classroom environment get more negative as their school year level goes down, which was considered as 'warning' by science educators. They also reported the variation of students' perceptions followed by gender factor by showing that girls usually had more favourable perception about their science classroom environments than did boys. It is noteworthy that these studies initiated the meaningful awareness of undesirable factors in science classrooms, which have not been clearly identified from research activities.

Kim and her colleagues (1995, 1996, and 1997) also used a single translated questionnaire, namely, the SLEI (Science Learn Environment Inventory). They especially have shown continuous effort in research on laboratory environment, which involved various levels of learners and teachers. In their studies, three levels of schools were involved such as junior high schools, senior high schools and universities. In addition to shed light on the different perceptions between samples from different school levels, they also compared Korean samples' perceptions with samples from other nations. In particular, they reported that students' perceptions from teachers' college (they are trained to become primary teachers) were far less favourable for their laboratory classroom environment than was the case of students from tertiary level in other nations. This concern about 'classroom' environment was extended to the effect of 'curriculum' reform, which can be characterised by constructivist approaches and the STS (Science-Technology-Society) spirit that have been formally and clearly reflected in the sixth science curriculum.

As described in this section, the academic efforts to identify the existing problem within affective aspects of classroom situations paved the way for building the new field of research, which can be entitled as 'the field of learning environment research'. In particular, most preliminary studies have reported the gap between 'actual happenings' and 'expected situations' in classroom situations. From those undesirable factors, the 'learning environment' has become one of the 'researchable' topics among Korean educators and researchers. The following sections show the continuous scenario which has been carefully planned, enthusiastically played and elaborated for the last decade in Korea.

3. Recent Curriculum Changes and Development

Science and technology education has been emphasised in Korean society for its contribution to the economic development and security of the country. This concern was formally described with the KEDI (Korean Educational Development Institute) needs assessment in 1984, which triggered governmental action in science education, such as putting a huge amount of funding into science and technological development (Mayer & Fortner, 1991). The nation-wide concern for science education has been continuously reflected in curricula. Since the fifth curriculum in Korea, the importance of science subjects has been identified in terms of preparing students for modern society, where science and technology are highly developed and have relevance to people's lives (http://www.moe.go.kr/english/edukorea/edukorea.html). Therefore, many efforts have been made to improve Korean science education, at least in documented statements. Basically, Korean curricula have been continuously changed according to the needs of societal change and philosophical trends in educational research. Through the previous six curriculum changes, science has been looked at as one of the most critical aspects in Korean education (Han, 1995). Within that context, laboratory activities have been dealt with as crucial aspects in science lessons. The emphasis on science in society is well-reflected in the way where students are classified into streams. Normally, students are allocated to one of three streams when they get to grade 10, depending on the extent of their interest in science. Although much effort has been put into developing appropriate curricula to manage the practical situation, it is not easy to find documentation of the extent to which the well-articulated curriculum has been implemented in classrooms where students and teachers co-exist. As one of the efforts for looking at the situations of science education, many studies have been conducted to assess the environment where science education occurs. Those studies have sought for the answers to the questions which have been raised about Korean science education. One of those questions is about the affective domain, which is normally considered as one of the important factors in education. In particular, students' attitudes towards specific subjects are believed to be related to the environment to which students are exposed. This concern about affective domain and the realization of the necessities for the research on that factor can be traced in the recently planned and partly being implemented curriculum. As our concern in this particular chapter is about the science classrooms in senior high schools, the following sections are dedicated to provide basic flavour of the new science curriculum in high school level, which was recently developed and partly implemented.

3.1. The Science Curriculum of Senior High School

There are nine courses in the science curriculum of the high school: General Science, Chemistry I, Physics I, Biology I, Earth Science I, Chemistry II, Physics II, Biology II, and Earth Science II. 'General Science' is a compulsory course for all high school students. This integrated course is designed to help students to develop inquiry process skills needed to solve everyday problems and to understand fundamental science concepts through inquiry activities.

The objectives of the 'General Science' course can be summarised as follows:

1. To understand natural phenomena and to solve problems scientifically in everyday situations by practising scientific inquiry methods.
2. To understand fundamental science knowledge through inquiry activities and apply it to solve problems creatively.
3. To build interest in natural phenomena and learning science and develop motivations to inquire continuously.
4. To understand the influence of science on the development of technology and the progress of society.

The content of 'General Science' consists of two areas:

1. The knowledge area including matter, force, energy, life, earth and the environment; and

2. The inquiry area including classification, measurement, prediction, experimentation, investigation and discussion, and interpretation of data. Students understand some fundamental concepts and strengthen their problem-solving abilities.

The objectives of the Chemistry I course can be summarised as follows:
1. To understand fundamental concepts in chemistry through inquiries into natural phenomena.
2. To acquire scientific inquiry methods and apply them to solving everyday problems.
3. To build interests in natural phenomena and chemistry learning and develop attitudes to inquire continuously.
4. To understand the development of chemistry knowledge and historical viewpoints on nature.
5. To understand the influence of chemistry in technological development and human life.

The Chemistry II course is designed to help science students (natural science and engineering) to be scientifically literate. It also serves as a preparatory course by providing fundamental knowledge and inquiry process skills necessary for majoring in science-related fields in the future. The objectives of the Chemistry II course are summarised as follows:
1. To systematically understand fundamental chemistry concepts and apply them to explaining natural phenomena.
2. To strengthen the ability to inquire about chemical phenomena scientifically and apply it to solve problems.
3. To build interest and curiosity in chemical phenomena and chemistry learning and to develop scientific attitudes.
4. To strengthen the manipulative skills needed in inquiries into chemical phenomena and matter.
5. To understand the development of chemistry knowledge and historical viewpoints on its nature.
6. To understand the influence of chemistry on the development of technology and human life.

Usually, the school classrooms in Korea are represented as 'overcrowded, run by examination-oriented teaching, ill-equipped and taught by the limited teaching strategies, no matter what subject students are supposed to learn. This situation is the worst in senior high school level. Recently, the desirable education environment for new generation has been indicated and discussed. In order to build the powerful academic suggestions, the rigorous studies are required in the field of learning environment research. Since the senior high school level is regarded as one of the critical turning points of individual future life in Korean society, it would be worthwhile to keep track of the ever-changing situations with continuous efforts. These efforts have been initiated and continued by several researchers as described in earlier sections. The following sections will describe more details about researchers and educators endeavours with this matter.

4. Curriculum Evaluation and Learning Environment Research

As described in previous sections, Korea has undergone the major curriculum changes seven times altogether, up to now. Before the new curriculum was introduced, usually evaluation procedure was undertaken so that it could be feedback for new curriculum. Since the sixth curriculum reform and evaluation movement, the concern with learning environment was initiated as one of the possible factors, which could indicate the effectiveness of currently implementing curriculum in practical situation. Initially, the concern about Korea Learning Environment was put within the learning context itself such as specific subject learning classrooms or other learning teaching places (Noh & Choi, 1996; Yoon, 1993). This concern has grown towards more complicated and present happening, namely, curriculum reform and new assessment system. To effectively perform the changed curriculum content within classroom contexts, the insights of learning environment — in which learning and teaching takes place — should be carefully investigated.

Kim, Fisher and Fraser (1999) reported their research, which was focused on the effectiveness of revised (sixth) science curriculum in terms of students' perceptions about their science lessons. Because the sixth curriculum was aimed at adding 'desirable' component to the existing/fifth curriculum with some aspects of constructivism, the Constructivist Learning Environment Survey (CLES) was translated and administered to students. The students involved in their study were grade 10 and grade 11, who were taught from two different curricula; old curriculum and new curriculum. Year 10 students and year 11 students from three different regions were involved in their study. Those students consisted of 2/3 boys and 1/3 girls, which was one of the aims of research such as gender effect on students' perceptions about science classroom environments. They found grade 10 students (who were taught with the guidelines from the new curriculum) perceived their lessons more favourably than did grade 11 students (who were taught by old curriculum based approach). They also used the translated TOSRA (Test Of Science Related Attitude) to investigate the possible association between their perceptions and their attitudes towards science in general. The potential of new curriculum had been investigated in several different ways, but this study was uniquely done by dealing with how students practically experienced their everyday lessons, which were constructed by the philosophy of new curriculum.

Another study involving the concern about curriculum evaluation was done by Noh and Kang (1997). They constructed their own instrument by selecting several items from several existing instruments (Individualised Classroom Environment Questionnaire, Science Laboratory Environment Inventory, and Classroom Environment Survey). They also employed the other instrument (VOST; Views On Science-Technology-Society) as well as learning environment instrument. And their main aim was to identify the aspects, which might have been affected by the new curriculum. They involved 211 students from year 10 (who completed science I course under 5th curriculum) and 216 students from year 11 (who took the 'general science' course under the 6th science curriculum) in order to find out whether the newly implemented 6th curriculum contributed to enhance students' perceptions about their classrooms. As in the case of Kim, Fisher and Fraser's study (2000), they reported that the new curriculum made students obtain more positive perceptions about their science classroom environment.

5. Classroom Situation (Teaching, Learning And Human Interaction) and Learning Environment Research

This category describes the studies conducted in practical situations, where students and teachers are actively and vividly involved in teaching and learning activities. The starting point of learning environment research in Korea was Yoon's study (1993) as mentioned earlier on. Her study was focused on the laboratory classroom situation in several classes of senior high school and junior high school. In addition to this earliest study by Yoon, several other research efforts within the field of learning environment research in Korea can be included in this category (Kim & Kim, 1995, 1996; Kim & Lee, 1997; Kim, Fisher & Fraser, 1999; Noh & Choi, 1996). They have undertaken several studies on learning environment within diverse contexts (primary, junior high and senior high, theory lessons, laboratory lessons). This section describes these studies with their details.

Noh and Choi (1996) investigated the theory classroom environment, by involving students from three different levels (primary, junior secondary and senior secondary) with the translated CES (Classroom Environment Survey). They reported that higher school level students perceived their classroom environment less favourably than did lower school level students. The conclusion from this study highlighted the current 'undesirable situation' of actual classrooms in terms of students' self perceptions.

Kim and her colleagues used a single translated questionnaire, namely, the SLEI. They particularly focused on laboratory environment, which involved various levels of learners (primary, secondary, tertiary) and teachers. Kim and Kim (1995) assessed the science laboratory environment with 148 students from the science education department and teachers' college, which train their students to be a primary school teacher. When they compared students' responses to the actual version and those to preferred version, they found that the differences between the two versions were statistically significant, meaning that students in universities were not satisfied with their laboratory environment with strong expectation towards better situation. Generally, the scores in open-endedness, integration and material environment were low. Also the mean scores of attitudes towards science were lower than those of elementary and secondary students obtained at other studies. Each scale of SLEI, except integration, showed significant correlation with the scores of attitudes toward science. In particular, open-endedness was found to account for a significant contribution to the affective outcomes.

They also investigated the students' (from middle and high schools) perceptions about their science laboratory environment using the SLEI (Kim and Kim, 1996). 276 middle school students and 263 high school students were involved in this study. These students were administered the actual version and preferred version of the SLEI. The responses from these middle and high school students showed similar patterns as the case of students in tertiary institutes as indicated by their previous study. That is, students from middle and high school also showed higher mean scores in student cohesiveness and rule clarity than the rest of scales. Generally, high school students showed more favourable perceptions about their science laboratory environments than did middle school students. In particular, the gap between actual version and preferred version was the biggest in the scale of open-endedness, meaning that students wanted to get a far more open-ended format of laboratory lesson than those lessons currently conducted.

Kim and Lee (1997) investigated science teachers' perceptions about science laboratory environment in schools where they were working by using the SLEI. They also sought the possible association of teachers' perceptions about laboratory with their belief of school science by employing the BASSQ (Belief About Science and School Science Questionnaire). These two questionnaires were administered to 157 teachers, who participated in re-training course for secondary school science teachers. The teachers' responses showed similar pattern to the students' responses as reported by previous studies, which focused mainly on students' perceptions. That is, teachers also perceived that their laboratory lessons are run as rather close-ended format with clear rules in ill-equipped room. However, teachers showed fairly different responses from students when they were asked about integration. Whereas students replied that their laboratory lessons are not effectively integrated with their theory lessons, teachers revealed that they run laboratory lessons with reasonably close link with theory lessons. According to their studies, students in Korea are usually not satisfied with their laboratory environment and it was also revealed that their perceptions were less favourable than the case of students in other nations. Kim, Fisher and Fraser (2000) recently investigated junior high school students' perceptions about the interaction behaviours with their science teachers. They used the 48-item version of QTI (Questionnaire on Teacher Interaction) and found classroom learning environment and teacher behaviour in 12 Korean schools through questionnaires administered to 543 eighth graders. Results, which support the cross-cultural validity of both measures, show positive relationships between classroom environment and interpersonal teacher behaviour and students' attitudinal outcome. Boys generally reported more favourable attitudes toward the classroom, teacher behaviour and science classes.

Lee's study (2001) was launched by Kim, Fisher and Fraser (1999)'s pioneering guidance about the direction of future research in Korea. In order to obtain significant meaning in her study within the international context, rigorous translation procedures were considered essential. This study (2001) involved students from three different streams in Korean high schools: the science-independent stream, the science-oriented stream and the humanities stream, by utilising survey with four questionnaires, interview and observation. These three different modes of inquiry provided an integrated image of Korean high school science classes. The following results were obtained from her study.

5.1. Survey

5.1.1. Instruments

The Korean version of the CLES exhibited the five-factor structure as originally intended. The factor analysis of SLEI and TOSRA data resulted in modified structures. In case of the conceptually unique QTI, the pattern of inter-correlations between scales was calculated to see if they reflected the circumplex structure as originally intended. Based on this validation, the internal consistency reliability of each scale of the CLES, SLEI, QTI and TOSRA and the discriminate validity of the CLES, SLEI and TOSRA were calculated to show that the scales within those three questionnaires are relatively reliable and independent for use among Korean high school students. The ability to differentiate between classrooms was investigated for each CLES, QTI and SLEI scale. Overall, the Korean version of CLES, SLEI, QTI and TOSRA were found reliable and valid when they were used with Korean high school students.

5.1.2. *General features of science classroom environments of high schools in Korea*

The survey with the CLES revealed that science lessons 'sometimes' conveyed the notions of constructivism. These results replicated a past study conducted in Korea (Kim, Fisher & Fraser, 1999) and provided further support for the reliability and validity of the Korean version of CLES. The survey results from the SLEI reflected highly structured laboratory lessons, focusing on correct and set answers instead of created ideas. It was also found that students perceived their science laboratory lessons to be more closed rather than open-ended and highly integrated with theory lessons. It reflects the general situation in Korean high schools, where laboratory lessons mainly serve to make the theory classes effective for examination preparation. The QTI results implied that the science teachers are directive, strict and not generous in allowing students' self-activities. This can be caused by the situation, where each teacher has to handle over 40 students. The TOSRA results revealed that students' attitudes towards science reflect their interests and academic abilities in science subjects.

5.1.3. *Findings concerning differences between streams*

For the CLES, students showed distinctive perceptions, depending on the stream which they were in. A comparison of the scale means between the three streams, it revealed that science-independent stream students perceived their science classroom more favourably than did students from the other two streams for all scales of the CLES. For the SLEI, science-independent stream students perceived more cohesiveness between themselves in their laboratory sessions and they also perceived their laboratory lessons to be much more open-ended than to be did students in the other two streams. The rules in laboratory classrooms were perceived by science-independent stream students to be less clear than did the students from the other two streams. Material Environment was perceived more positively in the science-independent stream than in the other two streams. It is noteworthy that science-independent stream students perceived more open-ended laboratory lessons, with less clear rules and better materials, than did students in the other two streams. The intention to deliver 'special' education for gifted students in science was verified with these results. In case of the QTI, it was revealed that each stream had its distinctive characteristics in terms of scales. And each pair of comparisons showed a statistically significant difference for many scales. The differences between streams reflected the unique nature of individual teacher, in terms of his/her interaction with students, rather than representing each stream's unique nature. As expected from the way in which the students were allocated to a particular stream (following their interest in science), TOSRA results were distinctive for each stream. In particular, Attitude to Scientific Inquiry and Interest in Science were different for humanities, science-oriented and science-independent streams.

5.1.4. *The associations between environmental perceptions and attitudes towards science*

Calculations based on data collected using both the CLES and TOSRA indicated that there were associations between students' perceptions of the learning environment and their attitude to science, especially Interest in Science. These results indicate that students' attitudes to science are more likely to be positive in classes where students perceive greater Personal Relevance, Uncertainty and Critical Voice. In case of the SLEI and TOSRA, calculations indicated that there were associations between students' perceptions of the laboratory learning environment and their attitude to science, specifically represented by Social Implications of Science. These results indicate that students' attitudes to science are more likely to be positive in laboratory classes where students perceive greater Student Cohesiveness, Integration and Rule Clarity. In order to determine the types of interpersonal behaviour that best promote students' attitudes to science, two types of analysis were undertaken using the data provided by the QTI and TOSRA. The implication of the simple correlation values is that, in classes where students perceive greater Leadership, Helping/Friendly and Understanding behaviours in their teachers, there are more favourable attitudes towards Social Implications of Science. Also, in classes where students perceive more Admonishing behaviours in their teachers, there are less favourable attitudes towards Social Implications of Science. Students seem to presume the image of science from the ways in which their teachers behave in classes and also they seem to construct their image of scientists from the experiences with their science teachers. That is to say, students can be given the initiative for their lessons are emotionally intriguing and comfortable to students.

5.1.5. *Commonality analysis*

In order to examine the magnitudes of the amounts of variance in student attitudes explained by two different instruments, commonality analyses were performed on the data. For the same scale in TOSRA, there were three pairs of environment instruments to analyse, namely, CLES and SLEI, CLES and QTI, and SLEI and QTI. The results of commonality analysis were different depending on the two instruments involved, as well as the specific scale in the TOSRA.

When the CLES and the QTI were analysed in the same pair, the findings suggest that there is little to be gained by including the CLES in a study of attitudes that also involves the use of the QTI. In the case of the SLEI and QTI, the findings support the usefulness of including both the QTI and SLEI within the same study of Interest in Science. In the case of the CLES and the SLEI, it was revealed that each instrument make a unique contribution to variance in Normality of Scientists scores.

5.2. Findings from Interviews and Observation

5.2.1. The extent of implementing constructivism

Generally, students in Korean high schools perceived that their classrooms involve a limited approach to constructivism, with personally relevant materials and active interaction between peers. For them, science classes are considered to be run mainly by teachers using planned materials, without students' involvement. It seems that they accept this didactic way of teaching as effective and natural. Students seldom experience any control over their lessons, but they can do some things for their teachers, which normally means simple assistance. Science-independent stream students showed the most positive perceptions of their classes, which are strongly associated with their interest in science. But shared control and critical voice were found to be practically not-existing, which is consistent with the Korean way of thinking and is characteristic of high schools in Korea. Practically, the national college entrance examination still rules over what and how teachers teach in the senior high schools in Korea. Even though this examination has been improving, teachers still feel that they must stress content so that students will get high scores in this examination, as pointed out by Cho, Yager, Park and Seo (1997). This trend has continuously existed in teachers' mind-sets even after the national curriculum explicitly emphasised constructivist approaches. The disparity between the responses from some scales and the responses from interview implied that the notions of constructivism were being displayed only with a narrower interpretation.

5.2.2. Happenings associated with laboratory classes

The findings from interviews and observations regarding happenings in laboratory supported the findings from survey with the SLEI. The responses of students in interview reflected that students are expected to follow these rules in the laboratory. It was also reported that experiments in laboratory lessons are normally organised with clear procedures, which causes 'closed' experiments. Relatively strong cohesiveness among students in the laboratory lessons was found as another characteristic of Korean high schools. In addition to these general conditions, some differences were also found among three streams. Compared to the students from the humanities and the science-oriented streams, students from the science-independent stream reported experiencing more frequent experiments with more abundant materials in their laboratory lessons.

5.2.3. *Interaction between teachers and students*

Students' responses reflected that the science teachers in Korean high schools are directive, strict and not supportive of students' self-activities. With this general impression, it was also found that students experience unique interaction in their science classrooms with their particular teacher. It was considered that this difference comes from the overlapping of a teacher's personal character with a stream's nature (e.g. curriculum, expectation etc).

In interviews, the differences between the three streams were clearly revealed, implying that the biggest difference between streams is the trust about students' self-study ability. In the science-independent stream's case, the teacher allowed students to do class tasks by themselves, based on the trust for students' self-study ability. The duration of teacher lecturing was relatively short. In the science-oriented stream classes, students were concentrating on the lessons but they showed some fear of being picked to give answers to the teacher's questions, because they did not want to be ridiculed because of wrong answers. In the humanities stream, students were very passive in the class. They were not confident in their answers when they were required to respond. The teacher did not wait for the students to respond to his questions. It was presumed that teachers did not expect responses from students. During observations, the researcher noted that in classes in the science-independent stream, teachers appeared more receptive of students' talking and the lessons were mainly run using group activities. Students' cooperation was natural and did not require explicit interception from the teacher. Interviews also indicated that students from the science-independent stream were more likely to interact actively with their teachers than were students from the other two streams.

Overall it was revealed that students in Korean high school are under pressure from highly-competitive university entrance examinations. This pressure has shaped various features of Korean high school science classroom environments: highly competitive, enormously teacher-centred, and limited students' self-activities. Although potentially ideal current notions (such as constructivism) have been discussed in order to improve the education in Korea, they have not overcome the restraints mainly coming from the examination-driven system. The dominant nature of the examination-driven style was illustrated from in terms of the aspects of science classroom environments.

One study by Lee (1998) which was recently done is worthy of being spotlighted here. The study was conducted based on self-developed questionnaires which could be sensitive to the Korean school context. The students from year 8 to year 11 were involved in his study. This study generated a comprehensive data set via several questionnaires.

6. Learning Environment Research embedded in the Paradigm of Alternative Evaluation or Assessment

Korea has an extremely centralized education system, which enables control over almost all the schools in the nation. In particular, new educational policies or recently adapted teaching strategies can make effect throughout the nation very easily and speedily. Recently, many educators and educational researchers in Korea have been concerned about the quality of assessment system in schools (Kim, 1999; Sung, 1999). They have criticised the current assessment system in schools, which can only evaluate the learning outcomes at surface level, by making students simply memorise what they have learned and reproduce them in the tests. Under this critic, new assessment system was introduced, which is called 'performance assessment' (Hart, 1994; Kim, 1999). Once it was introduced to several levels of schools (primary, secondary), the effectiveness has been actively studied by several researchers in diverse ways (Cho, Kim, 1999, 2000; Son, 1999). One of the big issues related to this evaluation system was and has been the impact on students' perceptions about their 'changed' classroom environments represented by this new evaluation scheme (Lee, 1998).

Cho and Kim (1999) investigated the impact of portfolio system on primary school children's perceptions about their science lessons' psycho-social environment. They designed comparative-experiment by using one control group (taught by traditional lecture-type lesson and assessed by only paper-pencil test) and the other treatment group (taught by portfolio instruction and assessed by several methods including portfolio). Year 5 students were involved in this study from two schools. After providing two different lessons (traditional lesson and portfolio-using lesson), the instrument (What Is Happening In this Classroom) were administered in order to obtain these children's perceptions about their lessons. They showed more positive perceptions on some scales in the WIHIC such as teacher support, task orientation, and equity.

Son (1999) reported similar study as done by Cho and Kim (1999). In his study, year 5 children participated in two groups: experimental and control group. He employed two questionnaires (the WIHIC and the QTI) in order to obtain the information about the impact of portfolio-leaded lessons on children's perceptions about their lessons. The group who was taught by portfolio-leaded lesson showed more positive perceptions on the WIHIC. In case of the QTI, there was only one statistical difference between experimental group and control group such as the uncertainty scale. This means that portfolio-leaded lessons encourage students to learn by themselves (rather than relying on their teachers). This also indicates that teachers can provide more effective support for their students' learning than does normal traditional lessons.

7. The Issue Surrounded Methodologies utilised in the Studies Conducted in Korea

The field of learning environment research in Korea has been maintained mainly by quantitative spirit, which is basically supported within positivistic paradigm. The quantitative spirit has contributed to create a large number of instruments for survey so that researchers can conveniently handle with their studies, including large sample sizes. One of the advantages of this methodology is that it can provide general view about targeted phenomenon, by involving large scales of population as samples. Many studies have reported this benefit from their own studies and still used one of the main tools within this field of research. This trend can also be traced in the studies conducted by other countries within the field of learning environment research. In Korea, Kim (1999) started to provide suggestion towards other methodological possibilities, by introducing recent recommendations by Fraser and Tobin (1998).

As age went by, certain groups of researchers appeared with critical view about this positivistic paradigm. They have pointed out the possible disadvantage of this paradigm, by mentioning implicitly and omitting significant aspects which should be dealt with by rather diverse approaches, such as multiple methodologies. Fraser and Tobin (1998) have recommended this trial by advocating possible benefit from this combining paradigm for the field of learning environment research.

The best choice would be to take the mild reformation from present status. In particular, the Korean academics which is mainly controlled by objectivistic paradigm, need to take some transitional period for paradigm shift. With this realization, the following would be one of the pathways for Korean researchers to take for their future research in the field of learning environment study.

As a transitional effort, Sunny Lee employed the combining technique for her own research methodology. She firstly introduced the dualistic point of view (Denzin & Lincoln, 1998; Howe, 1988), which presume that the two approaches (quantitative & qualitative) are incompatible. And then, she claimed that this dilemma can be resolved by replacing the dualistic notion with a rather practical notion for a particular study, by accepting Punch's notion (1998). Aldridge and her colleagues' study (2000) also support her claim for combining strategies for learning environment research. They did a fruitful task with this combining methodology in their cross-cultural study. Their study was benefited from this methodology by revealing some impressive factors, which are not usually expected from objectivist or quantitative spirit. Now, it is high time for Korean science educators to consider the potential of combining or employing the flexibility for their research especially within the field of learning environment research. This suggestion could go beyond the national boundary, meaning that international scholars in this field would expect benefit by employing this methodological strategy.

8. Suggestions and Implications

Although the studies on classroom learning environments in Korea have contributed to educational research and practice in diverse ways, there is still much room for further improvement and progress. At this stage, we can suggest several points as follows.

First, we need to enhance cultural adaptability of the questionnaires, which were originally developed in other languages. In fact, most of the studies in the field of learning environment research in Korea have been dependent on the adapted questionnaires by translating, which might not necessarily convey the cultural notions. Secondly, more qualitative spirit would enable many stakeholders (as well as researchers) to obtain more comprehensive and practical feature of current situation. Thirdly, for more comprehensive picture, especially about high school levels, the range of the sample needs to be extended to the non-academic stream. Also, if other year levels are involved, studies could investigate the spectrum across the levels in terms of their classroom environments. Fourthly, the perceptions of teachers and parents would also be valuable in future research for obtaining deeper insight about the classroom environments in Korea.

References

Aldridge, J.M., Fraser, B.J. & Taylor, P.C. (2000). Constructivist learning environments in a cross-national study in Taiwan and Australia. *International Journal of Science Education, 22*, 37–55.

Cho, S.H. & Kim, C.J. (2001). The effect of a portfolio system on elementary school students' socio-psychological classroom environment. *Journal of the Korean Association for Research in Science Education (in print).* (In Korean)

Cho, Kim (2000). The development, application and assessment of students' portfolio system for elementary science lessons. Research report submitted to Subjects' Research Institute. (In Korean)

Denzin, N. & Lincoln, Y. (1998). Entering the field of qualitative research. In N.K. Denzin & Y.S. Lincoln (Eds.), *The landscape of qualitative research: Theories and issues* (Vol. 1, pp. 1–34). London: Sage publications.

Hart, D. (1994). Authentic assessment: A handbook for educators. Addison-Wesley: Menlo Park, CA, USA

Howe, K.R. (1988). Against the quantitative-qualitative incompatibility thesis or dogmas die hard. *Educational Researcher, 17*, 10–16.

Han, J.H. (1995). The quest for national standards in science education in Korea. *Studies in Science Education, 6*, 59–71.

Kim, H.B., Fisher, D.L. & Fraser, B.J. (1999). Assessment and investigation of constructivist science learning environments in Korea. *Research in Science and Technological Education, 17*, 239–249.

Kim, H.B., Fisher, D.L. & Fraser, B.J. (2000). Classroom environment and teacher interpersonal behaviour in secondary school classes in Korea. *Evaluation and Research in Education, 14*, 3–22.

Kim, H.B. & Kim, D.Y. (1995). Survey on the perceptions towards science laboratory classroom environment of university students majoring education. *Journal of the Korean Association for Research in Science Education, 14*, 163–171. (In Korean)

Kim, H.B. & Kim, D.Y. (1996). Middle and high school students' perceptions of science laboratory and their attitudes in science and science subjects. *Journal of the Korean Association for Research in Science Education, 16*, 210–216. (In Korean)

Kim, H.B. & Lee, S.K. (1997). Science teachers' beliefs about science and school science and their perceptions of science laboratory learning environment. *Journal of the Korean Association for Research in Science Education, 17*, 210–216. (In Korean)

Lee, J.C. (1998). *The effects of psychological learning environment generated by science teachers upon students' affective perception and cognitive learning.* Unpublished doctoral thesis. School of Secondary Education, University of Teachers. Korea.

Lee, S.U. (2001). *Assessment, development and effects of high school science learning environments in Korea.* Unpublished doctoral thesis. Science and Mathematics Education Centre, Curtin University of Technology. Perth, Australia.

Noh, T.H. & Choi, Y.N. (1996). Primary and secondary school students' perceptions of science classroom environments and their relationships with science-related attitudes. *Journal of the Korean Association for Research in Science Education, 16*, 217–225. (In Korean)

Noh, T.H. & Kang, S.J. (1997). The effect of the general science course on the students' views about science-technology society relationship and their perceptions of science classroom environment. *Journal of the Korean Association for Research in Science Education, 17*, 395–403. (In Korean)

Punch, K. (1998). Mixed methods and evaluative criteria. In K. Punch (Ed.), *Introduction to social research: Quantitative and qualitative approaches* (pp. 239–263). Thousands Oaks: Sage publications.

Son, S.N. (1999). *Effects of portfolio system on socio-psychological classroom environment in elementary science class.* Unpublished Master project. Teachers' College. ChungJu University. ChungJu, Korea.

Sung, T.J. (1999). The change of educational evaluation and its validity. *Educational Research, 37*, 197–218. (In Korean)

Tobin, K. & Fraser, B.J. (1998). Qualitative and quantitative landscape of classroom learning environments. In B.J. Fraser & K. Tobin (Eds.), *International Handbook of Science Education.* London: Kluwer Academic Publishers.

Yoon, H.K. (1993). *The investigation on the relationship between psychological environment of science laboratory and learning outcomes.* Unpublished Master Project, Seoul National University, Seoul, Korea.

APPENDIX

SLEI

실험실 활동에서 경험한 사례에 대한 설문입니다.					
1. 나는 실험실에서 다른 학생들과 잘 지낸다.	1	2	3	4	5
2. 나는 실험실에서 내 흥미에 맞는 실험을 할 기회를 갖는다.	1	2	3	4	5
3. 정규 과학 수업에서 배우는 내용은 나의 실험 활동과는 무관하다.	1	2	3	4	5
4. 실험 수업에서는 명확한 규칙에 따라 내 활동이 진행된다.	1	2	3	4	5
5. 내가 실험을 할 때 실험실이 너무 혼잡하다고 생각한다.	1	2	3	4	5
6. 실험 수업에서 다른 학생을 알 기회가 거의 없다.	1	2	3	4	5
7. 실험 수업에서는 주어진 문제를 풀기 위해 스스로 실험을 계획한다.	1	2	3	4	5
8. 실험실 활동은 과학 수업 시간에 배우는 주제와 무관하다.	1	2	3	4	5
9. 실험 수업은 별다른 형식이 없고 지켜야 할 규칙이 별로 없다.	1	2	3	4	5
10. 실험 활동에 필요한 기구와 재료는 쉽게 얻을 수 있다.	1	2	3	4	5
11. 실험실의 학생들은 나를 도와준다.	1	2	3	4	5
12. 실험 과정에서 다른 학생들은 같은 문제에 대해 나와 다른 데이타를 모은다.	1	2	3	4	5
13. 정규적인 과학 수업은 실험 활동과 통합되어 운영된다.	1	2	3	4	5
14. 나는 실험실에서 특정 규칙에 따라야 한다.	1	2	3	4	5
15. 나는 실험실 모습에 대해 부끄럽게 생각한다.	1	2	3	4	5
16. 나는 실험 수업에 참여하는 학생들을 잘 안다.	1	2	3	4	5
17. 나는 정규적인 실험 활동을 벗어나서 나 자신만의 실험을 할 수 있다.	1	2	3	4	5
18. 나는 실험 활동 중에 과학 수업 시간에 배운 내용을 적용한다.	1	2	3	4	5
19. 실험실에서 안전하게 실험하는 방법이 잘 알려져 있다.	1	2	3	4	5
20. 실험실 기구들은 사용하기 좋게 배열되어 있다.	1	2	3	4	5

21. 실험 수업 동안 다른 학생들의 도움을 받을 수 있다.	1	2	3	4	5
22. 실험 수업 동안 나는 다른 학생들과 다른 실험을 한다.	1	2	3	4	5
23. 정규 과학수업 시간에 다루는 주제는 실험 시간에 다루는 것과 다르다.	1	2	3	4	5
24. 실험 시간에 내가 지키도록 하는 정해진 규칙이 별로 없다.	1	2	3	4	5
25. 실험실은 시원하고 통풍이 잘 된다.	1	2	3	4	5
26. 실험 시간에 짧은 시간 내에 모든 학생들의 이름을 안다.	1	2	3	4	5
27. 실험 시간에 내가 실험할 가장 좋은 방법은 선생님이 결정한다.	1	2	3	4	5
28. 실험 시간을 통해 과학 수업 시간에 다루는 내용을 더 잘 이해 할 수 있다.	1	2	3	4	5
29. 실험 시간을 시작하기 전에 선생님은 안전에 대해 주의를 준다.	1	2	3	4	5
30. 실험실은 내가 실험하는데 매력적인 장소이다.	1	2	3	4	5
31. 나는 실험 시간에 협동해서 일을 한다.	1	2	3	4	5
32. 실험을 수행하는데 있어서 가장 좋은 방법은 내가 결정한다.	1	2	3	4	5
33. 실험과 정규 과학 수업은 서로 관계가 없다.	1	2	3	4	5
34. 실험 수업은 다른 수업에 비해 명확한 규칙을 따르면서 진행된다.	1	2	3	4	5
35. 실험실은 개인이나 조별 실험을 하는데 충분한 공간을 갖고 있다.	1	2	3	4	5

QTI

교사의 행동					
1. 이 선생님은 자신의 과목에 대해 열정적으로 말씀하신다.	0	1	2	3	4
2. 이 선생님은 우리를 믿는다.	0	1	2	3	4
3. 이 선생님은 분명하지 않게 보인다.	0	1	2	3	4
4. 이 선생님은 예상치 못하게 화를 내신다.	0	1	2	3	4
5. 이 선생님은 명확하게 설명하신다.	0	1	2	3	4
6. 우리가 선생님에게 동의하지 않으면, 그것에 관해 말할 수 있다.	0	1	2	3	4
7. 이 선생님은 우유부단하다.	0	1	2	3	4
8. 이 선생님은 쉽게 화를 낸다.	0	1	2	3	4
9. 이 선생님은 우리의 주의를 사로잡는다.	0	1	2	3	4
10. 이 선생님은 기꺼이 다시 설명하신다.	0	1	2	3	4
11. 이 선생님은 자신이 무엇을 해야할 지 모르는 것처럼 행동하신다.	0	1	2	3	4
12. 이 선생님은 너무 성질이 급해서 우리가 규칙을 어겼을 때 고쳐주시지 못한다.	0	1	2	3	4
13. 이 선생님은 학급에서 일어나는 모든 일을 아신다.	0	1	2	3	4
14. 우리가 말할 것이 있으면, 이 선생님은 잘 들으려고 하신다.	0	1	2	3	4
15. 이 선생님은 우리에 의해 교실 분위기가 이끌어져가게 놓아둔다.	0	1	2	3	4
16. 이 선생님은 참을성이 없다.	0	1	2	3	4
17. 이 선생님은 좋은 지도자이시다.	0	1	2	3	4
18. 이 선생님은 우리가 이해할 수 없을 때를 잘 아신다.	0	1	2	3	4
19. 이 선생님은 우리가 잘못 행동할 때 무엇을 해야할 지를 확신하지 못한다.	0	1	2	3	4
20. 이 선생님과는 언쟁하는 일이 자주 있다.	0	1	2	3	4
21. 이 선생님은 신뢰성있는 행동을 하신다.	0	1	2	3	4
22. 이 선생님은 참을성이 많다.	0	1	2	3	4
23. 이 선생님은 불확실해 보이는 때가 많다.	0	1	2	3	4
24. 이 선생님은 비웃는 말을 하신다.	0	1	2	3	4

25. 이 선생님은 우리가 우리의 일을 하도록 돕는다.	0	1	2	3	4
26. 우리는 이 선생님의 수업에서 어떤 일을 결정할 수 있다.	0	1	2	3	4
27. 이 선생님은 우리가 속인다고 생각하신다.	0	1	2	3	4
28. 이 선생님은 엄격하시다.	0	1	2	3	4
29. 이 선생님은 다정하시다.	0	1	2	3	4
30. 우리가 이 선생님에게 영향을 미칠 수 있다.	0	1	2	3	4
31. 이 선생님은 우리가 아무 것도 모른다고 생각하신다.	0	1	2	3	4
32. 우리는 이 선생님의 수업에서 조용해야만 한다.	0	1	2	3	4
33. 이 선생님은 우리가 의지할 수 있는 사람이다.	0	1	2	3	4
34. 이 선생님은 우리가 수업에서 작업하는 시기를 결정하게 하신다.	0	1	2	3	4
35. 이 선생님은 우리에게 창피를 주신다.	0	1	2	3	4
36. 이 선생님의 시험은 난해하다.	0	1	2	3	4
37. 이 선생님은 유머 감각이 있으시다.	0	1	2	3	4
38. 이 선생님은 수업에서 우리 스스로 많은 것을 하도록 놓아두신다.	0	1	2	3	4
39. 이 선생님은 우리가 일들을 잘 할 수 없다고 생각하신다.	0	1	2	3	4
40. 이 선생님의 기준은 매우 높다.	0	1	2	3	4
41. 이 선생님은 농담을 하실 수 있다.	0	1	2	3	4
42. 이 선생님은 수업 시간에 우리에게 많은 자유를 주신다.	0	1	2	3	4
43. 이 선생님은 불만스러워 보인다.	0	1	2	3	4
44. 이 선생님은 가혹하게 시험 채점을 하신다.	0	1	2	3	4
45. 이 선생님의 수업은 즐겁다.	0	1	2	3	4
46. 이 선생님은 관대하다.	0	1	2	3	4
47. 이 선생님은 의심이 많다.	0	1	2	3	4
48. 우리는 이 선생님을 무서워 한다.	0	1	2	3	4

CLES

세계에 대한 학습					
이 수업에서					
1. 나는 학교 밖의 세계에 관해 배운다	5	4	3	2	1
2. 나는 학교 밖의 세계에 관한 문제로부터 새로운 학습을 시작한다.	5	4	3	2	1
3. 나는 과학이 학교 밖에서의 내 생활의 일부가 될 수 있음을 배운다	5	4	3	2	1
이 수업에서					
4. 나는 학교 밖의 세계에 대해 더 잘 이해하게 된다.	5	4	3	2	1
5. 나는 학교 밖의 세계에 관한 재미있는 것들을 배운다.	5	4	3	2	1
과학에 대한 학습					
이 수업에서					
6. 나는 과학이 시간이 지남에 따라 변화했음을 배운다.	5	4	3	2	1
7. 나는 과학이 인간의 가치와 견해에 의해 영향을 받음을 배운다.	5	4	3	2	1
이 수업에서					
8. 나는 다른 문화권의 사람이 사용하는 다른 과학에 관해 배운다.	5	4	3	2	1
9. 나는 현대 과학이 과거의 과학과 다름을 배운다.	5	4	3	2	1
10. 나는 과학이 이론을 창안해내는 것에 관해 배운다.	5	4	3	2	1
의견 제시에 대한 학습					
이 수업에서					
11. 나는 "이것을 제가 왜 배워야 합니까?"라고 선생님께 질문해도 좋다	5	4	3	2	1
12. 나는 내가 배우는 방식에 관해 질문을 해도 좋다.	5	4	3	2	1
13. 나는 혼동되는 애매한 활동에 관해 불평을 해도 좋다.	5	4	3	2	1
이 수업에서					
14. 나는 내 학습에 방해가 되는 어떤 것에 관해 불평을 해도 좋다.	5	4	3	2	1
15. 나는 내 의견을 말해도 좋다.	5	4	3	2	1

학습에 대한 학습					
이 수업에서					
16. 나는 선생님이 내가 학습하고자 하는 것을 계획하도록 돕는다.	5	4	3	2	1
17. 나는 선생님이 내가 얼마나 잘 학습하는 지를 결정하도록 돕는다.	5	4	3	2	1
18. 나는 선생님이 어떤 활동이 나에게 가장 좋은 지를 결정하도록 돕는다.	5	4	3	2	1
이 수업에서					
19. 나는 내가 학습 활동들을 하는데 얼마나 많은 시간을 들여야 하는 지를 선생님이 결정하도록 돕는다.	5	4	3	2	1
20. 나는 내가 어떤 활동을 할 것인지를 선생님이 결정하도록 돕는다.	5	4	3	2	1
의사소통에 대한 학습					
이 수업에서					
21. 나는 다른 학생들과 말할 기회를 갖는다	5	4	3	2	1
22. 나는 다른 학생들과 문제 해결 방법에 관해 말한다.	5	4	3	2	1
23. 나는 내 생각을 다른 학생들에게 설명한다.	5	4	3	2	1
이 수업에서					
24. 나는 다른 학생들에게 그들의 생각을 설명하도록 요청한다.	5	4	3	2	1
25. 다른 학생들이 내 생각을 설명하도록 요청한다.	5	4	3	2	1

Chapter 9

STUDIES ON LEARNING ENVIRONMENTS IN SINGAPORE CLASSROOMS

Swee Chiew Goh
Nanyang Technological University
Singapore

Research on learning environments in Singapore emerged recently in the last decade of the twentieth century and it has attracted considerable interest among educators. This chapter presents research in the field covering primary, secondary and tertiary levels. The research also involved the study of a wide spectrum of classroom learning environments in social studies, science, mathematics, computer classrooms, and that of science laboratories. These studies were carried out in schools, junior colleges, university and adult education classes. In general, the findings, through perceptions of students and teachers, attest to the importance of learning environments in terms of student achievement and attitude.

1. Introduction

The study of learning environments and their impact on the achievement and attitude of students began to emerge in Singapore in the early 1990s. Interest in this sphere of educational research has grown tremendously in the last decade, much of which is fanned by the recognition that the state of the classroom's learning environment may contribute to or hinder the learning process. The environment is considered conducive to learning when the students are happy, co-operative and absorbed in learning and their teacher enjoys facilitating and motivating them to learn (Goh, 2002). The nature of the learning environment is influenced by its psychosocial dimensions in terms of the degree of student cohesiveness, self-esteem and confidence, a sense of belonging and motivation to learn. In addition, a good teacher–student relationship is paramount to the creation and maintenance of a positive classroom environment.

The interest in learning environment research in Singapore is reflected in two ways. Firstly, studies in learning environment are carried out at all levels (primary, secondary, junior college, tertiary and adult education) and in different streams (normal, express, special and gifted). Secondly, studies are also done across the spectrum of disciplines; for example, curriculum areas in English Language, Social Studies, Science, Mathematics and Computers.

This chapter presents the study on learning environments in Singapore in three sections. The first section introduces the first studies while the second focusses on more recent investigations in different classroom contexts at the primary, secondary and post-secondary levels. The third section refers to other efforts; for instance, cross-national research in secondary science classrooms in Australia and Singapore and studies at the postgraduate level of teacher-training.

To provide a framework for an understanding of classroom environments in multi-racial Singapore, an overview of the education system is presented in the next section.

2. Overview of Education System in Singapore

The education system is structured in three main parts following a 6:4:2 model: six years of primary, four years of secondary and two years of pre-university or junior college education. The main aim of education is to provide the young with a balanced and well-rounded education so as to nurture the potential of every child or student in Singapore and to prepare him/her become a responsible and good citizen.

Formal education begins at the age of six and there are six years of primary and four to five years of secondary, making a total of ten to eleven years of general education. English Language is used as the medium of instruction in schools and mother tongue languages (Chinese, Malay and Tamil languages) are taught as a second language.

2.1. Primary Education

At primary school, students attend a four-year foundation stage (Primary 1 to 4) and a two-year orientation stage (Primary 5 to 6). At the end of Primary 4 (Grade 4), on the basis of achievement in a school-based examination in three subjects, namely, English Language, a mother tongue language (Chinese/Malay/Tamil) and mathematics, students are streamed into EM1, EM2 or EM3 classes. The better students are streamed into EM1 (where both English and mother tongue languages are taught at the first language level) or EM2 (where English Language is offered as a first language and the mother tongue as a second language) while the weaker students go to the EM3 (Foundation English Language, Aural and Oral mother tongue). This system also provides for lateral transfer of eligible students between streams.

At the end of Primary 6 (Grade 6), students sit for a national examination, the Primary School Leaving Examination, known commonly as the PSLE, in English and mother tongue Languages, Mathematics and Science. Based on performance in the PSLE, students are placed into one of the three secondary streams, the Special, Express and Normal (Academic or Technical). The fundamental principle underpinning this placement examination is that students are placed into a stream that suits their learning ability and aptitude.

2.2. Secondary Education

At secondary school, the Special and Express streams are four-year courses with similar curricular content except in the learning of languages. Students in the Special stream study both English and mother tongue languages at the first language level while students in the Express stream study English Language as a first language and mother tongue language as a second language. The Normal stream, subdivided into Normal (Academic) and Normal (Technical), each with a different curricular emphasis, has a fifth year for eligible students to move up to the standard of the Special and Express courses. As in the primary school, the system provides for lateral transfer between streams to allow students to progress at a faster or slower pace depending on their performance.

At the end of Secondary 4 (Grade 10), students in the Special and Express classes sit for the Singapore-Cambridge General Certificate of Education Ordinary Level (GCE "O" level) Examination. Based on academic performance and interest, students may select from post-secondary courses provided in junior colleges, centralised institutes, polytechnics and institutes of technical education. Students in the Normal stream sit for the Singapore-Cambridge General Certificate of Education

Normal Level (GCE "N" level) Examination. Students with better "N" level grades may sit for the GCE "O" level while others choose to study at the institutes of technical education.

2.3. Gifted Education

The Singapore education system also makes provision for the brightest students through the Gifted Education Programme (GEP) at selected primary and secondary schools. Screening is conducted at the end of Primary 3 (Grade 3) and eligible students are chosen to attend GEP classes in certain schools from Primary 4 (Grade 4) onwards. Top performing students in the PSLE, usually the cream of a cohort at Primary 6 (Grade 6), are also given the opportunity to study in GEP classes in selected secondary schools. The curriculum and teaching strategies are adapted to nurture and develop this group of gifted students.

2.4. Post-Secondary Education

At the post-secondary level, there are at least four pathways open to students. The 2-year Pre-University course at Junior Colleges (JC, Grades 11 and 12) is available to the more academically inclined students, at the end of which they take the Singapore-Cambridge General Certificate of Education Advanced Level (GCE "A" level) Examination. Many students enter the university at this point. There is also the 3-year Pre-University course offered by Centralised Institutes (CI) for those who cannot gain admission to the JC. Other students prefer to enter the Polytechnics that offer a wide range of courses in different fields to meet the increasing demands of industry. Courses at the Polytechnics are more practice-oriented, for example, electrical and electronic engineering, information technology, biotechnology/biomedical science, nursing or business. The least academically inclined students tend to enrol at the Institutes of Technical Education (ITE) for more skills-oriented courses, for example, the Industrial Technician Certificate (ITC courses) and Certificate in Business Studies (CBS courses) in preparation for entering the workforce. There are others who simply leave school and start working.

3. First Studies in Learning Environments

The first indication of studies on learning environment in Singapore emerged in 1993 (Lim, 1993, 1995) with a study of Secondary 4 (Grade 10) students' perceptions of their classroom environment. The target population were Secondary 4 students from different types of schools (Good, Average, and Below Average), streams (Gifted, Special, Express and Normal), subject specialisations (Arts, Science, Technical/ Commerce) and varied socio-economic backgrounds (high, middle and low). The Individualised Classroom Environment Questionnaire (ICEQ) was administered to a stratified random sample of Secondary 4 students from nine secondary schools to assess their perceptions of their actual and preferred classroom environments. This study was designed as part of a research on factors related to students' perceptions in learning.

The findings revealed that the school type, the stream, the subject specialisation and the socio-economic background of the students had an effect on the students' perceptions of all the dimensions of the preferred environment and some of the dimensions of the actual environment. Firstly, it highlighted the situation where students preferred a more positive and favourable classroom environment than was actually present. This data on the actual-preferred discrepancy made possible adjustments in the classroom environment and lessened the discrepancy so that students will learn better in their classes. Secondly, students in the good schools perceived their classroom environment favourably, reinforcing the idea that the person–environment fit is fine and these students view their environment more positively and learn better in it. This perception was also shared by students in the Gifted and Special streams as well as by science students. Thirdly, students in the below average schools tend to show that the person-environment fit is not that fine. They expressed stronger preferences for changes in their environment, for example, more opportunities to be able to learn on the basis of ability, learning style, interests and rate of working. This perception was also felt to be desirable by students in the Arts specialisation as well as in the Express and Normal streams. These findings were among the first to be documented in learning environment research.

At about the same time, Teh (1994) initiated a study of computer-assisted learning environment in secondary geography classrooms. This study examined the nature of the learning environment experienced by weaker Secondary 2 students in Normal (Academic) classes. A special CAL programme on the topic of "decision-making" was produced and a new questionnaire, the Geography Classroom Environment Inventory (GCEI) was developed and validated for this investigation. Findings indicated that the CAL programme resulted in better achievement and more positive attitudes among the slow learners. Thus, appropriate computer-based learning encouraged better performance among low-aptitude students in Secondary 2 Normal (Academic) classes. The GCEI was also found to be a reliable and valid instrument for studying classroom environment in Singapore.

These early efforts of studying secondary classroom environments, involving the use of an existing instrument and also the development and validation of a new questionnaire, are the forerunners of more studies in learning environments. The findings from these studies indicated that learning environments are indeed areas that could provide alternative perspectives to the effectiveness of the teaching and learning process in Singapore classrooms.

4. Recent Studies in Learning Environments

As a field of educational research, the study of learning environments has attracted considerable interest in Singapore. Recently, studies have been undertaken at both primary and secondary levels. The latest addition was an investigation into the learning environment of General Paper (English Language) classes in the junior colleges (pre-university level). One major concern of teachers and parents is that students should be given all available opportunity to excel both in and out of the classroom and their potential nurtured. Achievement or examination performance therefore tends to drive much of the learning that takes place in schools. As learning mostly takes place in the classrooms (be they the usual classrooms, special classrooms equipped for the teaching of art, music and home economics, science laboratories or workshops for technical education), the nature of the classroom environment will most likely influence the motivation and degree of students' learning. In turn, this generates interest towards the types of learning environment the students study in at primary, secondary and post-secondary classrooms, especially with the presence of computers in the classrooms. The focus is on the nature of the classroom environment and adjectives such as conducive, positive, productive and supportive are used to describe its state. Classroom practices and developments in the last three decades have indicated that a positive classroom climate is needed for effective learning (Brophy & Putnam, 1979; Emmer, Evertson & Anderson, 1980). Moreover, the availability of a range of questionnaires for various classroom environments (e.g., constructivist, computer-assisted and science laboratory) and the ease in use for examining different types of classrooms made the study of learning environments even more attractive.

It is within this context that research in learning environment began to make their presence felt in Singapore. The following sections highlight studies carried out at primary, secondary and post-secondary classes, each study being unique in its own right.

4.1. Primary Classrooms

Studies in learning environment in primary schools are fewer in number as the tendency is to investigate secondary classrooms. This sub-section includes studies conducted in Mathematics, Science and Social Studies classroom environments.

The first major study done at primary level is an investigation into mathematics classrooms in 13 government co-educational schools (Goh & Fraser, 1998, 2000). This study is distinctive in that it explored simultaneously two important aspects of the learning environment, namely interpersonal teacher behaviour and classroom climate. Two instruments, the Questionnaire on Teacher Interaction/Primary (QTI/Primary, Goh & Fraser, 1997) and the My Class Inventory (MCI), were used to explore the two aspects respectively. The QTI/Primary used in this study is a simplified version of the QTI (Wubbels & Levy, 1993). It measured interpersonal teacher behaviour based on the eight dimensions of leadership, helping/friendly, understanding, student responsibility/

freedom, uncertain, dissatisfied, admonishing and strict. Student attitude was measured through the Liking Mathematics Scale and achievement through a specially designed mathematics assessment. Findings revealed that student-teacher relationships and classroom climate were significantly related to students' achievement and attitude towards learning. One important result is that teacher leadership, being understanding, helpful and friendly are positive behaviours that teachers should demonstrate liberally in primary classrooms. It was also found that the classroom environment would be conducive to learning when there was a high degree of cohesion and little friction among students. The findings were encouraging and provided the impetus for more research at the primary level.

Another study into Primary 5 mathematics classrooms in one co-educational government school (Teng, 2000) focussed on the computer laboratory learning environment. The objectives of this study centred on the environment-outcome association, actual and preferred match and gender differences. The findings showed that there were positive links between the computer-assisted learning environment and students' attitude towards learning of mathematics. As for gender difference, the girls perceived their classrooms more favourably than the boys did.

Recently, a study looked at Primary 5 science classrooms in one co-educational government primary school (Chin, 2001). Seven classes took part in the study using instruments adapted from pre-existing ones. The main purpose was to examine the relationship between students' perceptions of their science classroom environment and their achievement and attitudes towards learning of science. There was also a comparison of the actual and preferred perceptions of the students and gender differences. Overall, the findings suggest that the better the learning environment, the better the students' academic performance and attitude towards learning. In terms of gender differences, the girls held more favourable perceptions than boys, a result that replicated the studies in primary mathematics classrooms.

Pang (1999) used a case study to explore the impact of a co-operative learning environment on underachievers in a Primary 4 (Grade 4) classroom. The spotlight was on three underachieving students — the nature and causes of underachievement and intervention in terms of modifying the classroom environment with co-operative learning strategies. The findings were fascinating and noteworthy as the underachieving students responded positively with more active participation in class activities, increased confidence and self-esteem and better relationships with peers. The qualitative data derived from systematic classroom observations, interviews with students, teachers and parents, journals of both the students and the researcher were rich and thick. Triangulation of the various sources of information made possible insights into the significance of classroom environment and learning, in particular, the alleviation of underachievement in a co-operative learning environment.

With reference to these studies conducted in primary classrooms, it is obvious that the learning environment is one critical factor in the learning process. This learning environment includes all the elements within the classroom, for example, the interactions between the teacher and students and classroom climate. Whether the teacher is being understanding, helpful or strict, whether the class is cohesive and has a sense of belonging, all contribute to a conducive classroom environment. This favourable classroom environment will most likely heighten the students' sense of wanting to learn and hence, the significant relationship between environment and learning outcomes. High achievement and a positive attitude are correlates of a productive learning environment.

These studies were also undertaken at the upper primary level when the students belong to the age-group 10–11. They are more mature and their command of the English Language better. The items in the questionnaires will be more easily comprehensible and the gathered data more meaningful. They also can keep journals of their classroom experiences and express themselves at interviews, albeit not in the best of English. On the whole, findings suggest that the learning environment is one crucial domain in the process of effective teaching and learning. The next section presents research in the learning environment of secondary classrooms.

4.2. Secondary Classrooms

In recent years, several studies were also conducted in secondary classrooms, examining the state of the learning environment for instance in Science, Mathematics, Geography and Chinese Language classes as presented below.

Science laboratory environments

There were two studies done in secondary chemistry laboratories, the first in Secondary 4 Express and Normal streams and the second in Secondary Gifted Education classes.

The first was a study of the determinants and effects of the chemistry laboratory environment (Wong & Fraser, 1997) using the Chemistry Laboratory Environment Inventory (CLEI, adapted from the Science Laboratory Environment Inventory) and the Questionnaire on Chemistry-related Attitudes (QOCRA). The sample was drawn from 56 secondary chemistry classes (both Express and Normal classes) in 28 secondary schools. The Actual and Preferred versions of the Class and Personal Forms of the CLEI were used in this study. In the examination of environment-outcome associations (Wong & Fraser, 1996), statistically significant findings were found between the CLEI and attitudinal outcomes, such as attitude to laboratory learning. More favourable attitudes towards laboratory work were found in classes that exhibited a higher degree of student cohesiveness and integration, that is, integration of laboratory activities with the theory learnt in non-laboratory classes. Gender differences in students' perceptions of the chemistry laboratory environment were in favour of girls, for girls tend to show more positive perceptions of their laboratory environment than the boys did. This finding replicates most of the learning environment research in this gender aspect.

The second study investigated the association between the chemistry laboratory environment and interpersonal teacher behaviour with student attitudes towards learning of chemistry (Quek *et al.*, 2001). The sample came from Secondary 4 students in the Gifted Education Programme and the Express stream. The Chemistry Laboratory Environment Inventory (CLEI) was used together with the Questionnaire on Teacher Interaction (QTI) to provide data for the laboratory environment and interpersonal teacher behaviour respectively, while the Questionnaire on Chemistry-related Attitudes (QOCRA) gave information regarding students' attitudinal outcome. One important finding of this study was the strong associations found between students' enjoyment of their chemistry classes and their perceptions of teacher interpersonal behaviour, especially in teacher's helping/friendly behaviour. The students' responses indicated that there should be more open-ended learning environments for the teaching and learning of chemistry. Students in both the Gifted Education and Express classes showed little difference in their perceptions towards teachers. However, it was found that in the Gifted Education classes, the females held more favourable perceptions of their teachers' interpersonal behaviour than did their male counterparts. In the Express classes, it was the female students who held less favourable perceptions of their teachers than the male students. Overall, the female students viewed their teachers more favourably than their male classmates.

Normal (Technical) & Normal (Academic) classroom environments

A special study into the classroom environment of Normal stream secondary classes, Normal (Technical) & Normal (Academic) was reported in 1997 (Goh, 1997a, 1997b). This was part of a major study to gather baseline data of this group of students in secondary school. A modified version of the My Class Inventory was administered to Secondary 1 and 2 Normal (Technical) and Normal (Academic) students in eight secondary schools. The purpose was to examine whether there were differences in students' perceptions of their classroom environment in the five psychosocial dimensions, namely cohesion, competition, friction, task orientation and satisfaction in terms of level, stream and gender. One important finding was that students from both levels enjoyed a relatively positive classroom climate with a high degree of cohesion and satisfaction and a low degree of friction in class. There was no appreciable difference in students' perceptions by virtue of the types of classes they come from. The analysis of students' perceptions by gender yielded interesting results. Boys seem to perceive their classroom as being more competitive while girls tend to view their classes slightly more favourably. Lastly, most students viewed their classrooms as not very task-oriented, and it was even less so in Secondary 2 classes. This suggested that as these students move up in their educational level they become less task-oriented, an undesirable trend that requires further investigation.

Mathematics and Geography classroom environments

Another study was carried out at upper secondary level examining the learning environment with a large sample in an unusual combination of Mathematics and Geography classrooms of the Express and Special courses (Chionh & Fraser, 1998, Fraser & Chionh, 2000). The What Is Happening In This Class (WIHIC) questionnaire was used to investigate relationships between classroom environments in Mathematics and Geography classes and three types of student outcomes (achievement in the Singapore-Cambridge General Certificate of Education Ordinary Level [GCE "O" level] Examination, self-esteem and attitudes towards learning). In assessing students' attitudes, the semantic differential technique was used (Osgood *et al.* 1957) to examine three attitude concepts: attitude towards subject-related lessons; attitude towards subject-related environment; attitudes towards subject-related work. For both Geography and Mathematics, better examination scores were found in classrooms with more student cohesiveness, whereas self-esteem and attitudes were more favourable in classrooms with more teacher support, task orientation and equity. Generally, students perceived their Geography and Mathematics classrooms in a relatively similar manner though they found their mathematics classrooms to be more positive than their geography classrooms.

Chinese Language classroom environment

Second language or mother tongue instruction is a pillar of the bilingual policy of the Singapore education system. Some information regarding second language classroom environment is provided by a study of the Chinese Language classroom environment. Chua *et al.*, (2001) reported that the goal of this study was to develop and validate an instrument for assessing secondary students' perceptions of their Chinese Language classrooms. The What Is Happening In This Class (WIHIC) questionnaire was selected for this study in Secondary 3 Chinese

Language classrooms because a Chinese Language version of the WIHIC had already been developed and validated for use in Taiwan (Chen *et al.*, 2000; Aldridge *et al.*, 1999). Owing to differences in language use, an adaptation was made of the Taiwanese version to produce another Chinese Language version that is suitable to the Singapore context — the Chinese Language Classroom Environment Inventory (CLCEI). In essence, the CLCEI is a bilingual questionnaire in both the English and Chinese Languages. Analyses of the data showed that the CLCEI is a reliable and valid bilingual instrument for use in Singapore.

4.3. Junior College Classroom Environment

Among the latest research is a study of the salient characteristics of the classroom learning environment for the subject of General Paper in Singapore's junior colleges (Wilks, 2000). The General Paper is a crucial subject in the 2-year Pre-University course and tests a student's understanding of and proficiency in the English Language. Data were gathered through quantitative and qualitative measures. The General Paper Constructivist Learning Environment Survey (GPCLES), modified from the new Constructivist Learning Environment Survey, provided the quantitative data while the qualitative information was obtained from student and teacher interviews, classroom observation, individual case studies and the researcher's personal journal. This study investigated the extent to which constructivist approaches are employed in the teaching of General Paper in Singapore junior colleges (Pre-University course for Grades 11 and 12). The data provided strong support for the validity and reliability of the GPCLES. No overall pattern of differences was apparent between male and female students. Educational and socio-cultural factors responsible for obstacles to constructivist changes were specified. This research, being the first of its kind conducted in Singapore, provides a rich source of data for those interested in the study of constructivism.

5. Other Studies

Apart from research at primary, secondary and post-secondary levels, there were reports of studies at postgraduate teacher education environments, adult learners' environments and cross-national collaboration.

5.1. Teacher-Training Learning Environments

Interest in learning environment has also extended into the area of teacher-training which is a vital link in the Singapore education system. Efforts are made to explore the nature of tutorial classrooms in teacher-training and the results are reassuring.

The College and University Classroom Environment Inventory (CUCEI) was used for the first time in Singapore to measure teacher trainees' perceptions of their university learning environment (Khine & Goh, 2001). The inventory was administered to graduate teacher education students enrolled on the one-year Postgraduate Diploma in Education (PGDE) Programme at the only teacher-training institution in Singapore, the National Institute of Education. Attitudinal perceptions were focussed on two factors, difficulty and speed of the education core course. The findings provided evidence of the cross-cultural validity and reliability of the CUCEI when used in the Singapore higher learning context. This confirmed the usefulness of the CUCEI as an instrument to measure learning environments in a university setting. Significant environment-attitude relationships were noticeable, for example, associations between student cohesiveness, innovation and satisfaction to that of difficulty, and between involvement and personalisation to that of speed. As reported by Goh and Khine (2001), this study also revealed gender differences among graduate teacher trainees in that female teacher trainees felt that they knew one another well and maintained good friendships among themselves within their classroom environment.

Another study shifted the focus from a tutorial classroom setting to an internet-based environment. The study was about teacher trainees' perceptions of synchronous internet-based learning environments (Teh, 2001; Teh & Fraser, 1999). The instrument used was the Internet Classroom Environment Inventory (ICEI) and the sample comprised postgraduate teacher trainees doing their social studies course in the PGDE Programme. The relevance of this study can be viewed in the context of the IT Masterplan in Education which is a blueprint for the integration of information technology in education to meet challenges of the 21st century. The synchronous internet-based learning was in real time mode, online and took the form of web-based conferencing and tele-computing approaches. The data yielded cross-validation support for the use of the ICEI in Singapore internet-based learning environments.

5.2. Adult Education Classroom Environment

Reviews of research in learning environment reveal that a study was undertaken to evaluate adult computer education classes taught by five separate private computer schools in Singapore (Khoo & Fraser, 1997). This attempt was the first to use a specially adapted learning environment questionnaire referred to as the Computer Classroom Environment Personal Form (CCEPF) in assessing the learning environment of computer education classrooms. The students perceived their learning environments favourably in terms of teacher support, task orientation and equity, and this pattern prevailed between different computer schools, age groups and gender. Students reported greater satisfaction in classes perceived to have a greater degree of teacher support, involvement and task orientation.

5.3. Cross-National Study In Secondary Science

In 1997, a team of two Singapore and two Australian researchers collaborated in a cross-national study into the learning environment of lower secondary science classrooms in Australia and Singapore (Fisher, Goh, Wong & Rickards, 1997). The focus was on the nature of interpersonal teacher behaviour and its impact on attitude and achievement. The QTI was cross-validated and showed good reliability and validity for use in both countries. This study showed that the eight dimensions of interpersonal teacher behaviour in the QTI (leadership, helping/friendly, understanding, student responsibility/freedom, uncertain, dissatisfied, admonishing and strict) and the attitude scores were significantly correlated for both Singapore and Australian students. In particular, students' attitudinal scores were higher in classrooms in which students perceived greater leadership and helping/friendly behaviours among their teachers. This study also revealed that Australian teachers were perceived as being more lenient towards the students, as well as giving more responsibility and freedom to their students, than was the case for the teachers in Singapore. These findings are not exceptional given the context of different cultural backgrounds and educational systems in Australia and Singapore.

6. Conclusion

Educational research in the field of learning environments in Singapore has made much headway in the last decade. Numerous publications and paper presentations at local and international levels indicate that learning environment research has indeed attracted significant interest in Singapore. The emphasis on achievement and examination performance has directed attention to classroom practices and events that could affect learning. This is supported by the assumption that a positive and conducive learning environment will enhance students' interest to learn.

Indeed, most of the research findings mentioned in this chapter attest to the importance of a conducive learning environment. The environment-outcome relationship is at the centre of all the studies to illuminate the learning process within each classroom. As the learning environment appears to exert impact on students' achievement and attitude, this relevant research finding is used to guide actions in the classroom.

Within the domain of teacher-training, as evidenced by courses taught in postgraduate programmes, emphasis is placed on teacher understanding of the nature and dynamics of various classroom environments. In addition, teacher trainees self-evaluate, through an online version of the QTI, their interaction patterns with their students based on the eight dimensions of the QTI. This understanding of self is encouraged and teachers are in a stronger position to ensure that their behaviours will not hinder their students' learning process. At the same time, a beginning is made in the use of a learning environment questionnaire in assisting teachers to be more aware of the significance of the learning environment and the pivotal role they play in the facilitation of students' cognitive and affective learning.

The field of learning environment research in Singapore will continue to grow in strength. It can be envisaged that more qualitative sources of information will be incorporated in the efforts to understand the impact of changing classroom environments. Through interviews with teachers and students, journals of teachers and students, and classroom observations, more information can be gleaned from those co-existing in the classrooms. The use of more qualitative sources of information in examining the nature and impact of the learning environment on students' learning is consistent with classroom epistemology and also appealing to the need to have more qualitative data to understand fully what happens in complex and dynamic classrooms. Singapore classrooms are multi-racial in character and unique in many ways. Therefore, it would be desirable to see more efforts made towards developing new instruments that will cater particularly to the local cultural and social nuances of Singapore classrooms.

References

Aldridge, J.M., Fraser, B.J. & Huang, I.T.C. (1999). Investigating classroom environments in Taiwan and Australia with multiple research methods. *Journal of Educational Research, 93*, 48–62.

Brophy, J. & Putnam, J.G. (1979). Classroom management in the elementary grades. In D. Duke (Ed.), *Classroom Management* (pp. 182–216) (Seventy-eight Yearbook of the National Society for the Study of Education, Part 2). Chicago IL: University of Chicago Press.

Chen D.T., Chua, S.L. & Wong, A.F.L. (2000, January). The development of a variation to the Chinese "What Is Happening In This Class" (WIHIC) for use in cross-cultural studies. Paper presented at the Second Conference on Science, Mathematics and Technology Education, Taiwan.

Chin, T.Y. (2001). *Pupils' Classroom Environment Perceptions, Attitudes and Achievement in Science at the Upper Primary Level.* Unpublished M Ed dissertation. Singapore: National Institute of Education, Nanyang Technological University.

Chionh, Y.H. & Fraser, B.J. (1998, April). *Validation and use of 'What is Happening in This Class' (WIHIC) Questionnaire in Singapore.* Paper presented at the Annual meeting of the American Educational Research Association, San Diego.

Chua, S.L., Wong, A.F.L. & Chen D.T. (2001, December). Validation of the Chinese Language Classroom Environment Inventory (CLCEI) for use in Singapore secondary schools. Paper presented at the International Educational Research Conference, Australian Association for Educational Research (AARE), Fremantle, Western Australia.

Emmer, E., Evertson, C. & Anderson, L. (1980). Effective classroom management at the beginning of the school year. *Elementary School Journal*, *80*, 5, 219–231.

Fisher, D.L., Goh, S.C., Wong, A.F.L. & Rickards, T.W. (1997). Perceptions of interpersonal teacher behaviour in secondary science classrooms in Singapore and Australia. *Journal of Applied Research in Education*, *1*(2), 2–13.

Fraser, B.J. & Chionh, Y.H. (2000, April*). Classroom environment, self-esteem, achievement, and attitudes in geography and mathematics in Singapore*. Paper presented at the Annual meeting of the American Educational Research Association, New Orleans.

Goh, S.C. (1997a, November). *Perceptions of interpersonal teacher behaviour in Normal (Academic) classes in Singapore*. Paper presented at the Annual Conference of the Educational Research Association, Singapore.

Goh, S.C. (1997b). Normal Technical students' perception of their classroom environment in Chang, A.S.C., Goh, S.C., Moo, S.N. & Chen, A.Y. *Report on Motivation and Classroom Behaviour of Normal Technical Students*, NIECER, Singapore.

Goh, S.C. (2002). *Classroom Management. Creating Positive Learning Environments*. Singapore: Prentice Hall.

Goh, S.C. & Fraser, B.J. (1997). Adaptation of the Questionnaire on Teacher Interaction for elementary grades. *Asia Pacific Journal of Education*, *17*(2), 102–116.

Goh, S.C. & Fraser, B.J. (1998) Teacher interpersonal behavior, classroom environment and student outcomes in primary mathematics in Singapore. *Learning Environments Research*, *1*, 199–229.

Goh, S.C. & Fraser, B.J. (2000). Teacher interpersonal behavior and elementary students' outcomes. *Journal of Research in Childhood Education*, *14*(2), 216–231.

Goh, S.C. & Khine, M.S. (in press). Classroom climate in Singapore higher education: a learning environment study. *Evaluation and Research in Education*.

Khine, M.S. & Goh, S.C. (2001). Students' Perceptions of the University Learning Environment in Singapore. *Journal of Applied Research in Education*, *5* (1), 45–51.

Khoo, H.S. & Fraser, B.J. (1997, March). *Using classroom environment dimensions in the evaluation of adult computer courses in Singapore*. Paper presented at the Annual meeting of the American Educational Research Association, Chicago.

Lim, T.K. (1993 September). *Secondary Four students' perceptions of their classroom environment*. Paper presented at the Annual Conference of the Educational Research Association, Singapore.

Lim, T.K. (1995). Perceptions of classroom environment, school types, gender and learning styles of secondary school students. *International Journal of Experimental Educational Psychology, 15*, 161–169.

Osgood, C.E., Suci, G.J. & Tannenbaum, P.H. (1957). *The Measurement of Meaning*. Urbana, IL: University of Illinois Press.

Pang, S.S. (1999). *Case Study of Underachievers in a Co-operative Learning Classroom*. Unpublished M Ed dissertation. Singapore: National Institute of Education, Nanyang Technological University.

Quek, C.L., Wong, A.F.L. & Fraser, B.J. (2001, December). *Determinants and effects of perceptions of Chemistry classroom learning environments in secondary school gifted education classes in Singapore*. Paper presented at the International Educational Research Conference, Australian Association for Educational Research (AARE), Fremantle, Western Australia.

Teh, G.P.L (2001, December). *Assessing students' perceptions of synchronous internet-based learning environments*. Paper presented at the International Educational Research Conference, Australian Association for Educational Research (AARE), Fremantle, Western Australia.

Teh, G.P.L. & Fraser, B.J. (1994). Development and validation of an instrument for assessing the psychosocial environment of computer-assisted learning classrooms. *Journal of Educational Computing Research, 12*(2), 177–193.

Teh, G.P.L. & Fraser, B.J. (1999). Assessing geography student perceptions of web-based learning environments in Singapore. In: J.A. Kesby, J.M. Stanley, K.F. McLean & L.J. Olive (Eds.), *Geodiversity: Readings in Australian geography at the end of the 20th century*. Canberra, Australia: Institute of Australian Geographers Inc.

Teng, L.K. (2000). *The relationship between the nature of the classroom learning environment and student attitudes in primary 5 computer-assisted mathematics*. Unpublished M Ed dissertation. Singapore: National Institute of Education, Nanyang Technological University.

Wilks, D.J. (2000). *An Evaluation of Classroom Learning Environments Using Critical Constructivist Perspectives as a Referent for Reform*. Unpublished PhD Thesis. Perth: Curtin University of Technology, Australia.

Wong, A.F.L. & Fraser, B.J. (1996). Environment-attitude associations in the chemistry laboratory classroom. *Research in Science and Technological Education, 64*, 29-40.

Wong, A.F.L. & Fraser, B.J. (1997). Assessment of chemistry laboratory classroom environments. *Asia Pacific Journal of Eduation. 17*, 2, 33–41.

Wubbels, Th. & Levy, J. (Eds.). (1993). *Do you know what you look like: Interpersonal relationships in education.* London: Falmer Press.

Chapter 10

INVESTIGATING FACTORS THAT PREVENT SCIENCE TEACHERS FROM CREATING POSITIVE LEARNING ENVIRONMENTS IN TAIWAN

Jong-Hsiang Yang
National Taiwan Normal University
Taiwan

Iris Tai-Chu Huang
National Kaohsiung Normal University
Taiwan

Jill M. Aldridge
Curtin University of Technology
Western Australia

As learning environment research is a relatively new field of research in Taiwan, it is hoped that the research reported in this chapter will pave the way for more such studies. This chapter reports a research project that investigated students' perceptions of learning environments in science classes in Taiwan. The researchers were involved in developing, modifying, translating and validating the *What is Happening in this Class* (WIHIC) questionnaire. The questionnaire, along with an attitude scale, provided the quantitative data for the study. Qualitative data were derived from classroom observations and interviews with teachers and students. The results indicate that social and cultural expectations of the teacher's role was one of the main factors preventing science teachers from creating more positive classroom environments in Taiwan. Based on results of the study, implications of the findings and suggestions for improvements in science classroom environments are introduced to the community of science educators in Taiwan.

1. Introduction

Students spend a huge amount of time at school. Rutter and colleagues' (1979) book *Fifteen Thousand Hours* suggests that this is as high as approximately 15,000 hours by the completion of secondary school. Students' reactions to, and perceptions of, their educational experiences are important. Clearly, it is assumed here that having positive classroom environments is a valuable goal of education. The classroom environment so strongly influences student outcomes that those wishing to improve the effectiveness of schools should not ignore it. A purpose of this chapter is to report the findings of a research project that investigated the social and cultural factors that are likely to prevent science teachers from creating a positive learning environment.

2. Past Research in Asian Learning Environments

This section places the present study of science learning environments in Taiwan into context by providing a review of previous learning environment studies that have been conducted in Asian countries.

Although a recent literature review (Fraser, 1998) shows that a majority of classroom environment studies involved Western countries, a number of important studies have been carried out in non-Western countries. Early studies established the validity of classroom environment instruments that had been translated into the Indian (Walberg, Singh & Rasher, 1977) and Indonesian (Schibeci, Rideng & Fraser, 1987) languages and replicated associations between student outcomes and classroom environment perceptions.

In Hong Kong, qualitative methods involving open-ended questions were used to explore students' perceptions of the learning environment in Grade 9 classrooms (Wong, 1996). This study found that many students identified the teacher as the most crucial element in a positive learning environment. These teachers were found to keep order and discipline while creating an atmosphere that was not boring or solemn. They also interacted with students in ways that could be considered friendly and showed concern for the students. Also, in 1993, Cheung used multilevel analysis to determine the effects of the learning environment on students' learning. The findings of this study provide insights that could help to explain why Hong Kong was found to rank highly in physics, chemistry and biology in international comparisons (Keeves, 1992).

Recently, researchers working in Singapore (Chin & Wong, 2001; Fraser & Chionh, 2000; Goh, Young & Fraser, 1995; Quek, Fraser & Wong, 2001; Teh & Fraser, 1994), Indonesia (Margianti, Fraser &

Aldridge, 2002; Soerjaningsih, Fraser & Aldridge, 2002), Korea (Lee & Fraser, 2001), and Brunei (Majeed, Fraser & Aldridge, 2001; Riah & Fraser, 1998) have each made important contributions to the field of learning environments.

3. Studies that used the *What is Happening in this Class* Questionnaire

The present study used the What is Happening in this Class (WIHIC) questionnaire to collect data pertaining to the classroom learning environment in Taiwan. The version of the WIHIC used in the present study has been cross-validated in high school chemistry classes in Brunei (Riah & Fraser, 1998), high school students in Singapore (Chionh & Fraser, 1998), high schools in Canada (Zandvliet & Fraser, 1998), Australia (Dorman, Adams & Ferguson, in press) and the United States (Moss & Fraser, 2002), and secondary science classes in Brunei (Khine & Fisher, 2001).

The studies in Singapore, Canada, Australia, USA and Brunei validated an English version of the WIHIC questionnaire, whilst a study in Korea (Lee & Fraser, 2001) validated a Korean version of the questionnaire. More recently, a study in Indonesia adapted the WIHIC for use at the tertiary level and validated an Indonesian version of the questionnaire (Margianti, Fraser & Aldridge, 2002). The findings in each study replicate those of past research, reporting strong associations between the learning environment and student outcomes for almost all scales. Whilst these studies provide useful suggestions to educators regarding classroom environment dimensions that could be changed in order to improve students' outcomes, they do not identify causal factors associated with the classroom environments.

4. Studying the Field of Learning Environments in Taiwan

Research within the field of learning environments is relatively new in Taiwan. The study reported in this chapter is one of the first to examine the nature of science classroom learning environments in Taiwan. This study is part of a larger cross-cultural study that examined a range of factors that might affect teaching and learning in science classrooms in Taiwan. She and Fisher (2000) developed an instrument that can be used to describe science teacher communication behaviour in Taiwan and Australia. The *Teacher Communication Behavior Questionnaire* (TCBQ) was administered to 30 classes in Taiwan and 12 classes in Australia. The results indicate that the reliability and validity of the instrument was satisfactory in both countries and that students' perceptions on four of the scales of the TCBQ were associated with their attitudes to their science classes. Wallace and Chou (2001) examined the way in which students cooperate in Taiwanese and Australian science classrooms. Data was collected using a survey instrument and in-depth interviews with students. In this study, the authors adopted the position that student cooperation is best understood by examining the patterns of variation within and between countries rather than trying to describe similarities and differences. The study found that students from Australia and Taiwan have a range of understandings and interpretations about what it means to cooperate in science classrooms.

5. The Present Study

The present study examined and explored learning environments in science classes in Taiwan. The study commenced from a more objectivist paradigm in which data were collected using a large-scale administration of a questionnaire. This phase sought to provide an overview of the learning environment in Taiwan that would provide a springboard for further data collection using different research methods.

It is widely agreed that multiple methods are useful in achieving greater understanding (Keeves & Adams, 1994; Tobin & Fraser, 1998). It was with this in mind that data collection for the present study involved different sources and kinds of information (as recommended by Erickson, 1998), including videotape recordings of science classrooms, field notes, interview comments and tape recordings of interviews. The idea of 'grain sizes' (the use of different sized samples for different research questions varying in extensiveness and intensiveness) in learning environment research (Fraser, 1999) has been used effectively in studies that combine different methodologies (Tobin & Fraser, 1998), and was used to guide the collection of data for this study.

During the progress of the present study, the researchers became aware of the importance of examining social and cultural factors that influence the learning environment. Culturally sensitive methods of collecting data, such as interviews with participants, narratives written by researchers and classroom observations, were used to help develop a clearer picture of such factors.

5.1. Developing a Mandarin Version of the WIHIC and Attitude Scale

The study involved the development of a Mandarin version of the WIHIC for use in Taiwan. The questionnaire was used to measure students' perceptions of their science classroom environment. The WIHIC was developed by Fraser, McRobbie and Fisher (1996) to bring parsimony to the field of learning environments by combining the most salient scales from existing questionnaires with new dimensions of contemporary relevance to assess seven dimensions of the classroom environment. In addition, an eight-item scale was used to assess students' attitudes in terms of enjoyment, interest and how much they look forward to science classes. This was based on a scale from the Test of Science Related Attitudes (TOSRA, Fraser, 1981).

For the purposes of this study, a Mandarin version of the WIHIC questionnaire and attitude scale were developed for use with students in Taiwan. The English version of the questionnaire was translated into Mandarin by educators in Taiwan and then translated back into English by an independent third party as recommended by Brislin, Lonner & Thorndike (1973). The back translations were checked, in collaboration with Taiwanese colleagues, to ensure that the Mandarin version maintained the original meanings and concepts as in the original English version.

A trial of the Mandarin version of the student questionnaire was carried out and this was followed by interviews about the readability and comprehensibility of items.

5.1.1. The questionnaire data

The WIHIC questionnaire and attitude survey were administered to junior high school students in 50 (25 biology classes and 25 physics classes) science classes. Two classes were selected from each of the 25 junior high schools considered to be representative of schools in Taiwan. These schools were drawn from different areas. Schools located in northern Taiwan were selected from Taipei, schools in central Taiwan were selected from the city of Changhua, and schools in southern Taiwan were selected from Kaohsiung.

Analyses of the data were conducted to determine the reliability and validity of the instruments, including factor structure, internal consistency reliability, and ability to differentiate between classrooms (Aldridge, Fraser & Huang, 1999).

5.1.2. The qualitative data

The data from the questionnaires provided a starting point from which other data could be collected. Analysis of the survey data revealed that, in some cases, the survey data were not congruent with what was observed in the classrooms, creating dialectic tensions that led to emergent research methods.

From this point, the study employed interpretative procedures to inform the inquiry. Using a recursive process (Erickson, 1998), involving observations and interviews (looking and asking), insights into the learning environments were sought. Observations were carried out in four classes and teachers were interviewed to seek their reasons for various actions and whether the classroom environments created by different teachers were influenced by social and cultural factors. Interviews of at least three students from each of the eight classes were also done. The multi-method approach allowed triangulation and cross-validation of the data. The data collected using the different methodologies complemented each other and together they formed a more complete and coherent picture of the learning environment (Denzin & Lincoln, 1994).

The following section outlines the factors related to the culture and education system in Taiwan and how these might impinge on the learning environment that is created. The bricolage method, described by Denzin and Lincoln (1994), was used to draw together the information collected using a variety of research methods. The following commentary attempts to bring together the pieces that form the bricolage.

The two themes that emerged are presented as 'educational aims and the nature of the curriculum' and 'pressures experienced by teachers'.

Theme 1: Educational aims and the nature of the curriculum

During observations and interviews, it appeared that the educational aims, reflected in the nature of the curriculum, were quite influential in the types of learning environments that teachers created. Teachers who were interviewed indicated that education was focused predominantly on the development of academic ability. "With the students, the examination results are most important. ... If they do not achieve well, then they cannot go on to university" (Taiwanese Teacher, Transcript 4.1.13). The social and emotional aspects of a student's development were generally considered to be the responsibility of the family and wider community rather than that of the school (Stevenson & Stigler, 1992).

The nature of the curricula in Taiwan appeared, in many ways, to reflect these academic aims. The nature of the curriculum tended to be examination-driven and highly competitive. Examination results were of paramount importance to students, as high achievement increased the likelihood of being allocated a position in a "star" school (i.e., a school with outstanding results as measured by the number of students who enter university).

It seemed that the educational aims considered important to the teacher and the nature of the curriculum together played a significant role, and in some cases acted as a constraint to the creation of the ideal learning environment. The competitive nature of the curriculum appeared to encourage teachers to concentrate on developing academic ability as efficiently as possible. Diversions from teacher-centred methods were viewed as off-task by many parents, teachers and students.

One such teacher, Mrs Lee, had a passion for biology and a love of teaching. However, when the conversation turned to the biology curriculum, it became clear that Mrs Lee was less than satisfied. Apparently the latest curriculum has been developed by scientists and much of the content is above the level of her students. The teacher explained that:

> "The textbook [upon which examinations are based] is very big and the teacher has to go through each stage. There is too much to teach ... and there isn't enough time to cover the content of the book. Ideally I would like to give students the chance to learn what is not in the textbook ... (but I) don't do that ... because of the shortage of time."

According to Mrs Lee, formal examinations in biology are held at least once a month in her school and she spends much time preparing her students for these. She went on to explain that, as a result, alternative methods were often not used in her class:

> "I try to include different methods in my teaching, but it depends on a lot of factors. I try to use a multimedia approach to keep my students interested but find that I constantly have to be aware of the time. Sometimes, I will prepare a lesson using a lot of different media but do not get the chance to use them because of the students' ability or the amount of content that needs to be covered."

The constraints that Taiwanese teachers experienced as a result of the examination-driven curriculum were also echoed by another teacher, Mr Cheung. He used the expression "time is tight" on a number of occasions to explain the predicament of teachers in Taiwan. Mr Cheung had explained:

> "The way we teach is constrained. Students have to do the entrance examination to senior high school and they like to be crammed ... The examinations, the [content of the] textbook and the amount of homework restrict how much work we can do outside of the textbook. Every aspect of science education is constrained."

The science curriculum (for both biology and physics) in Taiwan is presented to students in the form of textbooks and examinations are based on the content of these. As a result, it is important for teachers to cover all areas. Teachers explained that teacher-centred methods are the most practical way to cover the content in the given time frame, and that diversions are often not possible. Without exception, the classes that were observed were teacher-centred and there were generally few opportunities for discussions or questions. Initially, it was assumed that the teacher-centred nature of classes in Taiwan was the result of large class sizes, but speaking to more teachers convinced the researchers that class size was but one factor (among many) and the nature of the curriculum was another. When asked whether he used discussions in his class, Mr Cheung responded:

> "Usually no. I don't give them this kind of chance. In the beginning, in my first year of teaching, I tried this kind of teaching, but I found that it was too noisy and very difficult to control the class. Most of all, I found that this kind of chance [discussions] takes too much time, and sometimes the students are not on task. So, although I have tried, I don't use discussions in my teaching now ... Under the education system that we have in Taiwan, the lecture kind of teaching is the most efficient way to teach students and get a good score. ... The students' time is already very tight and they work too hard already. So [by teaching in this way] I can do something for them."

During classroom observations, it was noticed that teachers used rote learning on a number of occasions. The teacher would ask a question, and students would chorus back the answer. These sessions were used to revise the content of lessons, particularly when a test was close at hand. It became clear that what was perceived as rote learning (a mechanical procedure requiring little thought) could have actually been what is referred to as "deep memorization" (Biggs, 1996). Memorisation in the Confucian tradition is seen as a significant part of learning. It generally precedes understanding and is accompanied by reflection. When we asked students and teachers for their opinion about such rote sessions, they generally agreed that this was an effective method of preparing students for examinations. When asked about her opinion on rote learning, one teacher, Mrs Chou, commented: "In our situation, this kind of teaching is very helpful for preparing students for the examinations."

It is obvious that the nature of the curriculum tend to be examination-driven and highly competitive. This in turn appeared to be largely responsible for the type of teaching approaches used in science classrooms in Taiwan.

Theme 2: Pressures experienced by teachers

Teachers in Taiwan agreed that the pressures that they experienced (such as a lack of time) act as a constraint to the way in which they would ideally like to teach. Consequently, these constraints could negatively influence the learning environment that they would like to create. The teachers who were interviewed indicated that they experienced pressures from their principals, parents and other teachers to ensure that their students maintain high achievement.

In Taiwan, the principal, keen on schools to maintain or improve their position (according to the number of students who gain access into "star" schools), pressured teachers to push students towards improving their test results. The home-room teacher also pressured teachers to ensure that the grades of students in his/her class would not slip and, if the results were lower than those of other teachers, that they improve their performance.

Parents in Taiwan were keen that their children attend a "star" school to improve their chances of attending university. As a result, they also pressured teachers. Because the expectation of many parents was that their children would attend university (social mobility is available to students of any status through education), they exerted pressure on them to perform well in examinations and on teachers to ensure that their children's achievement was high.

The pressures of an examination-driven curriculum appear to encourage more traditional teaching methods, resulting in a more teacher-centred, lecture-style, learning environment.

6. Conclusion

The research described in this chapter is different from the majority of studies in science education in that it went beyond research restricted to translating a questionnaire developed in the West into another language, and then using it on another country to replicate previous research in

Western countries. This study used a multimethod approach in which the use of qualitative research methods (observations, interviews and narrative stories) augmented questionnaire data to provide richer interpretations and insights. Overall, the study highlighted the importance of including qualitative data to help our understanding of classroom environments and supported the value of using multiple research methods.

The quantitative data gathered from the What is Happening in This Class (WIHIC) questionnaire and an attitude scale in the first phase of this study supported the reliability and validity of a Mandarin version of all scales. The study provides strong support for the reliability and validity of a learning environment questionnaire that is suitable for use in Taiwan.

The initial data indicated that although Taiwanese students perceived reduced opportunities for investigations and involvement in their science classes, they held positive attitudes towards learning. To explore these findings in-depth, the researchers took the roles of 'bricoleur' as described by Denzin and Lincoln (1994) in that they pieced together the data collected using different methodologies to gain insight into the learning environments created in the classrooms.

It appears that the learning environments created in Taiwan were influenced by the nature of the curriculum. The examination-driven curriculum in Taiwan leads to more teacher-centred approaches in the classroom. Consequently, emphases considered important to science education in Western countries, such as involvement, are not always as important or possible in Taiwan. The pressures experienced by teachers in Taiwan appear to influence the learning environment. Many of the pressures were related to an examination-driven curriculum, in which students were competing strongly for positions at senior high schools.

Through examining the learning environment created by teachers in Taiwan, it was possible to identify barriers that might prevent teachers from creating their ideal learning environment and one which fosters positive attitudes and a love of learning. The present study of learning environments in Taiwan enables researchers, teachers and teacher educators to gain a better understanding about their own beliefs and the social and cultural restraints to their teaching.

References

Aldridge, J.M., Fraser, B.J. & Huang, T.-C.I. (1999). Investigating classroom environments in Taiwan and Australia with multiple research methods. *Journal of Educational Research, 93*, 48–62.

Biggs, J. (1996). Western misperceptions of the Confucian-heritage learning culture. In D.A. Watkins & J. B. Biggs (Eds.), *The Chinese learner: Cultural psychological and contextual influences* (pp. 45–68). Melbourne, Australia: Australian Council for Educational Research.

Brislin, R.W., Lonner, W.J. & Thorndike, R.W. (1973). *Cross-cultural research methods*. New York: Wiley.

Cheung, K.C. (1993). The learning environment and its effects on learning: Product and process modelling for science achievement at the sixth form level in Hong Kong. *School Effectiveness and School Improvement, 4*, 242–264.

Chin, T.Y. & Wong, A. (2001, December). *Upper primary pupils' classroom environment perceptions, attitudes and achievement in science*. Paper presented at the annual meeting of the Australian Association for Research in Education, Fremantle, Western Australia.

Chionh, Y.H. & Fraser, B.J. (1998, April). *Validation and use of the 'What is Happening in this Class' (WIHIC) questionnaire in Singapore*. Paper presented at the annual meeting of the American Educational Research Association, San Diego, CA.

Denzin, N.K. & Lincoln, Y.S. (1994). Introduction: Entering the field of qualitative research. In N.K. Denzin & Y.S. Lincoln (Eds.), *Handbook of qualitative research* (pp. 1–17). Newbury Park, CA: Sage.

Dorman, J.P., Adams, J.E. & Ferguson, J.M. (in press). Confirmatory factor analysis of the 'What is Happening in this Class' questionnaire and its structural invariance across groups. *Journal of Classroom Interaction*.

Erickson, F. (1998). Qualitative research methods for science education. In B.J. Fraser & K.G. Tobin (Eds.), *The international handbook of science education* (pp. 1155–1173). Dordrecht, The Netherlands: Kluwer.

Fraser, B.J. (1981). *Test of Science-Related Attitudes (TOSRA)*. Melbourne, Australia: Australian Council for Educational Research.

Fraser, B.J. (1998). Science learning environments: Assessment, effects and determinants. In B.J. Fraser & K.G. Tobin (Eds.), *The international handbook of science education* (pp. 527–564). Dordrecht, The Netherlands: Kluwer.

Fraser, B.J. (1999). 'Grain sizes' in learning environment research: Combining qualitative and quantitative methods. In H.C. Waxman & H.J. Walberg

(Eds.), *New directions for teaching practice and research* (pp. 285–296). Berkeley, CA: McCutchan.

Fraser, B.J. & Chionh, Y.H. (2000, April). *Classroom environment, self-esteem, achievement, and attitudes in geography and mathematics in Singapore.* Paper presented at the annual meeting of the American Educational Research Association, New Orleans, LA.

Fraser, B.J., McRobbie, C.J. & Fisher, D.L. (1996, April). *Development, validation and use of personal and class forms of a new classroom environment instrument.* Paper presented at the annual meeting of the American Educational Research Association, New York.

Goh, S.C., Young, D.J. & Fraser, B.J. (1995). Psychosocial climate and student outcomes in elementary mathematics classrooms: A multilevel analysis. *Journal of Experimental Education, 64,* 29–40.

Keeves, J.P. (1992). *The IEA study of science III: Changes in science education and achievement: 1970 to 1984.* Oxford, UK: Pergamon.

Keeves, J.P. & Adams D. (1994). Comparative methodology in education. In T. Husèn & T.N. Postlethwaite (Eds.), *The international encyclopedia of education* (2nd ed., pp. 948–958). Oxford, UK: Pergamon.

Khine, M.S. & Fisher, D.L. (2001, December). *Classroom environment and teachers' cultural background in secondary classes in an Asian context.* Paper presented at the annual conference of the Ausralian Association for Research in Education, Fremantle, Western Australia.

Lee, S. & Fraser, B.J. (2001, March). *High school science classroom learning environments in Korea.* Paper presented at the annual meeting of the National Association for Research in Science Teaching, St Louis, MO.

Majeed, A., Fraser, B.J. & Aldridge, J.M. (2001, April). *Learning environments and student satisfaction among junior secondary mathematics students in Brunei Darussalam.* Paper presented at the annual meeting of the American Educational Research Association, Seattle.

Margianti, E.S., Fraser, B.J. & Aldridge, J. M. (2002, April). *Learning environment, attitudes and achievement: Assessing the perceptions of Indonesian university students.* Paper presented at the annual meeting of the American Educational Research Association, New Orleans, MS.

Moss, C. & Fraser, B.J. (2002, April). Assessing and improving the teaching and learning environment in high school biology classrooms. Paper presented at the annual meeting of the National Association for Research in Science Teaching, New Orleans, LA.

Quek, C.L., Fraser, B.J. & Wong, A.F.L. (2001, December). *Determinants and effects of perceptions of chemistry classroom learning environments in secondary school gifted education classes in Singapore.* Paper presented at the annual conference of the Australian Association for Research in Education, Fremantle, Western Australia.

Rutter, M. et al. (1979). *Fifteen thousand hours: Secondary schools and their effects on children.* Cambridge, MA: Harvard University Press.

Riah, H. & Fraser, B.J. (1998, April). *The learning environment of high school chemistry classes.* Paper presented at the annual meeting of the American Educational Research Association, San Diego, CA.

Schibeci, R.A., Rideng, I.M. & Fraser, B.J. (1987). Effects of classroom environments on science attitudes: A cross-cultural replication in Indonesia. International *Journal of Science Education, 9,* 169–186.

She, H.C. & Fisher, D.L. (2000). The development of a questionnaire to describe science teacher communication behavior in Taiwan and Australia. *Science Education, 84,* 706–726.

Soerjaningsih, W., Fraser, B.J. & Aldridge, J.M. (2002, April). *Instructor-student interpersonal behaviour and student outcomes at the university level in Indonesia.* Paper presented at the annual meeting of the American Educational Research Association, New Orleans, MS.

Stevenson, H.W. & Stigler, J.W. (1992). *The learning gap: Why our schools are failing and what we can learn from Japanese and Chinese education.* New York: Summit Books.

Teh, G. & Fraser, B.J. (1994). An evaluation of computer-assisted learning in terms of achievement, attitudes and classroom environment. *Evaluation and Research in Education, 8,* 147–161.

Tobin, K. & Fraser, B.J. (Eds.). (1998). Qualitative and quantitative landscapes of classroom learning environments. In B.J. Fraser & K.G. Tobin (Eds.), *The international handbook of science education* (pp. 623–640). Dordrecht, The Netherlands: Kluwer.

Walberg, H.J., Singh, R. & Rasher, S.P. (1977). Predictive validity of students' perceptions: A cross-cultural replication. *American Educational Research Journal, 14,* 45–49.

Wallace, J. & Chou, C.Y. (2001). Similarity and difference: Student cooperation in Taiwan and Australian Science Classrooms. *Science Education, 85,* 694–711.

Wong, N.Y. (1996). Students' perceptions of the mathematics classroom in Hong Kong. Hiroshima Journal of Mathematics Education, 4, 89–107.

Zandvliet, D. & Fraser, B. (1998, April). *The physical and psychosocial environment associated with classrooms using new information technologies.* Paper presented at the annual meeting of the American Educational Research Association, San Diego, CA.

APPENDIX

班上發生了什麼事？

◎ 作答說明 ◎

座號：＿＿＿．　性別：＿＿＿．

1. 本量表包含56題，每題的敘述都和班級中各項活動情況有關。請仔細閱讀每一項敘述，並依據班上在上＿＿＿課時的情況來回答，在「答案欄」上適當的地方打圈選以表示你的看法。

   作答方式如下：
   (1)若你認為該項敘述在班級中幾乎「從來沒有」發生過，請圈選「1」；
   (2)若你認為該項敘述在班級中「很少發生」，請圈選「2」；
   (3)若你認為該項敘述在班級中「偶爾發生」，請圈選「3」；
   (4)若你認為該項敘述在班級中「經常發生」，請圈選「4」；
   (5)若你認為該項敘述在班級中幾乎每次上課時都會發生，請圈選「5」。

※ 例題：	從來沒有	很少發生	偶爾發生	經常發生	總是如此
20.學生在下課時，會到操場上去玩。	1	2	3	4	5

   ● 如果你認為這種情況在班級中經常發生，則應該在『答案欄』的 "4" 上圈選。

2. 本量表每一題都沒有一定的『正確答案』，因此，只要仔細閱讀每一項敘述，然後在『答案欄』上圈選，表示你的看法即可。
3. 本量表中有一些題目的內容看起來雖然十分相似，但並非完全相同，因此，每題均應作答。
4. 作答時間為25分鐘，請把握時間作答。

◎ 請等候指示，才開始翻頁作答 !!!

附錄一 科學（理化、生物）教室環境量表

同學的親和關係	從來沒有	很少發生	偶而發生	經常發生	總是如此
在上（理化、生物）課時：					
1. 我和班上同學能建立友誼。	1	2	3	4	5
2. 我和班上同學彼此熟悉。	1	2	3	4	5
3. 在班上我和同學間彼此很友善。	1	2	3	4	5
4. 班上的同學都是我的朋友。	1	2	3	4	5
5. 在班上我和其他的同學相處得很好。	1	2	3	4	5
6. 我會幫助課業上需要幫助的其他同學。	1	2	3	4	5
7. 班上的同學們喜歡我。	1	2	3	4	5
8. 在這班上我得到其他同學的幫助。	1	2	3	4	5

教師支持	從來沒有	很少發生	偶而發生	經常發生	總是如此
在上（理化、生物）課時：					
9. 老師會表現對我個人的關心。	1	2	3	4	5
10. 老師會停下進度來幫助我的問題。	1	2	3	4	5
11. 老師會留意我的感受。	1	2	3	4	5
12. 當我在功課上有問題時老師會幫助我。	1	2	3	4	5
13. 老師會和我談天。	1	2	3	4	5
14. 老師關心我的問題。	1	2	3	4	5
15. 老師會走到我的座位前和我說話。	1	2	3	4	5
16. 老師所問的問題幫助我的了解。	1	2	3	4	5

學生參與	從來沒有	很少發生	偶而發生	經常發生	總是如此
在上（理化、生物）課時：					
17. 在班上我會討論不同的想法。	1	2	3	4	5
18. 在班上討論時我會發表我的看法。	1	2	3	4	5
19. 老師會問我問題。	1	2	3	4	5
20. 在教室討論時，我的想法或建議會被採用。	1	2	3	4	5
21. 我會向老師問問題。	1	2	3	4	5
22. 我會向其他同學解釋我的想法。	1	2	3	4	5
23. 同學們會和我討論如何解決問題。	1	2	3	4	5
24. 老師會要求我解釋我是如何解決問題的。	1	2	3	4	5

探究	從來沒有	很少發生	偶而發生	經常發生	總是如此
在上（理化、生物）課時：					
25. 我用實驗活動來驗證我的想法。	1	2	3	4	5
26. 我會被要求對自己所做的敘述提出證據。	1	2	3	4	5
27. 我對討論中所產生的問題，會用研究方式來找答案。	1	2	3	4	5
28. 對我所提的敘述及圖表，我會說明其意義。	1	2	3	4	5
29. 我對疑惑的問題會用探究的方法找尋答案。	1	2	3	4	5
30. 我對老師所提的問題會用探究的方法來找出答案。	1	2	3	4	5
31. 我會做研究以發現問題的答案。	1	2	3	4	5
32. 我會用自己研究所得的資料以解決問題。	1	2	3	4	5

工作取向	從來沒有	很少發生	偶而發生	經常發生	總是如此
在上（理化、生物）課時：					
33. 對我而言在上課時要完成一些課業，是很重要的事。	1	2	3	4	5
34. 在班上我會盡力完成被交代的事。	1	2	3	4	5
35. 上課時我知道這一節課的學習目標。	1	2	3	4	5
36. 我已準備好準時上課。	1	2	3	4	5
37. 我知道自己在班上所要完成的事。	1	2	3	4	5
38. 我在上課時很用心。	1	2	3	4	5
39. 我設法了解這一門功課。	1	2	3	4	5
40. 我知道我該做多少功課。	1	2	3	4	5

合作	從來沒有	很少發生	偶而發生	經常發生	總是如此
在上（理化、生物）課時：					
41. 我會和同學合作完成老師所指定的功課。	1	2	3	4	5
42. 當我做功課時會讓同學享用我所蒐集的資料和書。	1	2	3	4	5
43. 當我在分組活動時，同學間都能以團隊方式合作。	1	2	3	4	5
44. 在班上我和同學合作進行實驗活動。	1	2	3	4	5
45. 在班上我能從別的同學學習到。	1	2	3	4	5
46. 在班上我和其他同學一起做功課。	1	2	3	4	5
47. 在班上活動時我和其他同學們互相合作。	1	2	3	4	5
48. 同學們和我一起努力以達成課業的目標。	1	2	3	4	5

平等	從來沒有	很少發生	偶而發生	經常發生	總是如此
在上（理化、生物）課時：					
49. 老師對我所發問的問題，與對其他同學所發問的一樣關心。	1	2	3	4	5
50. 在班上我從老師那裡所得到幫助和其他同學的一樣多。	1	2	3	4	5
51. 在班上我的發言機會和其他同學一樣多。	1	2	3	4	5
52. 在班上我受到的待遇和其他同學是一樣的。	1	2	3	4	5
53. 在班上我受到老師的鼓勵和其他同學一樣多。	1	2	3	4	5
54. 我對班上貢獻的機會和其他同學一樣多。	1	2	3	4	5
55. 我在課業上所受的稱讚和其他同學一樣多。	1	2	3	4	5
56. 我在班上回答問題的機會和其他同學一樣多。	1	2	3	4	5

Selected Bibliography

Aldridge, J.M., Fraser, B.J. & Huang, T.-C.I. (1999). Investigating classroom environments in Taiwan and Australia with multiple research methods. *Journal of Educational Research, 93*, 48–62.

Aldridge, J.M., Fraser, B.J., Taylor, P.C. & Chen, C.-C. (2000). Constructivist learning environments in a cross-national study in Taiwan and Australia. *International Journal of Science Education, 22*, 37–55.

Asghar, M. & Fraser, B. (1995). Classroom environment and attitudes to science in Brunei Darussalam. *Journal of Science and Mathematics Education in Southeast Asia*, XVIII(2), 41–47.

Fisher, D.L. & Fraser, B.J. (1981). Validity and use of My Class Inventory. *Science Education, 65*, 145–156.

Fisher, D.L. & Fraser, B.J. (1983). A comparison of actual and preferred classroom environment as perceived by science teachers and students. *Journal of Research in Science Teaching, 20*, 55–61.

Fisher, D.L., Goh, S.C., Wong, A.F.L. & Rickards, T.W. (1997). Perceptions of interpersonal teacher behaviour in secondary science classrooms in Singapore and Australia. *Journal of Applied Research in Education, 1*(2), 2–13.

Fraser, B.J. (1990). *Individualised Classroom Environment Questionnaire*. Melbourne, Australia: Australian Council for educational Research.

Fraser, B.J. (1994). Research on classroom and school climate. In D. Gabel (Ed.), *Handbook of research on science teaching and learning* (pp. 493–541). New York: Macmillan.

Fraser, B.J. (1998a). Science learning environments: Assessment, effects and determinants. In B.J. Fraser & K.G. Tobin (Eds.), *International handbook of science education* (pp. 527–564). Dordrecht, The Netherlands: Kluwer.

Fraser, B.J. (1998b). Classroom environment instruments: Development, validity and applications. *Learning Environments Research, 1*, 7–33.

Fraser, B. (1999). 'Grain sizes' in learning environment research: Combining qualitative and quantitative methods. In H. Waxman & H.J. Walberg (Eds.),

New directions for teaching practice and research (pp. 285–296). Berkeley, CA: McCutchan.

Fraser, B.J. & Chionh, Y.-H. (2000, April). *Classroom environment, self-esteem, achievement, and attitudes in geography and mathematics in Singapore*. Paper presented at the annual meeting of the American Educational Research Association, New Orleans, LA.

Fraser, B.J., Giddings, G.J. & McRobbie, C.J. (1995). Evolution and validation of a personal form of an instrument for assessing science laboratory classroom environments. *Journal of Research in Science Teaching, 32,* 399–422.

Goh, S.C. & Fraser, B.J. (2000). Teacher interpersonal behavior and elementary students' outcomes. *Journal of Research in Childhood Education, 14,* 216–231

Goh, S.C. & Fraser, B.J. (1997). Adaptation of the Questionnaire on Teacher Interaction for elementary grades. *Asia Pacific Journal of Education, 17, 2,* 216–231.

Hirata, S. & Sako, T. (1998). Perceptions of school environment among Japanese junior high school, non-attendant, and juvenile delinquent students. *Learning Environments Research, 1,* 321–331.

Khine, M. & Fisher, D. (2002, April). *Classroom Environments, Student Attitudes and Cultural Background of Teachers in Brunei*. Paper presented at Annual Conference of American Educational Research Association (AERA). New Orleans, USA.

Kim, H.B., Fisher, D.L. & Fraser, B.J. (2000). Classroom environment and teacher interpersonal behaviour in secondary school classes in Korea. *Evaluation and Research in Education, 14,* 3–22.

Lee, S. & Fraser, B. (2001b, December). *Science laboratory classroom environments in Korea*. Paper presented at the annual conference of the Australian Association for Research in Education, Fremantle, Australia.

Maor, D. & Fraser, B.J. (1996). Use of classroom environment perceptions in evaluating inquiry-based computer assisted learning. *International Journal of Science Education, 18,* 401–421.

Margianti, E.S., Fraser, B.J. & Aldridge, J.M. (2001, April). *Classroom environment and students' outcomes among university computing students in Indonesia*. Paper presented at the annual meeting of the American Educational Research Association, Seattle, WA.

Moos, R.H. (1974). *The Social Climate Scales: An overview*. Palo Alto, CA: Consulting Psychologists Press.

Moos, R.H. & Trickett, E.J. (1987). *Classroom Environment Scale manual* (2nd ed.). Palo Alto, CA: Consulting Psychologists Press.

Riah, H. & Fraser, B. (1998, April). *Chemistry learning environment and its association with students' achievement in chemistry*. Paper presented at the annual meeting of the American Educational Research Association, San Diego, CA.

Roth, W.-M. (1999). Learning environments research, lifeworld analysis, and solidarity in practice. *Learning Environments Research, 2,* 225–247.

Roth, W.-M., Tobin, K. & Zimmermann, A. (in press). Coteaching/cogenerative dialoguing: Learning environments research as classroom praxis. *Learning Environments Research*.

She, H.C. & Fisher, D.L. (2000). The development of a questionnaire to describe science teacher communication behavior in Taiwan and Australia. *Science Education, 84,* 706–726.

Taylor, P.C., Fraser, B.J. & Fisher, D.L. (1997). Monitoring constructivist classroom learning environments. *International Journal of Educational Research, 27,* 293–302.

Teh, G. & Fraser, B.J. (1994). An evaluation of computer-assisted learning in terms of achievement, attitudes and classroom environment. *Evaluation and Research in Education, 8,* 147–161.

Tobin, K. & Fraser, B.J. (1998). Qualitative and quantitative landscapes of classroom learning environments. In B.J. Fraser & K.G. Tobin (Eds.), *International handbook of science education* (pp. 623–640). Dordrecht, The Netherlands: Kluwer.

Walberg, H.J. & Anderson, G.J. (1968). Classroom climate and individual learning. *Journal of Educational Psychology, 59,* 414–419.

Walberg, H.J., Singh, R. & Rasher, S.P. (1977). Predictive validity or student perceptions: A cross-cultural replication. *American Educational Research Journal, 14,* 45–49.

Waldrip, B.G. & Fisher, D.L. (2000). The development and validation of a learning environment questionnaire using both quantitative and qualitative methods. *Journal of Classroom Interaction, 35*(2), 25–37.

Wong, A.L.F. & Fraser, B.J. (1997). Assessment of chemistry laboratory classroom environments. *Asia Pacific Journal of Education, 17,* 2, 33–41.

Wong, N.Y. (1993). Psychosocial environments in the Hong Kong mathematics classroom. *Journal of Mathematical Behavior, 12*, 303–309.

Wubbels, Th. & Levy, J. (Eds.). (1993). *Do you know what you look like: Interpersonal relationships in education.* London: Falmer Press.

Zandvliet, D. & Fraser, B.J. (1998, April). The physical and psychosocial environment associated with classrooms using new information technologies. Paper presented at the annual meeting of the American Educational Research Association, San Diego, CA.

Index

achievement gaps, 104
affective outcomes, 80
Asian studies, 1, 10, 14, 17
Assumptions of a linear, 106

Brunei, 131–144, 147–152

chalkboard, 108, 111–113, 116, 117, 124
classroom design, 51, 58, 69
classroom observations, 217, 221, 225
combining methodology, 187
computer science, 153, 155, 157
computers, 50, 52, 53, 58–61, 63, 65, 66, 71, 120, 122
conducive environment, 197, 203, 204, 205, 212
Constructivism, 69
constructivist, 203, 209, 215
cross-national, 198, 210, 211
CUCEI, 156
cultural
　capital, 110, 126
　enactment, 108, 111, 124
　field, 101, 107, 108, 109
　node, 111
　production, 108, 109, 119, 124, 126
cultural differences, 143, 146

culturally-sensitive factors of the learning environment, 27
curriculum development, 169

development and validation of a learning environment questionnaire, 45

educational aims, 223
emergent research methods, 222
environment-attitude, 210, 216
environment-outcome, 204, 206, 212
ergonomics, 50, 51, 70
evaluation, 2, 8, 11, 19–21, 23, 24

Gender differences, 145, 150, 152
gestures, 111–117

habitus, 113, 116, 119, 125

Indonesia, 153–158, 160–162
Influence, 76, 79, 80, 85, 94
information technology, 49, 66, 70, 155
interpersonal profiles, 77, 84, 89
interpersonal teacher behaviour, 203, 206, 211, 214
interpretative procedures, 222
laboratory activities, 103, 108, 111, 118–120

learning environment, 217–223, 226–230
learning environments, 1, 2, 12, 14–24
learning, 49–54, 56, 57, 59, 61–63, 66–70
    environments, 49–51, 56, 63, 67–70
learning environments
    actual, 106
    linear assumptions, 107
    preferred, 106
literacy skills, 27

mini-lectures, 113
Multilevel analyses, 85
multi-method approach, 222

nature of the curriculum, 223, 225, 226, 227
one-on-one interactions, 111, 122, 123
pedagogical, 76
pedagogy of poverty, 103, 128
perceptions, 89
    of students, 84
    of teachers, 84, 86
poverty, 102, 103
preferred and actual learning environments, 106
pressures, 223, 226, 227
problem-solving skills, 27
Proximity, 76, 79, 80, 87, 94

QTI, 141, 142, 144–147
qualitative, 205, 209, 213
quantitative, 209

Questionnaire on Teacher Interaction, 82
questionnaires, 1, 2, 6, 8, 11, 15–17

resistance, 109, 113, 124, 125, 127, 129
respect, 102, 109, 110, 112, 123, 126

science education, 131, 132, 134, 135, 137, 138, 143–145, 147–149, 152
scientific literacy, 125
secondary education, 79
Singapore education system, 200, 208, 210
small group activities, 108, 118
social and cultural factors, 218, 221, 222
social capital, 110, 123
strategies of action, 101, 107, 118, 125
student outcomes, 1, 8, 9, 10, 11, 17, 19, 20, 23
students' perceptions, 86, 90, 92

teacher-centred, 223, 225–227
teacher–student relationship, 74, 79
Teaching Career, 81, 85, 87, 89, 93
teaching out of field, 105
teaching, 49, 56, 67, 68, 70
Test of Computer Related Attitudes (TOCRA), 157
Test of Science Related Attitudes (TOSRA), 157
The model for interpersonal teacher behaviour, 76

Index

TOSRA, 142, 144
transitions, 111, 121, 122

urban
    high schools, 102, 103, 108, 125, 129
    shuffle, 122

validation, 4, 19, 20, 24

WIHIC, 141, 144–147, 153, 156–160